Making
Robust
Decisions

David G. Ullman is an active product designer who has taught, researched, and written about design and decision making for more than twenty years. He has published over twenty papers focused on understanding the mechanical design process and the development of tools that help support it. He is on the editorial board of four journals in this field and is the founder of the American Society of Mechanical Engineers—Design Theory and Methodology Committee. In 1998 he was honored as an ASME Fellow. He is Emeritus Professor of Mechanical Design at Oregon State University and the author of *The Mechanical Design Process* (2001) and *12 Steps to Robust Decisions* (2004). In 2001, he founded Robust Decisions, Inc., the leading provider of decision support solutions.

Dr. Ullman can be reached at ullman@robustdecisions.com.

Making Robust Decisions

Decision Management for Technical, Business, and Service Teams

Dr. David G. Ullman

Order this book online at www.trafford.com/06-2714
or email orders@trafford.com

Most Trafford titles are also available at major online book retailers.

First edition November 2006.
Design by Meadowlark Communications, Inc.
Accord™ and Bayesian Team Support (BTS)™ are registered trademarks of Robust Decisions, Inc.

Note for Librarians: A cataloguing record for this book is available from Library
and Archives Canada at www.collectionscanada.ca/amicus/index-e.html

ISBN: 978-1-4251-0956-1

*We at Trafford believe that it is the responsibility of us all, as both individuals and corporations,
to make choices that are environmentally and socially sound. You, in turn, are supporting this
responsible conduct each time you purchase a Trafford book, or make use of our publishing services.
To find out how you are helping, please visit www.trafford.com/responsiblepublishing.html*

*Our mission is to efficiently provide the world's finest, most comprehensive book publishing
service, enabling every author to experience success. To find out how to publish your book, your
way, and have it available worldwide, visit us online at www.trafford.com/10510*

 www.trafford.com

North America & international
toll-free: 1 888 232 4444 (USA & Canada)
phone: 250 383 6864 ♦ fax: 250 383 6804 ♦ email: info@trafford.com

The United Kingdom & Europe
phone: +44 (0)1865 487 395 ♦ local rate: 0845 230 9601
facsimile: +44 (0)1865 481 507 ♦ email: info.uk@trafford.com

10 9 8 7 6 5 4 3

When you get to a fork in the road, take it.
Yogi Berra

Contents

Preface

In the mid-1990s I was working as an engineer and teaching engineering design at Oregon State University. During that time, I became aware of the importance of decisions and the limitations of the methods available for making them. I was well aware of the best decision-making practices at the time, and found them wanting.

First, I couldn't understand how to compare a new idea to the current practice. For example, there were no tools to help me compare a new part to the one it might be replacing. Of course, I knew everything about the existing part: its cost, its good features, its problems—everything. The new concept, on the other hand, was fraught with uncertainty: There were many things I had to learn as I finished designing it, manufacturing it, and using it. Further, information about my new idea was incomplete, and often even conflicting. How, then, could I compare this varied information so I could choose whether or not developing the new part was worth the effort? No tools, no methods, no analysis that existed at that time could help me resolve this situation.

Second, virtually all the decisions I was involved in required input from many different people. I needed others to supply information that I didn't have and give me opinions from their unique viewpoints. The existing decision-making methods offered no way to merge the input of others with mine, no way to respect and account for differing perspectives.

The more time I spent digging through the library, the more I realized that many disciplines faced problems identical to mine, and that none of them had a good solution for how to support team decision making when the information the team had to rely on was uncertain, incomplete, inconsistent, and evolving.

Fortunately, I was in a position to research and develop methods to support these kinds of decisions. As I worked on these methods, the term "robust decision" evolved. By 2001, I had put what I learned in my first book on the subject, *12 Steps to Robust Decisions*. The book you now hold in your hands is the maturation of this earlier work.

The purpose of this book is to popularize the concept of a robust decision. Robust decisions stick: People buy into them and feel accountable for them. Robust decisions are made in a timely manner and with knowledge about the uncertainties and risks involved in the chosen course of action. Robust decisions include all the knowledge and information that is available, and point toward new information that may be important.

In this book I explore how to manage the information necessary to make the critical choices—those that determine success during product development, in everyday business, and in government.

Whatever decisions you're involved in—choosing the next product to develop, its configuration, or what machine to build it with; deciding on a new plant site, or which candidate to hire; whether to make or buy, or which proposal to select—the methods in this book will help you, the decision manager, ensure that you choose the best possible course of action and that you use your resources wisely.

Making Robust Decisions is designed for the team manager who is responsible for critical decisions. It develops an appreciation for decision management and achieving the best possible decision for any situation. The methods included in this book begin with those in common practice and build to more sophisticated ones based on new research and algorithm development. They are clearly explained so that you can select and apply the best ones for the specific situation you face.

Making Robust Decisions will be of particular interest to Design for Six Sigma professionals. The methods here extend the Six Sigma philosophy of managing uncertainty in the decision-making process. Decision support methods currently used in Design for Six Sigma are weak in their ability to support the uncertainty and conflict that are so common in product, service, and business systems development. The best practices shown here raise the art of decision management to a level equal to other Six Sigma tools. Further, Six Sigma practitioners will have an appreciation of the structure and the mathematical underpinnings, which are based on probabilistic methods that are an extension of what they currently use.

Finally, the book enables the OODA loop so that it can be applied to technology and business. The OODA loop—Observe, Orient, Decide, and Act—is a process developed by an Air Force fighter pilot to explain his split-second actions in combat. This model has been adopted by many governmental and commercial organizations to help them ensure that they decide on the best possible actions. But many decisions get stuck; the loop stalls at Observe and Orient, or "OO-OO-OO" (say it out loud for best effect), and Decisions get postponed. The methods in this book put the "D" back in the loop and lead to robust Action.

Making Robust Decisions presents methods that are easy to apply and show immediate results. What makes this offering unique is that it:

- Presents a clear and consistent decision-management strategy

- Develops the necessary tools for making robust decisions

- Includes methods that support consensus development: decision buy-in from all parties

- Provides strategies for resolving tough decision-making problems

- Explains why making estimates and decisions is hard work and prone to error

- Provides methodology for determining when a problem has been solved

- Includes techniques to clarify the problem

- Presents detailed methods to refine the requirements for a solution

- Shows how documentation can be generated with no additional effort

- Develops strategies for deciding what-to-do-next to resolve the problem

- Describes cost/benefit analysis for planning problem resolution

- Shows how to revisit decisions with evolving information

- Provides professional-level computer software called *Accord* to support individual and team decision making

- Provides Six Sigma tools for team decision management

- Provides details on how to unstick the OODA loop

Robust decision-making methods have been successfully implemented in a variety of technical, business, and service settings. As you explore the concepts and methods I present in *Making Robust Decisions*, I invite you to consider how you can put them to immediate and practical use in your own decision teams. Please let me know how they work for you.

David G. Ullman
ullman@robustdecisions.com
November 2006

Acknowledgements

This book has profited greatly from the help of others.

My long-term partnership with Dr. Bruce D'Ambrosio has led to most of the material in this book. He is the Bayesian brains behind the inner workings of the methods here. He sparked my interest in the concept of uncertainty, which has become an important part of my thinking. This focus was solidified by my interaction with Dr. Genichi Taguchi and his son, Shin Taguchi. Dr. Taguchi is the father of "Robust Design," a methodology that puts managing uncertainty first in the process of designing and manufacturing a product. All three of these experts truly solidified my understanding that managing uncertainty from the very beginning is vital to making robust decisions.

Larry Leach of Advanced Projects, Inc. is an expert in critical chain project management. This recently developed method also relies on understanding and managing uncertainty. My conversations with him have been a primary source of ideas and have expanded the scope of this book.

Arthur Chmielewski of the Jet Propulsion Laboratory greatly contributed to my thoughts on estimation and the difficulty of making accurate estimates.

Andy Schaefers was a student of mine in the 1980s who went on to become an engineering consultant and tool designer. He has great insight into how his customers fumble their way through their day-to-day decisions, and has added much reality to this book.

In addition to Andy, other readers of the original manuscript who made valuable comments were David Persohn, Mark Farley, Stephanie Ulbrich, and Thea Hardy. They all read from different viewpoints and forced me to better explain details and make the text more readable. I will treasure Mark's encouragement to make the book more "perky." Ex-engineering professors aren't supposed to write perky. But I tried to live up to his expectations.

I hired Sheridan McCarthy and Stanton Nelson of Meadowlark Communications, Inc. to be my editors and they proved to be much more. They bought into the content so eagerly and took their charge so thoroughly to heart that they did more than I contracted and paid for. Their help was outstanding and the quality of the book reflects this.

Frank Strickland of Edge Consulting supported this effort both financially and intellectually.

Finally, my wife Adele has never doubted that I could do anything that I put my mind to. This faith is scary but nice, and very supportive.

Robust Decisions
—Making choices you feel good about in the morning

1

Introduction

Do you frequently have to make difficult decisions? If so, this book will help you understand why they are so difficult. Then it will give you strategies for making those tough decisions with confidence, regardless of how uncertain, incomplete, inconsistent, or evolving your information may be and in spite of the personalities on your team.

The need to make good decisions is a never-ending issue in effective technology and business organizations, as it is in many other aspects of life. Yet we face numerous complex and interrelated problems in making even the simplest decisions. This book sheds light on the elements that make up effective decision making and offers a proven methodology for making better decisions—*robust* decisions. But before we get to the "how" of making robust decisions, let's look in on a team grappling with a typical workplace issue.

Anne is tasked with finding a new software system for her organization. To solicit proposals and select the best software vendor, she has created a System Selection Team—herself and three others: John from Engineering, Lisa from Human Resources, and Bob, who represents the end user of the software. The first thing the team did was to write a request for proposals (RFP). It was a long, very involved process and Anne still isn't sure if her team prepared it well enough to make selecting a vendor an easy process. Still, she hopes the meeting she scheduled for this morning will result in a final choice.

The team received seven proposals. All the team members have read them, and they have already agreed to eliminate four that did not even meet the basic specifications in the RFP. As Anne crosses into the conference area, she wonders whether choosing from the final three will be as easy as eliminating the first four. She doubts it…

The rest of the team is seated at the conference table when Anne arrives. "Okay, let's get started," she begins. "Our goal for the hour is this: Either choose to accept one of the proposals we received or decide to go back out for more. Now, to recap, we sent out the RFP in June, received seven proposals, and filtered out four that didn't meet the requirements in the request. Now let's see if we can choose from the three that remain: Grex, Able Industries, Inc., and Swale, Inc."

Anne looks around the room. She's worked with most of these people for years, yet she still has a nagging sense that she really doesn't know how to get the best out of them. They all work well together—there's not a lot of friction—but there are still too many budget overruns and miscommunications on important decisions that can, and often do, throw projects out of whack in the blink of an eye. There have been times when she has inwardly raged at all of them, but after she calms down she often feels that the blame lies on her shoulders; she needs to be a better manager.

John is the first to offer an opinion. "Speaking for Engineering, I say any of the three will do. They all meet the functional specs." John rarely makes eye contact, and Anne has always found this odd and a bit disturbing. And she knows from experience that John only considers his own criteria to be important, never looking beyond Engineering to any other concerns about a project.

Now Lisa speaks up. "After reading all three, I'm really concerned about training time. Even though we gave them a target number of hours in the request, I'm still very uncertain about what two of them are proposing in that area." She glances around, looking for support from the rest of the team. Ann notices a small nod from Bob, apparently in response, but as he speaks she realizes that it is only to voice his own concerns.

"Yes, Lisa," Bob says, "that seems important. But even more important than training time is ease of use. It's hard to know, with any of the proposals, just how easy the system will actually be to use." He surveys the faces at the table, wearing his best I-told-you-so look, then focuses his attention on Anne. "Remember, two years ago we bought that product from Grex, one of our current finalists here, and it was really hard to use!"

Anne remembers all too well. And she knows that if she lets Bob go on he'll start second-guessing everything in the current project because of the failures of the last one. "Bob, let's focus on the here and now, and what we can do to move ahead with the current project."

Bob interjects, "I'm just saying—"

Lisa interrupts, "But Grex has a great management team now. They hired a new managing director about a year ago. I went to school with him and he's very good. I have a lot more confidence in them now than I did then." Lisa looks pointedly at Bob, who shrugs.

Anne makes a mental note to get some objective references on the Grex team. But for the moment she'll give Lisa the benefit of the doubt. "I do think that the management team's experience is very important, as, obviously, is the cost." She turns to Bob. "Even though each proposal has a detailed cost sheet, with the areas of concern that Lisa and Bob have brought up, I'm still unclear exactly what the bottom line will be on this project in the end." Picking up a blue marker, she starts writing on the whiteboard. "Based on what I'm hearing, our important criteria appear to be…"

- Easy to use
- Short training time
- Reasonable cost
- High level of team experience

They all sit quietly for a moment, nodding at the list and making personal notes. The smell of the whiteboard marker is making Anne dizzy in the closed room. *I've got to remember to buy some non-scented markers while I still have any brain cells left*, she thinks. John begins tapping his pen on the table. "Anne, if this short list of criteria covers all we have to differentiate among the three proposals, this shouldn't be too hard." Anne tells her brain cells to brace themselves; she doesn't share John's sense of optimism.

Two hours later, sandwich wrappers litter the table and everyone is slouched down in their chairs, picking at the remnants of their lunches. The smells of luncheon meat and whiteboard marker in the closed room are overwhelming. Snatching a last bite of turkey pastrami, Anne stands up and addresses the group. "Well, guys, this has been fun, but we all have other things to do, and we still haven't selected a proposal. We're chasing our tails here. I made some notes while I was eating and I think I've figured out what our problems are with this selection process." She begins transcribing her notes to the white board.

- The information we have is uncertain
- We each have different interpretations of the information we have

•We each think different things are important

They have made many decisions together in the past, but suddenly Anne feels like she has a new grasp of their decision-making problem. The problem isn't with what they know about the proposals, and it's not with their experience. It's that they don't have a good strategy for reaching decisions. She looks around the room to find light dawning on the faces of her team. She adds to the list:

•We don't have a good decision-making strategy

Bob gets excited as these ideas begin to sink in. "Anne, can I add one item to the list?" Without waiting for permission, he jumps up and grabs the marker away from Anne. But instead of feeling offended, Anne is delighted. Bob writes this at the end of the list:

•It is not clear what to do next to reach a decision

John is sitting forward in his chair now, also engaged. "I think I see where you're going with this—this is good, you guys!" He actually smiles at his co-workers around the table. "I think one of the reasons that we can't agree on a proposal is that we just don't understand, or rather, we can't manage, the risks involved with each of them. So I suggest we add to the list, 'We don't understand the risks associated with each alternative'."

Anne takes the marker back from Bob and writes on the board:

•We don't understand the risks associated with each
alternative

Anne notices that now everyone is engaged, nodding their heads in agreement and smiling.

Bob adds, "One more, please! This decision has a fixed set of alternatives: the three remaining proposals or the option of going out for new ones." Everyone groans; no one is eager to start over with a new RFP. "For many problems we've dealt with in the past, we begin with a clean sheet of paper—we don't have any alternative solutions at all. And another thing, here we even have a list of criteria—cost, ease of use, etc.—but they seem to be changing as we talk. A lot of times, we don't even have a good idea what the criteria are—they evolve as we understand the alternatives. So..." He retrieves the marker and writes on the board:

- We must manage alternative and criteria evolution

Anne jumps in. "I want to add a very important item to this list." She writes:

- We must get buy-in on any decision we make

"This is key," she adds, "with no buy-in on a decision, everybody does their own thing and no one feels accountable for the consequences."

Decision-Making Challenges

The information we have is uncertain

We each have different interpretations of the information we have

We each think different things are important

We don't have a good decision-making strategy

It is not clear what to do next to reach a decision

We don't understand the risks associated with each alternative

We must manage alternative and criteria evolution

We must get buy-in on any decision we make

Lisa chimes in next, speaking rapidly: "This list is all the reasons we have such a hard time making decisions around this place! And it's why some projects wander off course. If we can solve these, maybe we actually could choose a vendor in a one-hour meeting, or maybe even without meeting at all." Everyone nods a yes vote for that.

Anne adds, "I need to go think about this list. Clearly, we didn't choose a vendor, but we may have done something even more important; we've itemized the limitations of our decision-making process. I agree with Lisa. If we can learn to manage these challenges then we should do a much better job of selecting vendors and making other important decisions."

If you face the same challenges Anne's team faces, then this book is for you. As the team discovered—and as is the case with most problems you face in business, industry, and your personal life—you base even the most key decisions on your interpretation of uncertain information. If you're part of a team, you need to work to develop a shared understanding of the information and decide *what-to-do-next* to reach a decision, with a known level of risk and with team buy-in. (The term "what-to-do-next" describes a key element of robust decision-making methodology and appears throughout this book.) Further, the foundation of your decisions lies in the evolution of the alternatives you consider and the criteria against which you evaluate them. If you approach these tasks skillfully, you have a strategy that works and meets all these challenges. Unfortunately, though, most organizations have no such strategy.

When you recognize how poorly most organizations make decisions, you come to appreciate just how difficult it is to make good ones. In _Why Decisions Fail_, author Paul Nutt describes his study of 400 decisions made by senior managers in medium to large organizations. The decisions these managers made included a mix of analytical and experimental information, expert opinion, and gut feel. His primary indicators of success were 1) whether or not anyone took action after the decision was made and 2) whether this action was still in effect two years later. He concluded that _fully half the decisions had failed:_ Either action was not taken, or it did not stick. Of the decisions that failed, the only effect he observed two years later was the use of resources—time, money, personnel, equipment, etc.—all expended without achieving success in attaining the original goals. In other words, fully half of the decisions made were not robust: They were not able to withstand uncertainty, conflict, and change, nor did they elicit the buy-in necessary to make them a success.[1]

According to Nutt, three main classes of "blunders" doom decisions. Decision makers' first blunder is that they use failure-prone practices in two out of every three decisions they make. Further, they seem oblivious to the poor track record of these practices and seldom study their failures.

The second blunder is basing decisions on premature commitments; decision makers jump on the first idea that comes up. In other words, many decision-making activities are actually only efforts to justify a premature conclusion, as opposed to using evidence to select the best possible alternative.

The third blunder is that people spend time and money on the wrong things: tasks that do not add value to making the best possible decision. In other words, they don't have a strategy that helps them determine what-to-do-next.

Where Nutt's book looks at why decisions fail, _Making Robust Decisions_ looks at how to make decisions succeed. It focuses on how to manage all the challenges that Anne's team has listed on the whiteboard. It is about managing the decision-making process so that decisions are as good as they can possibly be.

The methods you will find here are a combination of research results, tried and true wisdom, and some state-of-the-art analytical methods. Their goals are to give you tools that encourage success-prone practices, to help you know at what point to commit to a decision, and to guide you in knowing what-to-do-next to get to the commitment point as quickly as possible, with team buy-in and a known level of risk.

There are many other books on decision making. In fact, libraries often catalog decision-making books in six different sections: business, psychology, sociology, self-help, industrial engineering, and computer science. Many of these books are either highly mathematical, for solving well-formed analytical problems using professional analysts, or they focus on teamwork, explaining how to set up teams to support decision making. *Making Robust Decisions* goes beyond these general approaches, bringing together multiple facets of decision making to spell out a clear methodology on how to reach a robust decision. This methodology is based on a recently developed mathematical model, yet the methods can be used without doing any mathematics. Beyond the mathematics (which are only used in the last few steps), this clear strategy for reaching robust decisions is based on many existing technologies, blending them to be optimally useful and usable on a daily basis.

The methods contained in this book combine many diverse disciplines: teamwork, standard decision-support practice, cognitive psychology, Taguchi's method of robust design, and Bayesian probabilities. Most readers know little about these, and that's fine. I will discuss them as needed, but only in enough depth to be of practical use.

A note about terminology: Because decision making draws from so many fields and is of interest to so many different disciplines, there is great inconsistency in the terminology, or jargon, used. The terms I elect to use here are those that most closely agree with common usage, and are carefully defined.

Five Criteria to Determine If Your Problems Are Suited to Robust Decision Making

The strategies and methods in this book can help you with the solution to most, but not all, problems. Specifically, they are best suited for problems in which:

1. **The issue has known or discoverable boundaries.** This means that you can state the issue addressed in a manner that isolates it. For Anne's System Selection Team, the issue is to select a proposal to fund from the three finalist alternatives.

2. **There is more than one potentially acceptable alternative for resolving the issue.** More problems fall into this category than you may think, as even if there is only one proposed solution, you can either accept it or not, resulting in two alternative courses of action.

3. **It is possible to develop criteria that measure how well the alternatives resolve the issue.** Anne's team is concerned about cost, team experience, ease of use, and training. Some of these may have been clearly specified in the RFP, complete with ideal targets (e.g. the training time should be less than 4 hours). Other criteria, like team experience and ease of use, are harder to measure; they define qualitative criteria used to judge the alternatives. There is much work involved in creating a good set of discriminating criteria.

4. **At least one person has a stake in the solution to the problem.** If more than one stakeholder is involved, each may have expertise in different areas and may represent different, even conflicting, viewpoints, as we saw in the team's deliberations.

5. **All decision makers must be interested in solving the problem.** "Gaming" can short-circuit any effort. This occurs when decision makers are interested in solving the problem, but they believe the decision-making process will not yield a good result; hence, they undermine the process to get the "correct result" by adding unnecessary criteria, manipulating what is considered important so that only their pet alternative shines, only doing work that will support their position, etc. (The methods described in this book cannot eliminate this behavior, but can help dampen it.)

A wide variety of problems meets these broad requirements. The methods and strategies in this book can be applied to:

Business problems

Portfolio management

Choosing a new plant location

Deciding on which investment
  to make

Selecting the best proposal

Choosing a new employee

Product development
  problems

Concept selections

Design decisions

Vendor selections

Make or buy decisions

Trade studies

Service problems

Workforce deployment decisions

Personal problems

Finding a restaurant

Selecting a new car

Choosing a vacation spot

Choosing a new partner (though
    this is probably going too far)

Complicating the resolution of issues in any of these areas is that some of the criteria you develop are subjective and qualitative while others are quantitative. For example, let's say a team within a company needs to hire a Chief Technology Officer. After filtering the résumés they must either come to a decision and make an offer to one of the candidates or reopen the search. The team has already decided that the important criteria are:

• Compatibility with the current team
• Understanding of core technologies
• Proven ability to develop new technologies
• Good verbal communication skills
• Good written communication skills
• Good interpersonal skills

These criteria are all qualitative; rather than being subject to exact numerical measurement, they refer only to the personal characteristics of the CTO candidates. Certainly, it is possible to develop numerical scales for these characteristics, but that may not be a good use of time and effort.

At the other extreme is the task of choosing the optimum settings for a machine that extrudes a plastic part. To achieve quality parts, industrial engineers must choose parameters such as temperature settings and material flow rates. For this type of problem the alternatives and criteria are fairly well known and the system may be modeled with a set of equations and then optimized. If that is not possible, perhaps engineers can create a set of experiments to help find the best settings and rates to use. But even here things aren't simple, as it may be challenging to find a robust process, one that is least susceptible to both known and unknown uncertainties, and one that will still look good a week, a month, or two years later. There may also be differences of opinion about what elements to control and which are the important characteristics of the final product.

Most issues in technology and business are a mix of opinion-heavy, qualitative criteria, as in the "choose a CTO" example, and primarily quantitative criteria, as in the control of a manufacturing machine. Decisions about these issues are all based on the opinions, analysis results, and best guesses of a team of people, using information that is usually uncertain, incomplete, inconsistent, and evolving. One of the goals of this book is to give you tools to develop and manage decision-making criteria regardless of their type and certainty.

The Basics of Decision Making

Some of my earlier assertions may seem like overstatements, but in light of the high percentage of decisions that fail, they may not be. I will build on these assertions to refine the importance of decision making.

As you read the following, pay attention to whether the word "decision" describes an *event* or a *process*. An event statement is "I decided to buy the Porsche." To keep things clear, when I talk about the *event*, the "decision" will refer to the *choice*, as in "After considering many cars, I chose a Porsche." When referring to a *process*, it is common to add other clarifying terms such as "decision making" or "decision-making process." Later in this chapter, figure 1.2, which outlines the decision-making process and shows the final choice as just one small part of it, makes the relationship between these two concepts clear. But before tackling this diagram, let's look at some decision-making truths.

Decision-Making Truths

What were you taught about decision making in school? Probably not much. It's likely that the main thing you learned was that if you got an answer that matched the one in the book, you got the right one. Yet you later learned that when you went to buy a car, to design a product, or to make a business decision, there were no right answers. In real life:

There are no *right* decisions.
There are only *satisfactory* decisions.
Your goal is to find the best possible
   satisfactory decision.

In fact, most issues have multiple possible satisfactory solutions. The alternative potential solutions you consider often evolve as you work your way through a problem. As you learn more about the issue, the criteria used to evaluate these potential solutions also evolve. Note that the bigger the problem and the more people involved in making the decision, the harder it is to manage your alternatives, criteria, and evaluations. If you think of your alternatives, the criteria you use to judge those alternatives, and your evaluation results as information, then the following is generally true:

**Business and technical progress is the generation
and refinement of information, punctuated by
decision making.**

Take a moment to reflect on the process you used to make a recent decision to see if you can identify the methods or tools that helped you manage evolving alternatives and criteria, and evaluations of alternatives relative to those criteria. (Don't be surprised if you don't have one that you can articulate. You may have used failure-prone decision-making practices, the first blunder described in *Why Decisions Fail.*) Perhaps in the situation you recall, people tried to develop and share information that supported their favorite alternatives. In most organizations such activities are usually ad hoc, offering little help in ensuring that the knowledge and abilities of the participants are utilized. In fact, ad hoc processes result in unresolved issues and dissatisfaction with the results, and are at least a partial explanation of why people dislike meetings so much, especially those that are poorly structured and not clearly focused.

Decision making is of great importance because:

A decision is a commitment to use resources.

When you make a decision, choosing one of your proposed alternatives, all future activity focuses on that alternative: You begin using time, money, and other resources. For the most part, these resources cannot be recovered if you change your decision later. The choice to focus on one alternative precludes expending effort on the rejected alternatives. Part of decision making is determining how much commitment each alternative will require to bring it to fruition. Even procrastination—not making a decision—uses resources. Either the issue in need of resolution keeps wasting people's time or myriad other resource wasters continue to occur.

In fact, the previous truth leads to a working definition of "decision making," namely:

> ## Decision making is a process that commits resources to resolving an issue

Beyond the commitment of resources, note the two additional important parts of this definition. First, a goal of decision making is the *resolution* of an issue; thus, it is essential to know the issue being resolved. This seems obvious and perhaps trivial, but it is key. Second, as discussed earlier, making a decision is a *process*, not an event.

Finally,

> ## Decisions are based on
> ## uncertain,
> ## incomplete,
> ## inconsistent, and
> ## evolving information.
> ## You need to make the best of it.

A central focus of the methods in this book is the effort to manage the generally nasty nature of the information that characterizes most deliberations. Most information changes or evolves—even goals are often a moving target. Not only is information uncertain and evolving, it is also inconsistent, since teams make most business and technical decisions and teams usually feature people with differing backgrounds, loyalties, and opinions. The methods here help limit the conflict to the information itself, not the people who produce it. Finally, information about a decision problem is never complete; there is always information missing. And it will always cost time, money, or other resources to get more information on which to base your decision, if it exists to be found at all.

You may find this last "truth" to be an exaggeration. But no matter how sure you are about the information on which you base your decisions, there are always uncertainties. Not only that, but your information will look different to others than it does to you, and will even look different to you two weeks from now. Thus, it is imperative that you have strategies in place to make the best of the information you have.

The next truth is based on a quotation by Arthur C. Clarke, the author of *2001: A Space Odyssey*, who put it best when he said:

"The only real problem in life is what to do next."

In other words, it is not only important to select an alternative, it is arguably more important to decide what-to-do-next in your effort to get to the point where you can make a decision.

To sum up, most decision-making activities require:

Choosing a course of action from multiple alternatives and committing resources, using information that is
- Uncertain
- Incomplete
- Inconsistent
- Evolving

and based on input from stakeholders who
- Represent many different viewpoints, areas of expertise, and organizational functions
- Know only some of the relevant information
- May be distributed

The last bulleted item is new to this discussion. Team members may be distributed both by location and by time. Some of your team, for example, may be in other buildings, in other time zones, or on other continents. Managing a distributed group brings added challenges to the decision-making process.

The Value of Information

Focusing on decisions can help in managing information. The term "information" is used to mean many things, but it can be clarified by considering

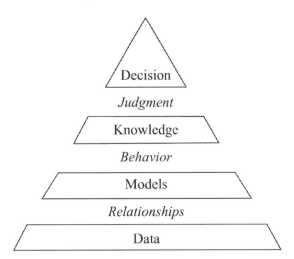

Figure 1.1: The Value of Information pyramid.

the Value of Information (VOI) pyramid as shown in figure 1.1. Let's explore the progression from the bottom of the figure to the top.

The simplest form of information, at the base of the figure, is raw **data**. Data are numbers, text, or other descriptive information about some object or idea.

Models define **relationships** between data. These relationships may be mental pictures of a situation, math equations, complete sentences or paragraphs, or graphic images that relate basic data and result in a richer form. These models are static relationships among the data and play a key role in evaluation.

You must understand and interpret the **behavior** of models to gain the **knowledge** necessary to evaluate information during the decision-making process. It is the knowledge gained during evaluation that you depend on to refine your alternatives and criteria.

Finally, when your knowledge is sufficient, you can make **decisions** using **judgment** based on this knowledge. According to this argument, the most valuable type of information is a decision, as it is based on all the less-valuable information types. In other words, supporting decision making requires that you manage data, models, and knowledge, as well as the associated judgment upon which your decisions are based.

If, for example, you are interested in buying a new computer system, you might look online or in a catalog and find all kinds of data on processor clock speed and memory size for each alternative computer you want to consider. If you know the relationships between these specifications, you have a model for how a potential computer might perform. In fact, some computer magazines generate measures based on such models. If you are familiar with computers, you can use the data and models to actually predict the performance of the computers you are considering. Furthermore, your knowledge helps you determine the criteria for selecting your new computer from the available alternatives. Based on this knowledge, the data, and the models, you use your judgment to make a decision about what-to-do-next. You accept your current level of uncertainty and select a computer to buy, or you iterate back to gain more information in an effort to reduce your risk before committing to a purchase.

As figure 1.1 shows, decisions are dependent on weaker types of information (data, models, and knowledge). As I stated earlier, business and technical progress is the generation and refinement of information, punctuated by decisions. Generation and refinement both use data, models, and knowledge coupled by relationships and behaviors. The flow that connects these types of information is the next topic to discuss.

Decision Flow

There are four main activities necessary for the generation and refinement of information (i.e., data, models, and knowledge) during the decision-making process: **understand, evaluate, fuse,** and **decide.** These occur unconsciously during decision making, no matter how small the problem addressed.[2] Helping decision makers become conscious of these four activities and providing support for each of them are both goals of this book.

Figure 1.2 shows the general relationships between these four activities and describes the process used throughout *Making Robust Decisions.* Note that the decision to choose an alternative—the last item in what-to-do-next—is only one activity of the decision-making process.

Let's look at the four rectangular boxes in this figure in more detail:

> It is necessary to **understand the problem** in order to resolve it.
> To understand you must:
> - Clarify the issue that needs a satisfactory solution.
> - Generate alternatives—the potential solutions for the issue.
> - Develop criteria, as they measure a satisfactory solution for the issue.

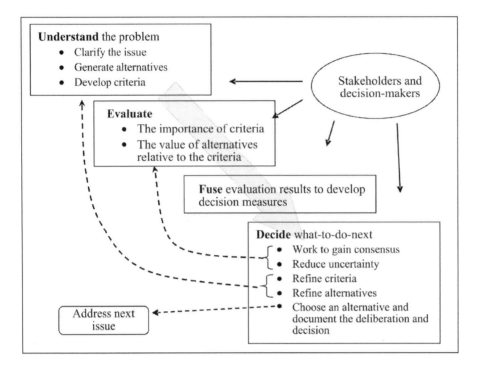

Figure 1.2: The Decision-Making Process.

The next major part of decision making is **Evaluation.** This includes two activities:

- Evaluate how important each of the criteria is relative to the others.
- Assess the value of the alternatives by comparing them to the criteria.

Decisions depend on **fused** evaluation results. Fusion is the combining of evaluation results. To manage what-to-do-next, managing fusion is critical. It is difficult for even a single decision maker to accomplish, and even more challenging for a team.

Based on the fused results, **decide what-to-do-next.** This decision will direct the process down one of three paths:

- Improve understanding
    Refine criteria
    Refine alternatives
- Refine evaluation
    Work to gain consensus
    Reduce uncertainty

- Choose an alternative—you've made a decision
  Document the decision
  Address other issues

One feature of the diagram is that two of the paths leading from "decide what-to-do-next" go back to earlier activities. These arrows emphasize the evolution and refinement of information that are inherent in solving most problems. This backtracking is often called iteration or recursion. Knowing what-to-do-next can keep your team from getting stuck in an iterative loop. By whatever name, it is a necessary part of the development of the relationships, models, behavior, and knowledge necessary for making a decision.

The diagram also shows that the stakeholders and decision makers are involved in all parts of the decision-making process.

The team we met at the beginning of the chapter followed this process up to a point. They did a good job of understanding the problem, at least initially. Anne stated the issue up front; the alternatives were obvious and some criteria were listed. Much of the evaluation information came directly from the proposals themselves—the proposed cost and training time in particular were specified in them. But it is clear that the team didn't have a good handle on the uncertainty associated with the information. Although we don't know what happened in the middle of their meeting, you can bet that they had difficulty fusing their evaluations and deciding what-to-do-next. They probably spent much of their time going around in iterative loops, with frustration building about their inability to converge on one proposal.

Five Decision Questions

As you work through the process, you consciously or unconsciously ask yourself five key questions:

1. Which is the best alternative?
2. What is the risk that our decision will not turn out as we expect?
3. Do we know enough to make a good decision yet?
4. Is there buy-in for the decision?
5. What do we need to do next to feel confident about our decision, within the scope of our limited resources?

If you are the only stakeholder in the decision, rather than a member of a team or group, just replace "our" with "my" and "we" with "I" in questions 2, 3, and 5, and eliminate the fourth question. It makes no difference what subject the problem addresses; the questions above all apply and they are generally not easy to answer. The quality of your decision will only be revealed by the passage of time (e.g., in Nutt's study, two years), and by then it is too late to change it. For example, after the team selects a proposal, it can't reverse its decision and select another one without major consequences. The goal, then, is to answer these five questions as part of the decision-making process, not as a post-mortem to a poor decision.

The first question, "Which is the best alternative?", implies that there is more than one alternative to choose from. Sometimes there are too many alternatives, as when deciding how to build an investment portfolio, but generally there are too few, which leads to the second *Why Decisions Fail* blunder—jumping on the first idea.

The second key question—"What is the risk that our decision will not turn out we expect?"—addresses the level of risk you are willing to accept when you make a decision.

The third question, "Do we know enough to make a good decision yet?", concerns the uncertainty of the information. The more you know, the less the uncertainty—sometimes; at other times you have to learn in order to know what you don't know.

The fourth question, "Is there buy-in for the decision?", focuses on the development of a shared understanding in team situations. What is important is that there is buy-in by all concerned, but not necessarily agreement. This occurs when:[3]

- Everyone can paraphrase the issue to show that he or she understands it.
- Everyone has had a chance to contribute to the solution to the problem.
- Everyone has had a chance to describe what is important to him or her.

If you can achieve these three goals, then those who do not agree with the final decision may still support the team because they have been a part of the decision-making process and they appreciate the compromise needed to reach a decision.

The fifth question—"What do we need to do next to feel confident about our decision, within the scope of our limited resources?"—addresses the third blunder, spending time and money on the wrong things.

I encourage you to keep these five questions in mind, as they form the backbone of this book. Note that they imply that making a decision is more than just choosing an alternative, which is only the first of the five questions. Making a robust decision requires answering all five of them.

The Concept of a Robust Decision

Why "Robust Decisions"? The name and methods begin with the field of "Robust Design" popularized primarily by Dr. Genichi Taguchi in the 1990s.[4] The essence of robust design is a two-step optimization process:

1 Find the alternative that is the least sensitive to noise (uncertainty) and then
2 Bring the design to its performance target.

This differs from what is generally taught and practiced—do deterministic analysis (ignore uncertainty) and then take into account the effects of uncertainty. Taguchi's point is that if you don't account for the effects of uncertainty from the very beginning, you may end up with a product that is great *if everything goes right*, but that may behave poorly if there is any change in the environment in which the product operates, as the product ages, or from one example to the next.

Robust decision making extends the "robust design" philosophy to general decision making with uncertainty considered from the beginning: controlling what uncertainty you can and finding the best possible solution that is as insensitive as possible to the remaining uncertainty. Thus, developing robust decisions depends on your ability to manage uncertainty:

> A robust decision is the best possible choice, one found by eliminating all the uncertainty possible within available resources, and then choosing with known and acceptable levels of satisfaction and risk.

There are three parts to this definition.

1 The end goal is to make the best possible choice. The view of which choice is the "best possible" may vary with different

stakeholders. Thus, a sub-goal is to support the development of best-choice buy-in by all stakeholders.

2   A major goal in making a robust decision is to eliminate all the uncertainty possible within the scope of available resources. This means improving the quality of the information used in making a decision by making optimal use of available people, time, and money.

3   The result of decision making is an option chosen with known and acceptable satisfaction and risk. This implies that you have a way to measure the satisfaction that you believe you can obtain with an alternative and that you know the level of risk that this may not be achieved.

"Decision management" is the decision-making process used to achieve these aims. The very name implies that you can control the process to ensure the most robust decision possible.

> ### Decision management is determining what-to-do-next with the available information in order to make the most robust decision as a part of standard work processes, and documenting the results for distribution and reuse.

The essential points in this definition are:

- *What-do-to-next*—as emphasized in figure 1.2. Identifying the next step in the deliberation process, one that helps obtain the highest return on investment (ROI), is often clouded by what is easy to do as well as other predispositions.
- *Available information* comes from many sources. Most of them are uncertain, incomplete, biased, conflicting, subject to change, and may be distributed to stakeholders over distance and time. Decision management supports the fusion of this information.
- Decision management adds capability while enhancing current work habits *as a part of standard work processes*. Ideally, the additional tasks suggested here become part of an organization's work ethic, adding little additional effort while improving the

quality of decisions and reducing decision-making time.

•Decision management supports *documenting the results for distribution and reuse*. Decision management is based on the belief that it is not only important to reuse information; it is essential to reuse the process that developed it.

There is one final term to define: uncertainty management—the activities undertaken to reduce the effect of uncertainties on decisions. What uncertainty you can't eliminate you must manage. This means making the best use of the incompleteness, the inconsistency, the evolution, and the lack of determinism (taking uncertainty into account) that plague all decisions. So:

> Uncertainty management is the effort to make the best possible use of the uncertainty that you cannot easily eliminate.

Managing uncertainty requires help; making complex, uncertain decisions is not easy.

Bayesian Team Support

Bayesian Team Support (BTS) is a mathematical method that is the basis of the robust decision-making process. BTS supports a team in making a decision as it collects evidence that supports or refutes alternative courses of action. BTS methods assume that the information collected will be uncertain, incomplete, inconsistent, and evolving. As evidence accumulates, the degree of belief in one of the alternatives will indicate the best choice. To help bring this process to closure, BTS provides graphical and textual feedback to the team to guide its deliberation.

Don't let the previous paragraph scare you. BTS mathematics is buried out of sight in these methods. I cover only enough of BTS for you to understand what is happening and apply the tools you need. You don't need to know about any advanced mathematics. In fact, I have taught this material in industrial settings to both technical and non-technical people. If you would like more detail on BTS, however, it can be found in appendix A.

BTS is an extension of Bayesian Decision Theory, a computational theory for applying general knowledge to individual situations characterized by uncertainty and risk. As classical statistics revolutionized the *discovery* of knowledge in the early twentieth century, so Bayesian decision theory is revolutionizing the *application* of knowledge in the twenty-first. The following indicate that this revolution is under way:

- Most major spam tools are based on Bayesian methods; it gives them the ability to learn which mail is spam and which isn't. As spam authors change their methods to get their messages to you, and you tag a new message as "spam," the spam tool updates its model. It is managing an uncertain and evolving model of what you consider to be spam.
- All speech recognition tools include some Bayesian methods to learn how you say certain words.
- In medical diagnosis, information (the symptoms and results of tests) is uncertain, incomplete, and inconsistent. Thus, recent diagnostic tools based on Bayesian methods have shown great ability to diagnose ailments.
- Information about terrorists is uncertain, incomplete, inconsistent, and evolving. This is why so many counterterrorism tactics use Bayesian methods.

Although most of the concepts of the BTS method can be implemented with paper and pencil, some of the team activities and BTS analysis need computer support. The next section introduces *Accord* software, which has been created for this purpose. It's the computerized version of robust decision making.

Accord: The Robust Decisions Software

Accord software helps support teams in making robust decisions based on the best available (however uncertain) information by seamlessly integrating new information and delivering results that include risk, probability of alternatives being best, and what-to-do-next analysis. *Accord* software supports:

- Making robust decisions by managing all available uncertain, incomplete, inconsistent, and evolving information
- Capturing qualitative and quantitative information through an easy-to-use graphical interface
- Getting the best possible information from your entire team

- Fusing all available information into decision measures that are easy to understand and use, including:
  - Levels of satisfaction for each alternative from multiple viewpoints
  - Probability of each alternative being the best
  - Decision risk
  - Level of consensus
  - What-to-do-next to ensure a robust decision
- Providing a rational decision strategy
- Recording the logic trail in a database for reuse and review
- Automatically generating decision reports

Additional details about *Accord* may be found at www.robustdecisions. com. You can download a free thirty-day trial copy there, complete with many of the examples from this book. See appendix B for further details.

How This Book Is Organized

I opened this introductory chapter with an example from everyday business life that gave some idea of the complexity of even the simplest decision-making activity. Throughout the book you will read many examples, some from commonly shared experience, some from business, and others from product development.

Industry and government have begun to realize the importance of expending energy on the decision-making process. In chapter 2, "A Focus on Decisions," I highlight popular best practices that contain decision management as an integral part of their philosophies, attesting to this importance. Each best practice gives a context for the use of the methods presented here.

Earlier in this chapter we were introduced to the pervasiveness of uncertainty in decision making. Chapter 3, "Often Wrong But Never in Doubt," more fully develops the definition and the causes of uncertainty, important issues in estimating uncertain information, and guidelines on how to get the best possible information.

Where uncertainty is one key theme, working with teams to get the best possible decisions is clearly another. Thus, chapter 4, "Teams Don't Make Decisions, But...," presents descriptions of how different individuals make decisions, the classes of people involved in decision making, and what happens to these individual styles when people form teams. The chapter also includes suggestions for managing stakeholders and decision makers and getting the best out of people and organizations.

The material in chapters 5 through 7 is all about setting up decision problems. Chapter 5, "Everyone Hears Only What He Understands," focuses on issue development, methods for developing alternatives, and how to structure a problem to get the best possible decision. Chapters 6, "Measuring the Ideal," and 7, "Importance Is in the Eye of the Beholder," explore establishing discriminating criteria.

Chapter 8, "Decisions Are Based on Your Belief About an Uncertain Future," introduces the concept of belief and how it affects decisions. Belief allows us to take uncertainty into account—a concept carried through into chapter 9, "Robust Decision Making"—developing the full capability of BTS.

The focus of chapter 10, "Decide What-to-Do-Next: Analyzing the Benefit of Further Effort," focuses on a key requirement of making robust decisions: knowing what-to-do-next. Also of importance is documenting the process and results, the topic of chapter 11, "Decision Documentation and Rationale."

Chapter 12, "Criteria Templates," offers a series of templates for common problems that you can use as a basis for making your own robust decisions.

Chapter 13, "Applications of Robust Decision Making," contains some short case studies. And finally, appendices A and B, for inquiring minds, explain the technical bases of BTS and introduce *Accord* software, respectively.

A Focus on Decisions 2

Why focus on decisions?

In business and technology, making good decisions is critical. This may seem obvious, but in spite of the fact, our educational system provides very little formal training in how to make robust decisions. And most businesses do a poor job of it. This is unfortunate, because a single poor decision early in a project can drive it over budget and behind schedule, and it can waste resources as decision makers find it necessary to go back and revisit their earlier efforts.

Although interest in decision making goes back at least as far as the Greeks, it is only now becoming a focus of business and technology. To be sure, many businesses have used analysts to perform formal decision analysis in the past, and certain sectors have used other formal methods, but until recently there has not been a general focus on decision making as the critical skill it is.

So why the recent interest? Many companies spent the 1990s coming to understand and evolving their business and technology processes. It was a time of ISO–9000 and measurement of process quality. *Making Robust Decisions* itself grew out of the 1992 text titled *The Mechanical Design Process*, which is now in its third edition and is used at many universities to teach about the process of product design.[1] It ties together all the popular best practices in a process that flows from customer need to final product. I debated the use of the term "process" in the title when the book was first published, as the word primarily described physical activities, not business and development activities. But its usage proved to be correct, because focus on processes became important in product development, business, and service activities.

Then in 1994 the Project Management Institute published the first edition of *A Guide to the Project Management Body of Knowledge (PMBOK*

Guide).[2] It's a collection of best business management practices, written so as to link them into a process. PMBOK is still maturing and is very much in use today.

As organizations become more mature in understanding their processes, this statement from chapter 1 becomes more appropriate: "Business and technical progress is the generation and refinement of information, punctuated by decision making." Processes control the generation and refinement of information, as well as products (which are a manifestation of information). And mature process descriptions recognize the importance of decision making.

This chapter explores some recent and not-so-recent models of the decision-making process. In fact, it starts with a model that Benjamin Franklin developed over two hundred years ago, then progresses through another model developed by a modern fighter pilot. It then presents an evolving best practice commonly used in technology and business. A brief description of an evolving standard leads to a concluding section that contains a flow chart to guide you in selecting the best decision-support method for your particular issue. The methods themselves are detailed throughout the rest of the book: a mix of old methods and others that I introduce in this book for the first time.

We begin with Benjamin Franklin.

The Ben Franklin Method

Benjamin Franklin considered the decision-making problem over two hundred years ago. In a 1772 letter to Joseph Priestley,[3] Franklin explained how he analyzed his problems when intuition failed him:

> *Dear Sir: In the affair of so much importance to you, wherein you ask my advice, I cannot, for want of sufficient premises, advise you what to determine; but, if you please, I will tell you how. When those difficult cases occur, they are difficult, chiefly because, while we have them under consideration, all the reasons pro and con are not present to the mind at the same time; but sometimes one set present themselves, and at other times another, the first being out of sight. Hence the various purposes or information that alternatively prevail, and the uncertainty that perplexes us.*
>
> *To get over this, my way is, to divide a sheet of paper by a line into two columns; writing over the one pro and over the other con; then during three or four days' consideration, I put down under the different heads*

short hints of the different motives, that at different times occur to me, for or against the measure. When I have thus got them all together in one view, I endeavor to estimate their respective weights; and, when I find two (one on each side), that seem equal, I strike them both out. If I find a reason pro equal to, some two reasons con, I strike out the three. If I judge some two reasons con, equal to three reasons pro, I strike out the five; and thus proceeding I find at length where the balance lies; and if, after a day or two of further consideration, nothing new that is of importance occurs on either side, I come to a determination accordingly. And, though the weight of reasons cannot be taken with the precision of algebraic quantities, yet, when each is thus considered separately and comparatively, and the whole lies before me, I think I can judge better, and am less liable to make a rash step; and in fact I have found great advantage from this kind of equation...

Franklin considers whether to accept or reject a single alternative. This is really a choice between two alternatives: Do this, or do something else (including nothing). Franklin advises five steps for making a decision:

Step 1. Make two columns on a sheet of paper and label one "Pros" and the other "Cons."

Step 2. Fill in the columns with all the Pros and Cons of an alternative.

Step 3. Estimate the importance of each Pro and Con.

Step 4. Eliminate Pros and Cons this way:
   a) When two are of about equal importance, cross them both out and
   b) find other importance equalities of Pros and Cons—e.g., the importance of two pros equals three cons—and then strike them out.

Step 5. When one or the other column becomes dominant, then "come to the determination accordingly."

You can extend the idea of using Pro and Con lists to include more than one alternative, but the balancing step quickly becomes complex. Still, NASA frequently uses this approach to help organize experts when evaluating multiple proposals. For each proposal the experts list the Pros and Cons. They then informally balance the Pros and Cons to differentiate among the alternatives. This helps to tease out the good and bad points.

Although Franklin's method doesn't formally itemize criteria, each Pro or Con is a statement about the alternative relative to some measure: an *implied* criterion. These criteria are primarily qualitative, with Pro statements like "It is fast," implying that speed is a criterion with an implied target of being fast, and that the current alternative meets this ill-defined target.

As I stated earlier, Franklin's method can be extended beyond a single alternative and a single person, but it is not well suited for complex problems with teams of people and a high degree of uncertainty.

From this very practical colonial-era method, we leap ahead to a modern model of the decision-making process created by a jet fighter pilot. While Franklin gave us a step-by-step recipe, Colonel John Boyd offers a framework for understanding and managing complexity.

The OODA Loop

While flying combat missions in Korea and Vietnam, Colonel John Boyd, U.S. Air Force fighter pilot ace, noticed that he could think and react faster than his opponents. In fact, he was so good at it that he became known throughout the Air Force as "Forty-Second Boyd" because he had a standing offer to all pilots that if they could defeat him in simulated air-to-air combat in under forty seconds he would pay them forty dollars. He never lost a simulated—or real—dogfight.

Over the years he reflected on what happened in air combat when he made rapid life-or-death decisions. As he won dogfights in Korea and Vietnam, his decision-making model matured, and he later used it to describe how to gain a competitive advantage in any situation. He referred to the model as an "OODA Loop" (Observe, Orient, Decide, and Act).[4] Until his death in 1997 he spoke to military and business audiences about the importance of the OODA loop. These talks fueled the recent interest in applying the OODA Loop to business and product development as a way to describe decision-making cycles.

The OODA Loop is a succinct representation of the natural decision cycle seen in every context—war, business, product development, and life in general. Boyd diagrammed the OODA Loop as shown in figure 2.1. In it, all decisions are based on observations of an evolving situation. These observations are oriented to the problem being addressed. The oriented observations are the raw information upon which decisions and actions are based.

You need to process the information you observe and orient to it before

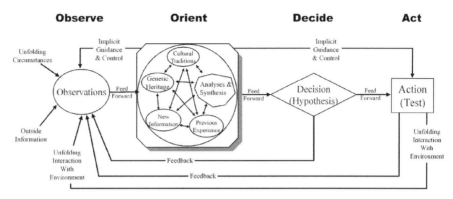

Figure 2.1: Boyd's original OODA Loop

you can proceed further in making a decision. In notes from his 1987 talk, "Organic Design for Command and Control," Boyd wrote, "The second O, orientation—as the repository of our genetic heritage, cultural tradition, and previous experiences—is *the most important part* of the OODA loop, since it shapes the way we observe, the way we decide, the way we act" (the emphasis is Boyd's).[5] As he said, and as you can see in the Orient box, there is much filtering of information that needs to go on: through our culture, genetics, ability to analyze and synthesize, and previous experience. Since the OODA Loop was designed to describe a single decision maker, the situation is usually more complex than the illustration implies. Most business and technical decisions involve a team of people observing and orienting, each bringing his or her own cultural traditions, genetics, experience, and other information to the task. It is no wonder that we often get stuck here, and find that the OODA Loop has been reduced to the stuttering sound of "OO-OO-OO."[6] Getting stuck means no decision, thus no action. But in reality, when you're stuck you've made a decision: to do nothing. Time keeps moving along, and by doing nothing, you waste resources. In Boyd's world, the pilot who hesitates gets shot out of the sky. In business, the competition keeps taking action and you keep using your resources without adding value. In other words, getting stuck at the decision point can have severe, even grave consequences.

The organizational responses to being stuck are often doing more analysis, gathering more data, conducting more simulations, or doing "decision making by wringing of hands." Sometimes these activities help, if directed at the right sticking point, but more often they only result in postponing decisions until some external event occurs that forces a decision. The result? "Decision by running out of time" or, if the action is dictated by a superior,

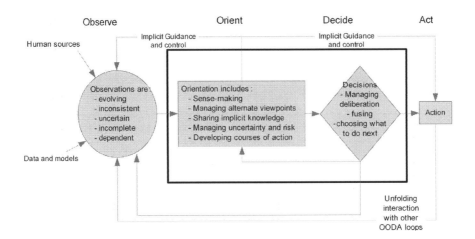

Figure 2.2: The Expanded OODA Loop.

"decision by fiat." Neither of these methods offers much chance of leading to a robust decision.

An important feature of the OODA Loop is that it *is* a loop; it is not static. Your orientation efforts affect what you observe and how you implement your actions. Each decision and action changes the context for subsequent observations, and the result of the action on the environment causes a push-back from it that affects the information being observed. Competitive advantage comes from quickness over the entire loop: With each iteration the changes are smaller (being modifications to an increasingly well-understood situation) and can be more easily managed, helping you stay ahead of the competition.

To explore why we get stuck in this process, consider an expanded OODA Loop, figure 2.2.

Here, the OODA Loop elements are detailed, and the dark box around Orient and Decide emphasizes where we will focus the bulk of the discussion.

Observations originate from human sources, data, test results, and models about the situation. There are many types of information included in observations: criteria for choosing a course of action (either formal or informal); the importance of, targets for, and other details about the criteria; and evaluation results (ranging from gut feel to formal simulation results and measurements). Regardless of the types of information or level of formality, this information is *uncertain, incomplete, inconsistent,* and *evolving,* and it is *dependent* on who is doing the observing (e.g., two intelligence sources may give conflicting information, two engineers may interpret the results of a simulation differently). Further, some of the information is qualitative and some is quantitative. This informational mess is characteristic of most critical combat, technical, and business situations.

The goal of **Orientation** is to make sense of your observations. This requires understanding them as a basis for choosing the best course of action. In many cases, formal analysis can help reduce the fog, but much information cannot be easily modeled. Thus, managing information to match the human decision maker's needs is crucial.

Orientation is also dependent on *viewpoint.* Even within the same team, how the observations are understood depends on who is trying to understand them. As Boyd pointed out, understanding is dependent on previous experience, cultural traditions, and genetic heritage. Beyond these, understanding is also dependent on one's role in the organization and the team's objectives. Helping a team make sense of the situation and develop a shared understanding, while honoring members' differing viewpoints, is a challenging but necessary part of getting team buy-in and arriving at a robust decision.

Orientation should aid in the sharing of *implicit knowledge and assumptions.* By this I mean that in the effort to make sense of the situation, some of the *implicit* knowledge must become *explicit* and be communicated to others.

Often the OODA Loop stalls because the decision makers are not comfortable with the uncertainty and risk involved. *Managing uncertainty and risk* implies that to resolve such discomfort there is an effort to: 1) measure uncertainty and risk, 2) control as much of it as you can, and 3) minimize the effect of what you cannot control. Traditionally, assessment of risk has been based on past statistics that convey information on the probability of an occurrence (i.e., the uncertainty) and the consequence of it. But many decisions require a look into the evolving future, and such traditional methods for managing risk and uncertainty do not apply. Recently, Bayesian methods have been used to help manage these situations. You will see them in action in chapters 8 through 10 and can explore them in greater detail if you wish in appendix A.

A key part of Orientation is *developing alternative courses of action.* In the words of the French philosopher Emile Chartier, "Nothing is more dangerous than an idea when it is the only one you have."

Making a **Decision** is not a single action; rather, it is a process of *repeatedly deciding what-to-do-next*—Observe more information, do further

Orientation, or take Action. A major component of this is *managed deliberation*, which is synergistic with Orientation, as it is part of sense-making and can help lead to a shared vision of observations. Managed deliberation implies:

- Identifying the areas on which you will focus, based on the benefit of further effort. This is a major sticking point in the OODA Loop. It is often difficult to see where you need to focus more work. The benefit of further work is usually hard to measure, but it should be considered in terms of: 1) anticipated change in the level of satisfaction resulting from a course of action, 2) anticipated change in the risk associated with a course of action, or 3) anticipated consensus or buy-in by management or team members.
- Identifying the cost of further effort: another major sticking point in the OODA Loop. The cost of doing more work is usually measured in the time used and the expense of research, testing, or consultants.
- Identifying areas where consensus is low and impact is high. Often, sticking points are not critical to the decision but people argue over them anyway.
- Finding OODA Loops within OODA Loops, as the decision about what to work on next requires its own OODA activities.

Deciding what-to-do-next requires the *fusion* (i.e., combining or blending) of the orientation results. As is the case with observations, the result of orientation is usually uncertain, incomplete, inconsistent, evolving, and dependent on who is doing the orientation. Somehow, oriented information must be fused to develop a picture of the situation that is cognitively small enough so the team can decide what-to-do-next.

Fusion may be both an analytical effort and a consensus-building effort, so analytical methods range from formal optimization to those that combine the subjective opinions of team members. More important is building a consensus through collaboration, so you can get buy-in on the action you choose. Consensus doesn't necessarily mean locking people in a room until they agree, but it does call for collaboration. As I explained in chapter 1, collaboration requires that the following conditions be met:

- Everyone can paraphrase the issue to show that he or she understands it.
- Everyone has had a chance to contribute to the solution of the problem.
- Everyone has had a chance to describe what is important to him or her.

Those who don't agree with the final decision will be more likely to support the team anyway because they've been included in the decision-making process; they can appreciate the compromise necessary to reach a decision.

The proof of the success of the OODA Loop is in the success of the **Action** taken. The results of this action affect future observations and other adjacent (both concurrent and subsequent) OODA Loops. The action determines the success of the whole process. But as I've said before, many organizations get stuck in a stuttering "OO-OO-OO" and never get to the point of taking action.

The OODA Loop is a handy, informal model for thinking about decision making. To make any decision, you need to Observe and Orient so you can understand and evaluate the situation. Then you need to Decide before taking Action. The majority of this book focuses on the two middle elements of the loop: Orient and Decide. It is here that sticking occurs. We will revisit the OODA Loop in chapter 11, where you will find guidelines for unsticking it.

Decision Matrices in Design for Six Sigma

A very different model of decision making has evolved in product development and is moving rapidly into the business sector. It is called Design for Six Sigma (DFSS), but the methods that make it up have little to do with either design or Six Sigma. In fact, DFSS is a compilation of best practices. One of these, the Decision Matrix (known as Pugh's Method in the DFSS literature), is a very powerful model of formalized decision making. After offering some background on DFSS I will describe this best practice in detail, as it is one of the foundations of the robust decision-making methods developed in this book.

DFSS grew out of traditional Six Sigma quality control efforts. Six Sigma was developed at Motorola in the 1980s and popularized in the 1990s as a way to help ensure that products were manufactured to the highest standards of quality. It uses statistical methods to account for and manage product manufacturing uncertainty and variation. Key to Six Sigma methodology is the five-step DMAIC process (Define, Measure, Analyze, Improve, and Control). Although Six Sigma did bring improved quality to manufactured products, quality begins in the design of products and processes, not in their manufacture.[7] Recognizing this, the Six Sigma community began to emphasize quality earlier in the product development cycle, evolving DFSS in the late 1990s. More recently, it has moved into business and service processes, and DFSS is still an emerging discipline.[8] Based on the demonstrated success of the Six Sigma concept, it has grown rapidly and has become a collection of best practices that go far beyond its original statistical methods.

The phases or steps of DFSS are not universally recognized or defined; almost every company or training organization defines DFSS differently. Like Six Sigma, DFSS is organized into a set of DMAIC-like steps. The problem is that there is little agreement about what these steps are. The acronym DMADV (Define, Measure, Analyze, Decide, and Validate) is commonly used.[9] Drawing a parallel to the OODA Loop, Measure = Observe (most observations are measures of the situation), Analyze = Orient (both reduce the amount of information required for decision making), Decide = Decide and Validate = Act (in the OODA loop, the actions validate the results). There are many acronyms other than DMADV for this evolving discipline. But regardless of their details, all point to the development and optimization of new solutions, with the goal of managing uncertainty throughout the evolution process.

Regardless of whether DFSS is used to develop a product, service, or process, the first steps focus on developing criteria and alternative concepts to evaluate. A major milestone in DFSS is selecting the best concept to develop, the one that best meets the criteria. It is generally agreed that the results at that point greatly affect all quality downstream. Most books and consultants recommend using Pugh's method, a form of Decision Matrix, to support the decision-making process. These methods are very powerful, but they are inconsistent with the DFSS philosophy of measuring and managing uncertainty. As we shall see, they provide no way to account for uncertainty, which is a dominant factor in most decision making.

I will explore the strengths and weaknesses of the Decision Matrix and Pugh's method, as both are simple to use and have proven effective for comparing alternative concepts. The basic forms for the method are shown in figure 2.3, with the Decision Matrix on the left and Pugh's modification on the right. Regardless of which form you use, in essence the method provides a means of scoring each alternative concept in its ability to meet a set of

Criteria	Wt	Alternatives		
		Vendor 1	Vendor 3	Vendor 4
Cost	.30	4	4	4
Response time	.17	3	3	5
Training time	.17	2	4	5
Ease of use	.17	1	4	4
Strong team	.10	3	4	
Team experience	.10	3	4	
Total				
Weighted total				

Criteria	Wt	Alternatives		
		Vendor 1 (Datum)	Vendor 3	Vendor 4
Cost	.30		+	S
Response time	.17		+	+
Training time	.17		-	S
Ease of use	.17		+	+
Strong team	.10		-	-
Team experience	.10		S	-
Pluses	1.0		3	2
Minuses			2	2
Overall total			+1	0
Weighted total			+.37	+.14

Figure 2.3: The two forms of a Decision Matrix.

criteria. Comparing the scores you develop gives you insight into the best alternatives and the most useful information for making your decision.

The Decision Matrix method is an iterative evaluation tool that tests the understanding of criteria, rapidly identifies the strongest alternatives, and helps foster new alternatives. It is most effective if each member of the team performs it independently and the individual results are then compared (*not* averaged—more on this later). The results of the comparison lead to a repetition of the technique, with the iteration continuing until the team is satisfied with the results.

This method consists of five steps that can be easily managed on a computer using a common spreadsheet program. A spreadsheet allows for easy iteration and comparison of team members' evaluations. We will look at the five steps and the difference between the two forms using an example. Initially, we will follow the five steps through the Decision Matrix; then we will see how they are modified in Pugh's variation.

As you read through the steps, you will notice several references to future chapters. This is because, even though this method is quite powerful, it raises many issues that must be addressed further if you are to truly make robust decisions.

We'll use the system selection team's issue introduced in chapter 1: "Select a vendor for a system from among three that remain after filtering out weaker alternatives."

		Wt	Alternatives		
			Vendor 1	Vendor 3	Vendor 4
Criteria	Cost	.30	4	4	4
	Response time	.17	3	3	5
	Training time	.17	2	4	5
	Ease of use	.17	1	4	4
	Strong team	.10	3	4	2
	Team experience	.10	3	4	2
	Total	1.0	16	23	22
	Weighted total		2.8	3.8	3.9

Figure 2.4: Sample Decision Matrix.

Step 1: Develop criteria that measure how well the alternatives resolve the issue. The criteria are listed in rows (seen in figure 2.4). Here the criteria measure cost, response time, etc. Chapter 6 develops more detail on formulating a good set of criteria.

Step 2: Develop importance weightings. This method allows one set of weightings per evaluator. Weights can be set using any of the methods described in chapter 7.

Step 3: Select the alternatives to be evaluated. You would like all the alternatives to be at the same level of abstraction, e.g., all concepts or all refined to practice. If some of the alternatives are refined and well known, and others are less so, you have a problem. For example, how do you compare your current product or process to a new idea when you know only the current product very well—warts and all—and know very little about the other? All newborn babies and ideas are pure, and their weaknesses only become evident as they age and are refined. Using these methods, you cannot account for disparities in levels of knowledge about the alternatives. Chapter 8 further addresses this problem.

There are three alternatives, three vendors, being considered in our example. Vendor 2, conspicuously absent, has been eliminated in screening; it was much weaker than the three remaining alternatives.

Step 4: Evaluate the alternatives. Here, you have some choices to make. One way of evaluating the alternatives versus the criteria is to use a 5-point scale:

5 = meets the criterion very well
4 = meets the criterion well

3 = meets the criterion somewhat

2 = meets the criterion poorly

1 = does not meet the criterion at all

Using this method, figure 2.4 shows one evaluator's results.

Step 5: Compute the level of satisfaction.

For the decision matrix in figure 2.4, two totals can be calculated: the direct sum and the weighted sum. The direct sum is found simply by adding the evaluation scores. The weighted total is the sum of each score multiplied by the weight. Thus, the weighted total for the first alternative, Vendor 1, is:

$$.3 \times 4 + .17 \times 3 + .17 \times 2 + .17 \times 1 + .1 \times 3 + .1 \times 3 = 2.8$$

Both of these totals are measures of the evaluator's level of satisfaction with each alternative relative to the targets implied in the 1-to-5 scale. For Vendor 3, satisfaction is 77%: 23 ÷ 30 (where 30 is the highest possible total) or 76%: 3.8 ÷ 5 (where 5 is the highest possible weighted total). Based on this interpretation, Vendor 3 is slightly better than Vendor 4 using the sum, and slightly worse using the weighted total, and Vendor 1 appears to be out of the running. As we shall see, there is more to be learned here.

Stuart Pugh proposed a second way to do this.[10] He disliked the 1-to-5 scale because it required absolute comparisons to targets that may not be clearly understood or stated. His way around this problem was to consider one of the alternatives as a datum and compare the other alternatives to it.

This doesn't indicate how good any one alternative is relative to any target, only how well the current set of alternatives compare to each other on a feature-by-feature basis. Using Pugh's approach, rather than the 1-to-5 scale, each alternative being evaluated is judged to be either better than, about the same as, or worse than a datum. If the concept is better than the datum, it is given a plus (+) score. If it is judged to be about the same as the datum or if there is some ambivalence, an S (same) is used. If the concept doesn't meet the criterion as well as the datum does, it is given a minus (-) score. If you do this on a spreadsheet, then +1, 0, and –1 can be used for scoring. Some evaluators extend the method and use "++" for alternatives that are much better and "– –" for those that are much worse. The sample problem is shown in Pugh's format in figure 2.5, in which Vendor 1 is considered a datum.

Using Pugh's formulation, you can generate four scores: the number of

		Wt	Alternatives		
			Vendor 1	Vendor 3	Vendor 4
Criteria	Cost	.30	**Datum**	+	S
	Response time	.17		+	+
	Training time	.17		-	S
	Ease of use	.17		+	+
	Strong team	.10		-	-
	Team experience	.10		S	-
	Pluses	1.0		3	2
	Minuses			2	2
	Overall total			+1	0
	Weighted total			+.37	+.14

Figure 2.5: An example of Pugh's Matrix.

plus scores, the number of minus scores, the overall total, and the weighted total. The overall total is the difference between the number of plus scores and the number of minus scores. This is an estimate of the decision-makers' satisfaction with the alternative relative to the datum. You can also compute the weighted total. This is the sum of each score multiplied by the importance weighting, in which an S counts as 0, each + as + 1, and each – as –1. Neither the weighted nor the unweighted scores are to be treated as absolute measures of the concept's value; they are relative to Vendor 1 and for guidance only.

The scores can be interpreted in a number of ways:

- If a concept or group of similar concepts has a good overall total score or a high + total score, it is important to notice what strengths it exhibits—that is, which criteria it meets better than the datum. Likewise, groupings of scores will show which requirements are especially hard to meet.
- If most concepts get the same score on a certain criterion, examine that criterion closely. You may need to develop more knowledge in the area of the criterion in order to differentiate between alternatives. It may be that the criterion does not measure anything that can help you differentiate among the alternatives. Or the criterion may be ambiguous, interpreted differently by different members of the team, or unevenly interpreted from concept to concept. If the criterion has a low

importance weighting, then don't spend much time clarifying it. But if it is important, you need to either generate better concepts or clarify it.

- To learn even more, redo the comparisons, with the highest-scoring concept used as the new datum. This iteration should be redone until a clearly "best" concept (or concepts) emerges.
- Develop new alternatives by using the high scores or pluses to identify features of the current alternatives that might be combined to develop new, even better alternatives.

After each team member has completed this procedure, the entire team should compare individual results. The results can vary widely, since neither the concepts nor the requirements may be refined. Discussion among the members of the group should result in a few concepts to refine. If it doesn't, the group should either clarify the criteria or generate more concepts for evaluation. Warning! Do not average evaluations, as it is like mixing paint and you will only get brown.[11] It's better to discuss the differences and iterate.

The Decision Matrix and Pugh's variation on it work quite well and can be done on a spreadsheet. Their strengths are:

- They force you to itemize and articulate your criteria. This provides a forum for team members to ensure that they use the same basis for their evaluations.
- They force you to consider all of the alternatives relative to a consistent set of measures.
- They provide a way to include the relative importance of the criteria, offering a viewpoint with which to weight the evaluation results.
- They provide a way to combine the evaluations into a single satisfaction score, helping team members to visualize the relative value of each alternative.
- They are flexible. Adding or deleting alternatives or criteria is not difficult.
- They give some limited guidance about what-to-do-next to reach a decision.

The limitations of these types of decision matrixes are:

- They can't include uncertainty, or the fact that you may know more about some of the alternatives than you do about the others. This limitation is not consistent with Six Sigma robust decisions philosophies of managing uncertainty and variation.
- They can't manage incomplete information; you have to evaluate against all the criteria regardless of whether or not you know anything about them.
- It is difficult to mix qualitative and quantitative evaluation results. Where some features may be evaluated qualitatively and others may be the result of simulations and analysis, there is no way to fuse these results, and all must be reduced to qualitative evaluations.
- It is difficult to combine different team members' evaluations.
- It is assumed that all criteria can be traded off. Poor performance relative to one criterion can be traded off for good performance relative to another criterion. There is no way to manage critical criteria (discriminating criteria that cannot be traded off), as satisfaction is measured as either a sum or a weighted sum. This will be further addressed in chapter 9.
- The underlying mathematics can lead to a less-than-best result. This shortfall is addressed in subsequent chapters.

In summary, the Decision Matrix is very powerful, but limited. In fact, in 1995, my dissatisfaction with the Decision Matrix was what led me to develop the methods in this book.

Matching the Method to the Issue

I began this chapter with Franklin's method and then described the OODA model of the decision-making process. I followed this with the Decision Matrix and Pugh's method. These are examples of how to support the Orientation and Decision elements of the OODA Loop. In fact, as we progress through this book, we will encounter other methods to accomplish this. Some are the works of others and some are introduced here for the first time.

With such a variety of decision-making methods available, it is a challenge to select the best one to use. There are ten measures that can help you choose. The first five focus on the characteristics of the issue being addressed and the second five focus on the desired results. Taken together, these ten measures can help in choosing the best possible support system for making a particular decision.

The following measures characterize the issue you need to solve:

1   Available time

There are some decisions you need to make in a heartbeat: fight or flight; jump out of the way of the speeding car or save the baby; respond to your boss's stupid statement; or bite your tongue. For other decisions, you may have minutes or hours, and spending any more time may begin to use resources beyond the value of the decision. In some cases there may be a trade-off between the quality of the decision and the time taken to support it. In technology and business it is sometimes perfectly acceptable, even mandatory, to spend weeks or months doing simulations and optimization to ensure the best possible decisions. Based on this discussion, one measure for choosing the most appropriate method is to answer this question: When is the decision needed—instantly, in an hour, tomorrow, next week, or later?

2   Issue size

Some problems have very few alternatives and important criteria to consider, whereas others are more complex. Fight or flight offers two alternatives, while deciding which new product ideas to invest in may have hundreds. There are methods that work best with small problems and others that are appropriate for more complex issues.

3   Information distribution

For many problems, you have all the information you need, you require minimal outside input, and you are empowered to carry out the decision. In other situations, the information you need to make a decision is distributed among many people in an organization, and/or you need others' buy-in to implement the decision. Further, in many modern organizations, decision making is done by people in different locations and time zones. Based on these factors, to choose a decision-support methodology it is important to know how many people will contribute to the deliberation and their distribution by time and distance.

4   Evaluation support

Some problems are purely qualitative—pick the prettiest flower, the most suitable house to live in, etc. Others are quantitative and can be reduced to a set of equations. A decision-support method must be compatible with the type of evaluation information being used. Some can work only with qualitative information, others only with the results of numerical simulations (i.e., qualitative information), and still others with a mix of the two.

5   Information certainty

This book focuses on the importance of information certainty, or rather the general lack of certainty. Decisions based on certain information are generally easier to make than those characterized by high uncertainty (although you can still get stuck when choosing a new car, even with all the specification sheets in front of you). Most decision-management methods assume that all information is deterministic; it has no variation or uncertainty. Some methods add a form of sensitivity analysis to the results to check for the effects of uncertainty; but doing this is too little and too late. A few methods (those developed in this book) assume that all information is uncertain and that this uncertainty must be accounted for from the beginning. It is critical to match the level of uncertainty in the situation to the method used. Many methods that ignore uncertainty will inspire a feeling of confidence about a potentially wrong choice.

There are an additional five measures of desired results. These help you answer the Five Decision Questions that I posed in chapter 1:

1   Which is the best alternative?
2   What is the risk that our decision will not turn out as we expect?
3   Do we know enough to make a good decision yet?
4   Is there buy-in for the decision?
5   What do we need to do next to feel confident about our decision, within the scope of our limited resources?

Based on these five questions, an ideal decision-support system provides:

6   Identification of the best alternative

Ideally, a decision-support system will guide you to the best possible choice from among the alternatives considered. It may not directly say "Choose option A," but it will guide you to it.

7 Identification of the risk involved in accepting the choice

Ideally, you would like to know how much risk there is that you are going to make an inferior choice.

8 Understanding of the level of knowledge that supports the choice

It is imperative that you understand what the choice is based on. If it is based on uncertain, incomplete, and conflicting information, then you need to know how uncertain, incomplete, and conflicting it is and how this affects your decision.

9 Indication of team consensus

The term "consensus" is a catchall term for how well the system helps build a shared understanding of the problem and creates buy-in and accountability among team members.

10 Guidance about what-to-do-next

Knowing what-to-do-next is as important as knowing what to choose. An ideal system offers a strategy that will guide you though the decision-making process and lead you to a robust decision.

You can use these ten measures as a basis for choosing the most appropriate method to address any problem. In a rough sense, the flowchart in figure 2.6 is based on the most important measures. If the uncertainty is anything but "very low," only the methods in the dashed box, those developed in this book, can help. But each of the methods suggested in the diagram is covered in this book, at least on an introductory level. Table 2.1 serves as a guide to where you will find a discussion of each method.

Note that the Analytical Hierarchy Process is listed in the table but not shown on the flow chart.

Method	Chapter
Intuition	8
Franklin	2
Evaporating Cloud	5
Optimization	8
Decision Matrix	2
Analytical Hierarchy Process	7
Decision Matrix with Belief Maps	8
Bayesian Team Support	9-10

Table 2.1: Methods by chapter.

Although it has features worth studying and understanding, it has serious drawbacks and I don't recommend it; hence, it does not appear in the diagram.

Two major points that the flowchart raises are *uncertainty* and *teams*. These are so important that both are covered in subsequent chapters. Only after we consider these can work begin on structuring the decision-making process to support the OODA Loop and DFSS, and to develop robust decisions.

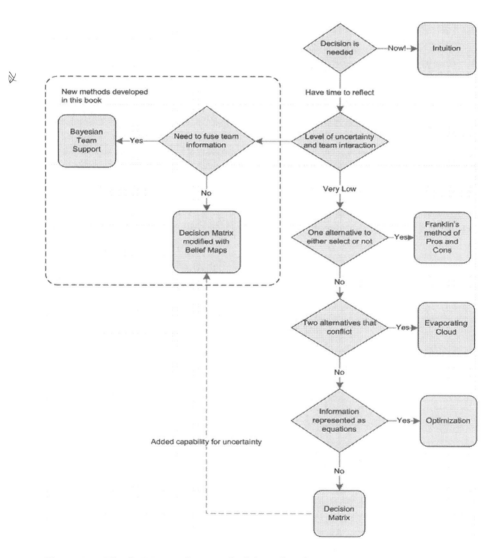

Figure 2.6: The decision-making methodology flowchart.

Often Wrong But Never in Doubt
—Making Estimates in an Uncertain World

3

*I*n Benjamin Franklin's letter to Joseph Priestly from chapter 2 he describes a decision-making method to address "the uncertainty that perplexes us." Franklin recognized that making good decisions was all about managing uncertainty. But few books or methods really address how to support information that is based on best estimates of past performance, assessments of the current situation, and visions of the future. **Where past performance may be known, the present is obscured by its immediacy and the future is a best guess.** In other words, very little is known with certainty; everything else is an uncertain estimate. The robustness of any decision and the level of risk incurred in making it can only be as good as the estimates upon which it is based. Some examples will help set the stage for examining estimation in detail, as well as the uncertainty that makes it difficult and the risks that are incurred.

For the first example, let's say that you're in the market for a new car. You're considering several, and have test driven a couple of them. You have just found out about a new model that will be introduced next year. You saw a fuzzy photo of this concept car in the newspaper, along with an article containing a vague description of its performance and an implication that it will be in your price range.

Suppose your main criteria for a new car are: initial cost, quality, mileage, and visual appeal. Your immediate decision is whether to add this car to your list of alternatives, realizing that it won't be available for a while (availability is another criteria that may be important to you).

Obviously, there is high uncertainty in your estimates of all the important criteria. For example, the car appears to be in a class that gets in the range of 25 to 28 miles per gallon (mpg), but the article said that, due to some new technologies, this car will do better. Based on all the information you have, your best guess is that it will get 30 mpg. It may do as well as 35 mpg or as poorly as 27 mpg. These three values—30, 35, and 27—indicate your uncertainty about mileage.

The manufacturer of another car you are considering lists its mileage at 27 mpg on its Web site. But your estimate of the mileage based on this information may still be uncertain; you may not trust manufacturer's numbers. You may conclude that your best estimate is 27 mpg, that it certainly won't be any better, and that, based on your knowledge about this manufacturer, it may be as low as 24 mpg.

Say that an independent consumer's group has tested a third car on your list, and that your buddy owns one. All data from these sources point to a mileage of 29 mpg ±1 mpg.

If you assume that all the data on these cars represent a distribution of uncertainty, they would look something like figure 3.1.

There are similar uncertain data available to use in evaluating the other measurable features of the cars you are considering buying. Additionally, subjective factors such as visual appeal will also be uncertain, especially since you have only seen a single, poor-quality picture of Car 1, the concept car.

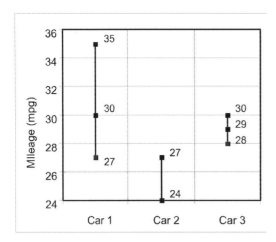

Figure 3.1: Mileage.

There are three key points to consider in this example:

1   High uncertainty can be caused by lack of knowledge, as is the case with Car 1. While the uncertainty might easily be reduced by speaking to experts or reading reports, sometimes it can only be reduced by research and extensive effort, and sometimes it can't be reduced at all.

2   When something is well known and understood, as with Car 3, the uncertainty will be in the variation between individual cars. I will discuss this further later in the chapter.

3 As is often the case, with Car 2 you have a mix of lack of knowledge and variation.

Before you write this example off as too simplistic, or not representative of the kinds of information on which you base decisions, itemize a couple of important factors you used in a recent real-life decision and note the most likely estimate—the best you can expect, and the worst. Then note whether the uncertainty you faced was due to lack of knowledge or just the natural variation among things.

A Simple Estimation Problem

You have just had a dinner party and the stir fry, salad, fresh bread, apple pie, and coffee were all great. Your guests have gone and it's time to clean up. Your dishwasher is broken and you need to hand-wash the dishes, silver, and pans listed below and put them on the drying rack next to the sink. The dishes have been sitting stacked randomly in the sink and on the counter for a couple of hours, but no food is burned on.

You need to clean:

- 4 large dinner plates
- 4 dessert plates
- 4 sets of silver (2 forks, knife, and spoon each)
- 4 sets of coffee cups and saucers
- 4 salad bowls
- 2 serving bowls
- Salad tongs

- Bread knife
- Pie serving knife
- 1 wok
- 1 sauce pan
- 1 pie pan
- 1 bread pan
- 1 cream pitcher
- 1 serving spoon

You have a sponge, scrub brush, dishwashing soap, and plenty of hot and cold water. After stacking the clean dishes in the drying rack, you need to make sure that the 40-inch (100cm) square countertop and sink are also clean.

Estimate how many minutes it will take you to clean up the kitchen. _____

How many times have you hand-washed dishes in the last 100 days? _____

Thank you for your estimate.

Name_____ Organization _____

Email _____ Phone _____

Figure 3.2: Sample questionnaire.

Another example demonstrates the difficulty in estimating the time it takes to do an easy task that you have not done before. I have done a simple experiment, using the questionnaire shown in figure 3.2, in which I ask people to estimate how long it would take them to clean up a stack of dishes.

Before you read on, I suggest you make your own estimate about cleaning the number of dirty dishes listed in figure 3.2. Then, to put it in perspective, reflect on the complexity of this task relative to other tasks you are involved in.

I gave this questionnaire to a group of fifty people and reduced the results to find the best normal distribution curve for the data, which is shown in figure 3.3.[1] The mean estimate of this distribution is 32 minutes and the standard deviation is 10 minutes. This result implies that, assuming the normal distribution shown, there is 50% chance that it will take longer than 32 minutes and a 50% chance that it will take less time. Further, there is an 84% probability that the dishes will take less than 42 minutes to do (the mean plus one standard deviation, or 32 +10 min) and there is a 90% chance that they will take less than 45 minutes to do.

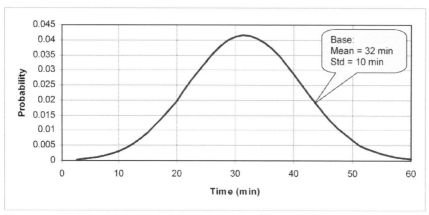

Figure 3.3: Estimates in response to questionnaire (figure 3.2).

These results bring up many questions. First, if you made your own estimate as I suggested, where does it fall on this distribution curve? Then, is the 32-minute estimate any better or worse than yours? And how long will it actually take someone to do these dishes?

One aspect of figure 3.3 should be troubling to you. Washing dishes is a simple task that has been done many times. In fact, in my experiment, 60% of the respondents had hand-washed dishes more than twenty times in the preceding 100 days. Yet there was a wide variation in the time estimates among respondents. How does that make you feel about estimates for more complex tasks? With this experiment in mind, how confident do you think you'll feel next time a colleague or a vendor says, "It will take about two weeks"? What does such an estimate mean? And if you asked another person who gave you a different value, what could you say about these two values? It gets even worse; we will revisit the dish washing experiment later in this chapter and you will see additional effects of uncertainty on the estimated time needed to complete the task.

Certainty Is an Error on Your Part

I borrowed the title of this section from a quote by Richard Feynman: "If you thought that science was certain—well that is just an error on your part." A central premise of this book is that the information on which most decisions are based is uncertain; there is uncertainty in everything.

The following pages define some of the terminology used throughout the rest of the book. I must state up front that the word "uncertainty" has multiple meanings and can get entangled with "variation" and "risk." Let's clarify these terms.

I have established that decisions are based on uncertain information. In this context, "information" is any data, models, opinions, or knowledge and "uncertainty" is any doubt, variation, change, or inconsistency in the information. The information in question can be of any kind—written, drawn, verbal, or even knowledge that is implicit and not articulated.

Information uncertainty has three main sources, as shown in figure 3.4: human cognition, the environment, and variation. The categories listed on this map were developed from many different fields and sources.[2]

Cognitive Sources

The mental or cognitive information that people bring to each decision is uncertain. This uncertainty is caused by five factors. The first three apply to both individuals making decisions and to teams. The last two apply only to teams.

1   Knowledge limitations: The more knowledge you have, the higher the certainty in your estimates—sometimes. (Sometimes more knowledge opens your eyes to uncertainty you were not even aware of.) The less knowledge you have, the higher your un-certainty, always. Sometimes this form of uncertainty is called

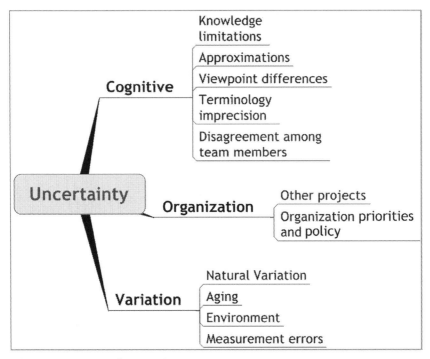

Figure 3.4: Sources of uncertainty

"ambiguity" or "epistemic uncertainty" (*episteme* is Greek for knowledge). If you try to determine the cost of Car 1 from its description in the newspaper, you can only guess; this is highly uncertain. You can gain more knowledge by looking up the price at the manufacturer's web site. This will give you a better idea, but there is still some uncertainty. When the car is available, you can go to a dealer and further refine the price, but until a contract is signed there is still a level of uncertainty about the price. In general, you can only reduce knowledge uncertainty by more modeling, additional expertise, or other forms of learning. However, as I will discuss in an example in chapter 8 taken from the Wright Brothers' notes, sometimes more knowledge opens your eyes to additional uncertainty. All efforts to reduce uncertainty require time and other resources. Later, also in chapter 8, I will address this question: When is it worthwhile to expend additional resources to improve the certainty of your knowledge?

2 **Approximations**: Approximation uncertainty arises because mental, analytical, and physical models are only simplified versions of the real world. Often, the level of approximation of

an analytical model is referred to as its **fidelity**.
Fidelity is a measure
of how well a model or
simulation represents the
state and behavior of a
real-world object. For example, up until the late
seventeenth century, all
military calculations of
cannonball trajectories
were computed as if the

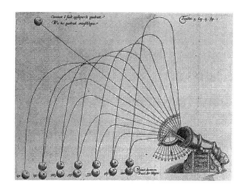

Figure 3.5: Trajectories.

projectile went up in a straight line, then followed a circular
arc, and then followed another straight line straight down to the
target (see figure 3.5). These were low-fidelity simulations. However, in the late fifteenth century Leonardo da Vinci knew this
model was wrong—that the trajectory was actually parabolic—and
developed more accurate methods to compute the impact point.[3]
Even though he didn't have the mathematics to write the equations to describe his conclusions, his simulations were of better
fidelity than preceding ones. It wasn't until Galileo that the parabolic model was developed and higher-fidelity estimates could
be made. These were later refined by Newton, and even later by
the addition of the effects of aerodynamic drag and higher-order
dynamics.

Back-of-the-envelope calculations are low fidelity, whereas
detailed simulations—hopefully—have high fidelity. Experts often
run simulations to predict performance and cost. At the early
stages in projects, these simulations are usually at low levels of
fidelity, and some may be qualitative. Increasing fidelity requires
increased refinement and increased project costs. Increased
knowledge generally comes with increased fidelity, but not
necessarily; it is possible to use a high-fidelity simulation to
model "garbage" and thus do nothing to reduce uncertainty.

3 Viewpoint differences: People's estimation of any situation is col-
ored by their viewpoint—the organization or field they represent.
The marketing manager thinks that look and feel is most important, the engineer thinks it's functionality, and the CFO is sure

it's cost. None is right and all are right, and this results in an uncertain picture of what is important. There are ways to make use of viewpoint differences to strengthen buy-in, which I describe later in the book.

4 **Terminology imprecision**: Imprecision arises when inexact terms are used to describe things when communicating about a project. Since each discipline may use different jargon, it is often a challenge to find out, for example, that one person's net cost is another's gross cost.

5 Disagreement among team members: Team members' interpretations of the available information may be different or conflicting. Conflicting interpretations occur naturally due to differences in background, role in the project, interpretation of the information, expertise, and problem-solving style. Conflicts are neither good nor bad; they are just different interpretations of the available information. Conflicting interpretation is different from conflicting viewpoint, and we will handle them differently.

Organization Sources

The second source of uncertainty is the organization itself.

- **Other projects:** Dependence on other projects or tasks adds uncertainty because of the availability, certainty, and quality of information derived from them.
- **Organization priorities and policies:** Organizations create uncertainty both through their procedures and their instability. We have all been on projects that were cancelled or radically altered by an organization. Although it may seem difficult to insulate a project from organizational changes, well-defined projects that are making good progress—on schedule, within cost, and headed toward their expected features and functions—are least likely to be cancelled, changed, or otherwise tinkered with.

Variation Sources

Variation occurs in all information, even if the level of knowledge is high and the organization is stable. Variation has four causes.

- **Natural variation** (i.e., stochastic uncertainty or statistical variation): Natural variation is the result of the fact that all things behave in random ways. The weather will change, material properties are not constant, even the time it takes to do the dishes will vary. In manufacturing, the term "variation" is the actual fluctuation in measured output as a process is repeated. In projects that have not occurred before, the **variation is the *anticipated* fluctuation in output as the process is repeated**. In our example earlier in this chapter, the anticipated variation in Car 3's mileage is expressed as a standard deviation.
- **Aging**: Often duration, cost, performance, or another property will vary with time. For mechanical products made of plastics, for example, strength will usually degrade. For business processes, the time an activity takes may shorten with repetition.
- **Environment**: Environmental effects can cause properties to vary. These may be changes in temperature, wind, the organization in which the decision is made (as discussed above), which engineer you get on the project, who is sick this week, etc.
- **Measurement errors**: Statistical variation arises from random error in measurements of a given quantity.

Common Cause and Special Cause

Superimposed on this list of uncertainty causes are the concepts of "common cause" and "special cause." W. Edwards Deming, one of the fathers of modern product quality, popularized these terms to force differentiation between uncertainties that can be controlled and those that can't. Here, I apply these definitions to all the causes of uncertainty, not just variation. According to Deming's model:

> **Common Cause** is uncertainty resulting from chance causes in the system. Common causes are the noises that cannot easily be controlled. For example, it may take you five minutes to process certain paperwork one day and six the next. Or, the car you design may be driven by a teenager sometimes, and a little old lady at other times. Resources put into managing common cause uncertainty are generally wasted. Instead, you should make decisions that are as insensitive as possible to common causes.

Special Cause is uncertainty resulting from an assignable cause. Special causes are generally controllable—if you know about them.

There are really two types of special causes, known-unknowns and unknown-unknowns (commonly called "unk-unks"). The known-unknowns, such as the possibility of bad weather causing shipping delays, you can plan for. The unk-unks—a change in direction by management, or a competitor developing a new technology—are more difficult to foresee and are directly tied to a lack of knowledge about the future.

Each type of uncertainty may have both common and special parts. The challenge is to tease these apart. In general, you can't control common cause uncertainty, and attempting to control it is a mistake. Since common cause is just chance effects in the system, it will be expensive or impossible to control, and not possible to eliminate. You can control special causes to some degree if you expend enough resources on doing so and build in enough buffers to reduce their impact. You must determine the cost/benefit of doing so before you commit resources to try to control special causes. Table 3.1 lists examples of the types of uncertainty we have discussed, and whether they are common or special cause uncertainties.

Uncertain situation	Type of uncertainty	Common or special cause
You have decided to develop a new system and only have textbook knowledge about the discipline	Knowledge limitation	Special cause
You develop a set of equations that represent the economics of a proposed business unit	Approximation—depends on fidelity	Special cause
You write a set of equations that well represent the time it will take to do a well understood task and run these across many different likely situations (e.g. Monte Carlo simulations)	Approximation	Common cause
You and Fred disagree about which is most important, cost or speed	Viewpoint differences or disagreement among team members	Special cause
A project that was going to supply you information is behind schedule	Other projects	Special cause
The time it takes a fast food chain to make a hamburger	Statistical variation	Common cause
The time it takes you to go up a flight of stairs	Aging	Common cause

Table 3.1: Examples of uncertainty.

All of the causes of uncertainty **evolve** with time; thus, their effect on decisions changes. Figure 3.6 shows a graphical way to visualize this. Here uncertainty is plotted against the time, money, or effort necessary to reduce it. Starting at the left, early in a decision, cognitive uncertainty is generally dominant, but as you learn more and put decisions into action, variation becomes the dominant uncertainty. Organization uncertainty can have an effect throughout a project's evolution.

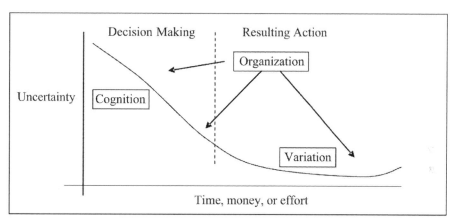

Figure 3.6: Uncertainty through time.

To illustrate the interplay of uncertainties, let's say that you need to develop a process for handling some function within your organization. This is a new function for both you and the organization. Early on, you develop three concepts from which to choose. Then you need to learn enough about these concepts to make the decision. After you choose one and begin to refine it, your knowledge increases, and as you put it into practice any uncertainty you encounter is now due to variation. But at any time, another project or some other organizational factor can greatly alter the robustness of any decisions you have made.

As uncertainty decreases, there is still some common-cause uncertainty, with its lower limit being the boundary between common and special causes. In other words, there will always be some common cause variation, no matter how refined the system or process. Any additional effort you make to reduce the common causes will have little effect. At the right end of the plot, the tail increases just to remind us that aging, organizational effects, and other factors may increase uncertainty at any time.

Estimates of the Unknown Future

All decisions are based on best estimates. It makes no difference whether you are estimating time, cost, performance, or any other factor; in order to make robust decisions it is essential to understand how much uncertainty there is in them. Next, I will explain why estimates are so difficult to make and offer a vocabulary for managing them.

Types of Estimates

Not all estimates are alike. Estimating your friend's weight is not the same as estimating the time required to design the *Cassini* spacecraft. It's important to classify estimates in order to understand what you can control and what you can't, and how estimates impact your decisions.

Fact Estimates

In the opening of his book *The Wisdom of Crowds*, James Surowiecki relates the story of Francis Galton observing a contest at a country fair.[4] The crowd was asked to wager on the weight of the meat that would result when an ox was slaughtered. They wrote their estimates on cards and submitted them with the understanding that the closest estimate would get part of the meat. Galton took the 787 total estimates and averaged them. The average estimate was 1,197 pounds, compared to the actual weight of 1,198 pounds.

This is a good example of estimating a simple fact—something that has already happened or already exists. Other examples are estimating the number of beans in a jar, the number of trees in a forest, or another parameter that can later be checked. The tendency for group estimates to be superior to individual estimates is well documented. One of Surowiecki's premises is that crowds can do a pretty good job of estimating facts even if they are not particularly expert in the field—if there are enough estimates to average. While this is not particularly germane to most business or technical decisions, it is the most basic form of estimation.

Analysis Estimates

Some fact estimates go beyond a single value, requiring not only an estimate of multiple values, but also of the physics or economics involved. These types of estimates generally require some form of analysis or simulation, or may be based on the results of experimentation. What is most frightening about many analytical estimates is:

- They are sometimes done with little awareness of fidelity.
- They are usually done deterministically (based on a single value), with little modeling of uncertainty (which requires a distribution).
- The results are usually believed regardless of fidelity or uncertainty.

The following example should help clarify these concepts. A theory has been proposed that you can estimate the closing value (CV) of a stock on a given day based on the opening value (OV) and the midday value (MV). This theory suggests that you plot a straight line through these two points, OV and MV, to estimate the CV. So the model is CV = 2*MV − OV. Let's say that this morning GE opened at $34.05 and by midday it was up to $34.27. Using the formula, GE should be $34.49 by closing. Unfortunately, though, it falls to $33.90. Why? Because this crude model is a very low-fidelity (linear) model of a complex situation. Further, if you did want to develop a model that used a straight line, which may not be bad in and of itself, you should base it on the distribution of the difference between the midday value and the opening value taken over some time rather than a single, current day's value. This way, you will have an idea about the probability that $34.49 will be achieved and, if it is sufficiently high, how much you might want to invest.

For many estimates it is not possible to write a set of equations that represents its physics, but other forms of analysis may help. In May 1968 the nuclear submarine USS *Scorpion* (SSN-589) failed to arrive as expected at her home port of Norfolk, Virginia. The United States Navy was convinced that the vessel had been lost off the Eastern seaboard, but an extensive search based on the best estimates of its position failed to discover the wreck. As is detailed in the book *Blind Man's Bluff*, John Craven, a naval intelligence officer, used Bayesian probabilistic method to estimate its location—some distance from where the Navy had been searching.[5] He developed this model by asking many experts what they thought had happened to the submarine and fusing their opinions to develop a probabilistic grid of where to search. Craven was able to identify a most likely location, and after much reluctance the Navy searched the area and found the wreckage within 220 yards (200 meters) of where it was estimated to be. Craven's problem of not having a simulation to rely on is common to many business and technical situations. Yet he was able to combine estimates by a team of experts to develop a probabilistic model that led the Navy to the location.

Craven used the wisdom of an expert "crowd" and analytically combined their best estimates of the situation.

Common Process Estimates

Process estimates are about time and money. Some processes are common enough—they have occurred enough times—that there is statistical data on how long they take or how much they cost. These processes are dominated by common-cause variation. When you take your car in to a shop to get it repaired, an "estimator" gives you a cost estimate for the repair. This estimate is based on statistics about how long the same type of service has taken over an extensive history of prior repairs, multiplied by the hourly salary of the shop's technician. Companies compile historical data and supply single values to shops so they can safely estimate how long your repair will take. The single number is one that predicts the time it will take to make the repair with a 70 to 80% probability. Sometimes (20 to 30% of the time) it will take longer and the shop will lose money. Most of the time, the repair takes less time and the shop makes a little extra. These percentages are found in a manner similar to the dish washing estimate we saw earlier, but are based on historical data, not estimated times. Building cars, making hamburgers, and many other common activities can be estimated fairly accurately this way.

However, for many public works projects, estimates for common tasks are much worse than they should be. One study of 258 projects found that public works projects' costs average 28% higher than estimated, with the likelihood of actual costs being larger than estimated at 86%, and lower than or equal to estimated costs at 14%. As of 2002, Boston's Big Dig was 300% over estimated cost.[6] These results are partly due to the dominance of special-cause variation (think politics) and partly due to the fact that low estimates are made on purpose. If accurate estimates were made initially, many public works projects would never be approved for funding.

Even though engineers should have been able to develop fairly accurate estimates for these projects, other factors intervened. We will explore these later in this chapter.

New process estimates

If the estimates you are making are for a new process, estimating the time and cost for activities you have never undertaken before, then they are likely to be fairly poor.

Consider the following. An annual analysis of IT projects, called "The Chaos Report," shows that for 2004, 51% were delivered late or over budget and an additional 15% were cancelled. Further, projects completed by large companies had only 42% of the originally designed features and functions.[7] And in fact, features and functions are often jettisoned during a project to help meet schedule and budget. This is often referred to as "de-scoping," and some organizations build de-scoping into their original plans. It should be noted that "The Chaos Report" numbers may actually be worse than stated, as they are self-reported and therefore self-serving.

Project type	Average Overrun
Very Small	31%
Small	19%
Medium	34%
Large	81%
Very large	315%

Table 3.2: Cost overruns

In one large government agency that develops new technologies with high uncertainty, cost overruns have historically been as high as 315%, as shown in Table 3.2.[8] This is approximately a factor of pi (3.1415); thus, an inside joke was embodied in the adjacent icon, which one staff person devised.

Unfortunately, when vendors saw this they were led to assume that overruns of this size were to be expected. This is a form of *anchoring*, which I will discuss shortly.

The dish washing estimate you made earlier was an example of a new process estimate because it was new to you.[9] If the identical stack of dishes had been washed repeatedly and the washing timed, then it would be a common process and you would have data to estimate the expected time.

The key point here is that estimates about new processes made with low-fidelity analyses are dominated by uncertainty. Since most important decisions in business and technology concern the development of new products and processes, uncertainty must be a major consideration in any deliberation.

Causes of Estimate Inaccuracy

The major factors that affect estimations can be seen as the layers of an "onion" in figure 3.7. By exploring these you can develop the rationale behind many of the inaccuracies described earlier and set the stage for how to best manage information to keep errors to a minimum. In this section, each of the layers of the onion will be broken down to show the major causes of estimation error.

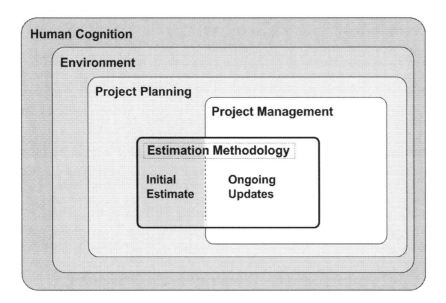

Figure 3.7: The Estimation Onion.

Human Cognition

Cognitive limitations affect every estimate, and thus every decision. There are five major cognitive limitations shown in figure 3.8. The first cause of estimate inaccuracy is **weak accounting for uncertainty.**

The examples of estimates I've given so far in this chapter are not very accurate; the initial estimates do not compare very well with the actual final values. However, this definition of an "accurate estimate" is flawed, and the flaw is important to understand. When asked to estimate something, people generally respond with a single value: "three days," "two weeks,"

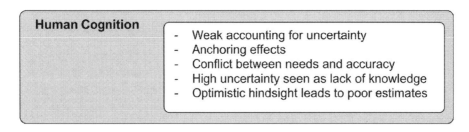

Figure 3.8: Human Cognition.

etc. Sometimes they add a qualifier that communicates something about the certainty of the estimation (e.g., "about," "in the range of," "near," "should be"). Even dictionaries are not clear about the need for this uncertainty qualifier. Merriam-Webster gives as part of its definition of "estimate" 1) "an opinion or judgment of the nature, character, or quality of a person or thing," 2) "numerical value obtained from a statistical sample and assigned to a population parameter," and 3) "a statement of the cost of work to be done." Note that although the first and third definitions suggest that an estimate is a single value, the second definition implies that there is distribution associated with it, requiring the need for information about its certainty.

Further, the statement "It will take three days" does not convey whether this is a 50% certain estimate (half the time it is estimated to take longer, half shorter), a 90% certain estimate (with a 90% chance it will be done in three days) or some other percentage.[10]

To explore this shortcoming, let's reconsider the dish washing problem. Rather than asking respondents to "estimate how many minutes it will take you to clean up the kitchen" as before, I asked a new group of people to "estimate how many minutes so that you are 50% sure you will be finished cleaning up the kitchen." Their results, and those for a third group who was asked to "estimate how many minutes so that you are 90% sure you will be finished cleaning up the kitchen," are shown in figure 3.9.

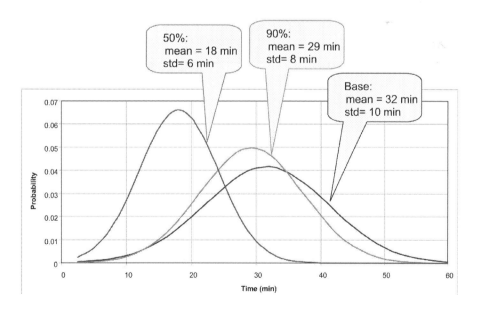

Figure 3.9: Probability and time

Here, for the limited sample, the initial question and the 90% question elicited approximately the same mean and the 50% estimate was about half as much. There are two conclusions to draw from these results. First, when only asked to make an estimate for a simple task, people generally give a result they are fairly sure they can meet: i.e., about 90% sure. Second, if you force people to give you a 50%, they do so fairly well at about half the 90% estimate. But all these estimates are very noisy and these conclusions are based on very sparse data. However, statistically this is consistent if the mean values are normally distributed.[11]

So the estimate that you get is highly dependent on how you ask the question. Does any of this tell you how long it will actually take to *do* the dishes? Not really, because in the final analysis it depends on who does them, the pressure to get them done, the quality of the final job, how much the person is interrupted, and many other factors. Actually, the situation is even worse than this simple example implies, as I will demonstrate when we look at more factors that affect estimates.

All this leads to the conclusion that the term "estimation accuracy" is problematic. Nonetheless, it is in common use and generally defined as the difference between the initial **mean estimate** and the final actual value (or mean value if the task is done more than once). This definition applies to time, cost, performance, and all other factors that must be estimated to make a decision. Note that the mean estimate can be for 90% surety, 50% surety, or any other stated or unstated percentage.

Anchoring sets a biased context for estimation.[12] Anchoring occurs, for example, when a manager asks for an estimate via a question or statement that includes a predetermined amount for the estimate: "I don't see how we could commit more than $10,000 to this." $10,000 now becomes the anchor point. This stated amount biases all the following estimates that are generated.

Anchoring can happen in subtle ways. Let's say you are bidding on a project and you have been led to believe that the customer has a ceiling of, say, $10,000. You are now anchored to this value and will try to force your project to fit it. This only seems logical, but it has interesting effects, as I will show in the "W" model discussed in the next section.

To demonstrate anchoring, I modified the dish washing experiment again. I asked a group of subjects how long it would take to clean the dishes as before, but this time with the addition of "Your partner has told you that the kitchen needs to be clean in 15 minutes." This anchoring resulted in a

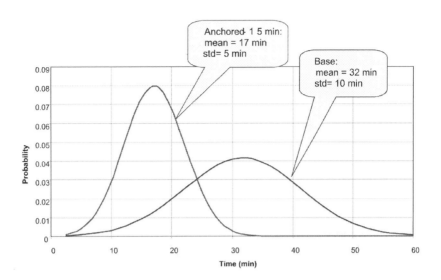

Figure 3.10: Probability and time with anchoring

new distribution with a mean of 17 minutes and a smaller standard deviation, as shown in figure 3.10.

This effect can even be subtler. In another experiment, 150 students watched a one-minute film about a car accident. They were then asked "How fast were the cars going when they _____?" The blank was filled in with one of five different words, and each of the five versions of the question was handed out to thirty students. Their average responses were: "smashed"—40.8mph, "collided"—39.3mph, "bumped"—38.1mph, "hit"—"34.0mph, and, "contacted"—31.8.[13] The more dramatic the word, the higher were the students' estimates of speed.

A final example is the "stamp out pi" icon shown in the previous section (page 75). It anchors vendors about expected cost overruns.

In all these examples we have seen how anchoring biases people to a potentially false estimate. Clearly, we must take care in how we word information and develop icons.

Another cognitive effect is that **needs are often in conflict with estimation accuracy.** You can always improve your accuracy by estimating wider intervals.[14] For example, an estimate that claims "I am 90% sure I can do the dishes in the interval between 5 and 50 minutes" has a high probability of being correct. However, this kind of overly wide interval is so broad that it conveys nothing useful and is in conflict with management's desire to have minimal uncertainty when planning.

The following incident is supposed to have actually occurred; it illustrates both uncertainty and our human unwillingness to accept it.[15] Some military officers were assigned the task of forecasting the weather a month ahead, but they found that their long-range forecasts were of low accuracy; in fact, they were no better than numbers pulled out of a hat. Since their estimates were useless, the forecasters asked their superiors to be relieved of this duty. The reply was: "The Commanding General is well aware that the forecasts are no good. However, he needs them for planning purposes."

Estimation needs in conflict with estimation accuracy are demonstrated graphically in figure 3.11, where management wants a single-point estimate for planning purposes, and estimators want little estimated uncertainty so they don't show a lack of knowledge by describing a larger uncertainty. These pressures may both occur despite a much different objective reality

This mismatch between what is desired in an estimate and what is real is often fostered by economic or political pressures. In "Underestimating Costs in Public Works Projects: Error or Lie?" the authors conclude that the main reason for the discrepancy between estimates and reality is that we often lie to get a project approved and started.[16] Later we rely on long hours, sunk-cost arguments to get more money, de-scoping the project to fit the money available, or some combination of the three, to finish the project.

Another result of uncertainty is that since **higher uncertainty is seen to indicate less knowledge,** it is often not shared with others. We are not willing to show our ignorance because it implies that we don't know enough to do our jobs. Since "poor" perceived ability is bad, we often hide uncertainty instead of disclosing it for further discussion and investigation. But hiding uncertainty often results in problems later. As we will see, in order to make a robust decision, uncertainty must be made visible in a non-threatening environment.

Last in the list of human cognition factors is **optimistic hindsight,** which often leads to poor estimates. Hindsight usually paints a picture that is rosier than reality. We tend to forget our bad experiences or assume

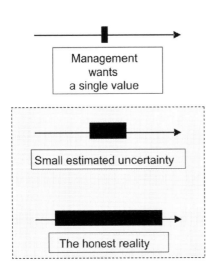

Figure 3.11: Management vs. reality.

that they won't occur again. This leads to overconfidence in our ability to complete projects within the time and cost we estimate and with the features we think we can achieve.[17]

Beyond being optimistic, most hindsight is just plain wrong. In one experiment, a group was asked two weeks after a meeting to recall specific details of it.[18] In recounting the meeting they:

- Omitted 90% of the specific points that were discussed.
- Recalled half of what they did remember incorrectly.
- Remembered comments that were not made.
- Transformed casual remarks into lengthy orations.
- Converted implicit meanings into explicit comments.

The conclusion we can derive from the discussion of human cognition factors is that we all come to our estimating tasks with much cognitive baggage and must do everything possible to compensate for our limitations. At the end of the chapter, I offer a list of estimation improvement guidelines to help accomplish this.

The Estimation Environment

Where cognitive factors influence individuals, the environment in which they create estimates has an equal or greater effect on their estimates. Part of the environment is company culture; with effort, you can change it. Other environmental factors are created by external expectations and are much more difficult to control. There are seven environmental factors that affect estimates.

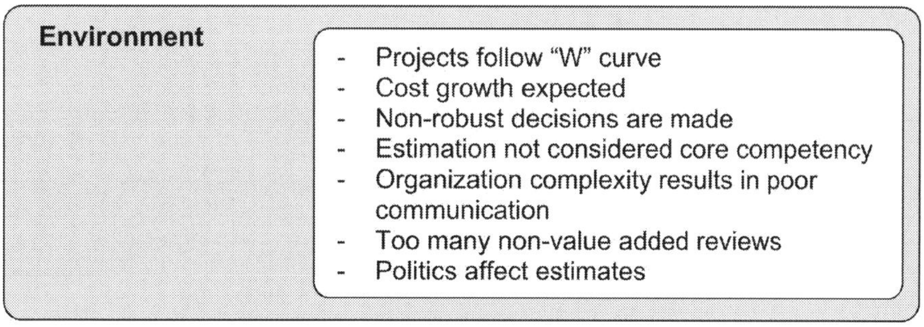

Environment
- Projects follow "W" curve
- Cost growth expected
- Non-robust decisions are made
- Estimation not considered core competency
- Organization complexity results in poor communication
- Too many non-value added reviews
- Politics affect estimates

Figure 3.12: Environmental effects on estimation.

For many projects, the effect of the environment can be visualized as a **"W" curve**, a plot of project scope versus cost, as shown in figure 3.13.[19] Here, "scope" refers to the functional capabilities of the product or project. This model was developed after studying an organization that created very high technology systems. The chronological flow is from right to left, as the scope of the project is decreased—the de-scoping referred to earlier. Starting on the right, the engineers estimated the cost of the project they envisioned. They then realized that their initial cost estimate was too high to get funded, and they responded by de-scoping the project and discounting their new estimates by decreasing their optimism about what it would take to deliver their de-scoped vision. This scope and the resulting cost are what they proposed. The cost level was anchored by the cost cap, which was either set by the engineers' perceptions or imposed by management.

If their proposal was accepted, then they got to develop a feasibility report. During this period of effort, they still held to what they perceived as the cost cap; they further de-scoped the project as they reduced their uncertainty, learning more about what they knew and didn't know.

Assuming that the engineers successfully demonstrated feasibility,

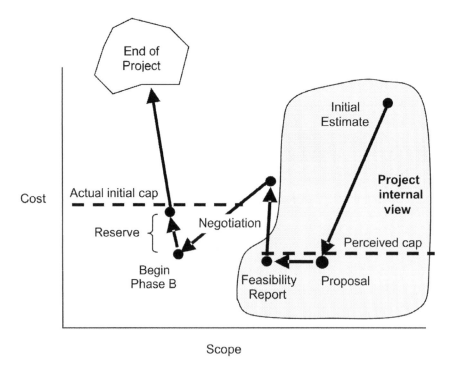

Figure 3.13: The "W" diagram of scope vs. cost.

management developed a cost estimate based on the proposal during a negotiation phase with the engineers. This estimate would usually show that the cost was low for the scope proposed. Thus, the project was further de-scoped (or more funds were found to move the perceived cap upward). Also, even though the engineers may have included a cost reserve in both the original proposal and feasibility report to account for their uncertainty, management would generally increase it relative to the actual initial cost cap. This cap may be higher or lower than that perceived by the engineers.

By the time the project is completed, the cost has increased and, quite possibly, more scope has been lost. Since this behavior is seen so often, **cost growth is expected**. In fact, the system of allocating "reserves" is an admission that this behavior will occur and costs will grow.

Plotting cost versus scope does not always lead to a "W" shape. As figure 3.14 shows, the relationship between cost and scope can follow many patterns. (These are based on actual observations.)

The goal is that the project ends exactly where the original estimate was made and the plot looks like a single point. Pattern A is even better; cost goes down and scope goes up. Pattern B is more likely; the project oscillates

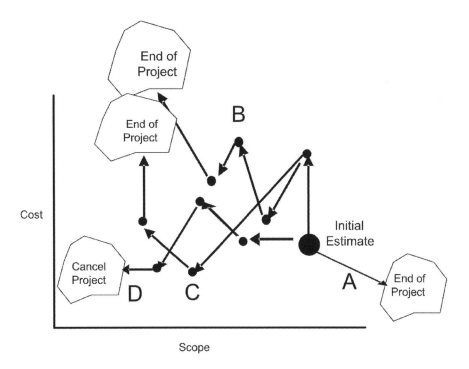

Figure 3.14: Alternative "W" diagram patterns.

between periods of rising cost and de-scoping. Pattern C is a variation in which the project begins and ends with periods of increasing costs after a mid-course effort to bring costs under control by de-scoping. Finally, pattern D shows a project that is heavily cost constrained and de-scoped to the point that it is cancelled.

Many organizations repeat the same pattern over and over, which leads to an important point: **If an organization repeatedly shows the same cost/ scope behavior, it is *designed* to create that behavior.** Put another way, most organizational structures are unintentionally designed to yield missed estimates. At first read this may sound very harsh and perhaps even untrue, but the conclusion, while difficult to admit, is inevitable.

Decisions made during the planning stage and early in the execution of a project are key to managing uncertainty and minimizing the potential for overruns. Thus it is critical to make **robust decisions** in these early phases. Remember from chapter 1: A robust decision is resistant to uncertain estimations; it looks good a year later; it promotes buy-in and accountability; and it gives guidance about what-to-do-next to make the best possible decisions with measured satisfaction and risk. (It must be noted, however, that a broken organization, or one in which lying is necessary to get decisions made, can undermine robust decision making.)

The estimation accuracy environment sets the overall context in which people make and live with estimates. If estimation accuracy is valued, it is treated as a **core competency.**[20] Just like any other management or technical skill, accurate estimation skills need to be developed and appreciated. Organizations demonstrate an appreciation of estimation accuracy as a core competency when they invest in estimation accuracy training, and reward estimation accuracy in performance evaluations.

Organizational complexity sometimes leads to **poor communication**. Managers sometimes use project reviews as a method to try to improve it. But these are often perceived as **non-value-added** exercises. One staffer I interviewed claimed that he had to prepare for four unexpected reviews and he felt he was "reviewed every time I sneeze." The decision structure described in this book can help make reviews, other meetings, and communication in general more efficient and productive.

The last environmental factor is **politics.** Many public works projects are underbid just to get them through the political system. This may be necessary, but down the road headlines are going to read, "Project X is 30% over budget." This reflects an *expected* growth in cost or other measures of accuracy. The uncertainty caused by the environment surrounding an estimate is, for the most part, special-cause uncertainty and can be managed. Guidelines to address this appear at the end of the chapter. But first, let's peel back the estimation onion another layer.

Project Planning

This is not a book about project planning, but I will touch on the topic here. There are two aspects of project planning that affect the ability to meet estimates, as shown in figure 3.15.

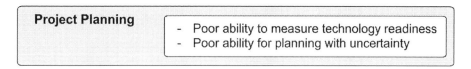

Figure 3.15: Project planning effects on estimation.

The first of these focuses on understanding the current state of a project. The term **technology readiness level** (TRL) is used in aerospace and the military to describe the maturity of a technology. This pertains especially to product development projects, but can be generalized to others. Generally, TRLs range from 1 (a first demonstration in the lab) to 9 (a technology that is proven in its use environment). Many technical projects have as their goal the development of a new product based on an immature technology. Misassessment of the TRL during planning sets up a poor base upon which project cost and time estimates are then built. One project I reviewed was composed of software and hardware components. The software was the team's primary interest. The hardware was to be supplied by another project. In the original proposal, the hardware was claimed to be at TRL 4, near the software's rating, but in an interview the hardware project manager said he thought it was closer to TRL 1; this may have been more accurate. The level of skill and care with which TRL was assessed was not very high, and the project had to be cancelled about halfway through. Assessing TRL is a type of decision-making effort, namely: Based on the state of technology, choose the most accurate TRL to represent it. TRL assessment is covered in detail in chapter 8.

Most projects begin with planning but virtually ignore **planning with uncertainty**. The best that planners usually do is to insert a buffer in the schedule, but this is often not managed or controlled. Planning includes the development of tasks, estimates for the time needed to accomplish the tasks, their organization, and possibly the personnel needed for each one. These are often plotted as Gantt charts showing the organization of the tasks, their start dates, and their due dates. In spite of this planning effort, virtually no projects end ahead of deadline. Estimates of the time needed are nearly always too low. Generally, the higher the uncertainty, the farther off the mark are the estimates. This observation leads us to the next layer of the estimation onion, project management.

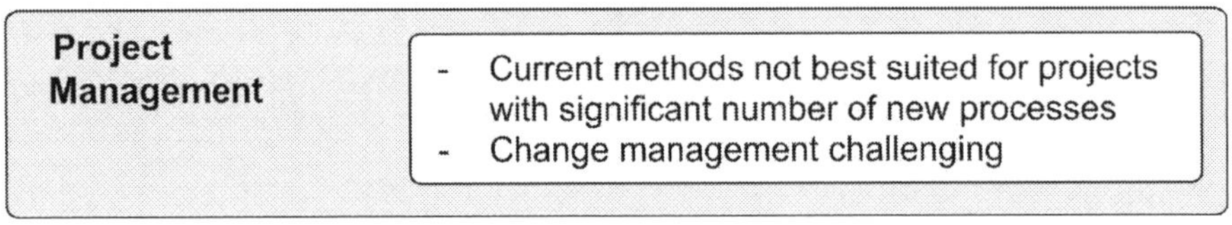

Project Management	- Current methods not best suited for projects with significant number of new processes - Change management challenging

Figure 3.16: Project management effects on estimates.

Most project management methods are designed to manage cost, not uncertainty; thus they are **not well suited for projects involving a significant number of new processes.** Since estimates and planning are uncertain, project management determines whether schedules and budgets are met or overrun. Fortunately, methods that are designed to manage high-uncertainty projects have recently been developed. One of these, Critical Chain Project Management, is gaining favor for complex projects.[21] A recent U.S. Air Force study[22] found that companies using Critical Chain Project Management methods benefited from:

- Projects coming in on time; the method is schedule-focused
- People working on "red" (critical) tasks
- People no longer being afraid to expose problems or their own uncertainty
- Less confusion
- Meetings being focused on problems and how to fix them
- Organizations being forced to decide what is most important

These results appear to be critical for effectively managing projects that involve a high level of uncertainty.

One of the hallmarks of uncertain projects is change. **Managing change** on projects that entail concurrent development processes is especially challenging.[23] As I noted earlier, using buffers and reserves as a change management methodology does not appear to work very successfully.

Estimation Methodology

Even though estimate accuracy is limited in ways we've already discussed, it is imperative to develop and maintain the best possible estimates throughout a project. The ability to do this is limited by poor estimation and estima*tor* practice and poor tools to support estimation.

Poor estimation practice and poor tools

Poor estimation practice occurs when estimators make unrealistic estimates, use single-value estimates (as discussed earlier), and fail to clearly define their estimates, as seen in figure 3.17. Interviews I conducted for a large organization brought up all of these factors:

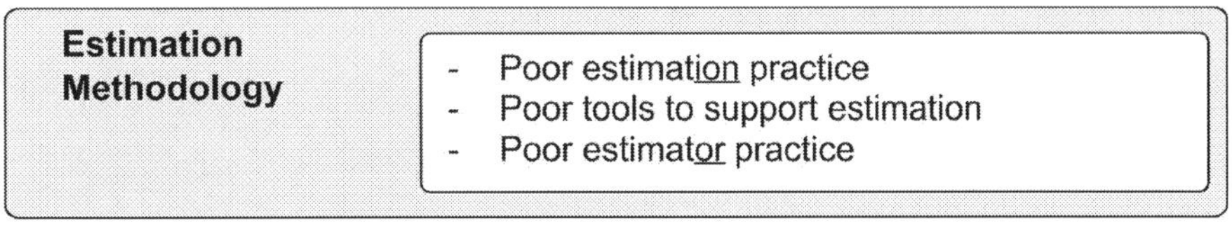

Estimation Methodology	- Poor estimation practice - Poor tools to support estimation - Poor estimator practice

Figure 3.17: Estimation methodology effects

- Unrealistic estimates resulted from one person's assumptions about goals and the ability to reach them. These assumptions were neither reviewed nor justified, and existing resources and information were overlooked. It is essential to be clear on what type of estimate is preferred—the worse case (e.g., 90%), the average case (e.g., 50%), or the best case, depending on the project.[24] In the dishes experiment, asking the question in different ways (e.g., give the 50% estimate, the 90% estimate) elicited significantly different results.
- In the projects I reviewed, the few tools used to make estimates were primarily those designed for software development time estimates. Most of the estimates were based on memory of past projects. As we know, hindsight estimates tend to be optimistic: "What happened often seems more likely afterwards than it did beforehand, since we fail to appreciate the full uncertainty

that existed at the time. Hindsight instills an illusion of omniscience."[25]

- There seemed to be no easy-to-query tool for historical cost and schedule data that enabled estimators to have empirical data on which to gauge the accuracy of estimates, or to define a base set of information on which to build estimates.[26]

Poor estimator practice

In the projects I studied, I generally found **poor estimator practice**. In many cases there was a single estimator with little estimation training. In some cases the estimator was not the person who was going to participate in the completion of the task, which led to a lack of the closure needed to measure his or her estimation accuracy.[27]

This completes our discussion of the estimation onion. Considering all the factors we have covered, it seems amazing that estimates are as good as they are. If we follow guidelines for making the best estimates, they can be much better. But first, a discussion of risk is in order.

Risk: A Code Word for Uncertainty

Like other terms in this chapter, the term "risk" has many different meanings. If you enter "risk definition" into Google you will get over twenty-five definitions; some are redundant, but there is little consistency. A few definitions that are important here are:

- In technology and economics, risk is expressed as an expected value that an event will be accompanied by undesirable consequences.[28] It is measured by both the probability of the event and the seriousness of the consequences. For example, the probability that a bearing will fail in five years is .001%. The consequence of the bearing failing is that the engine it bears will stop running. These two combine in a single value that communicates risk.
- In planning, risk is what can happen that will cause the project to fall behind schedule or go over cost. During planning, the known-unknowns are risk.
- In management, risk is the possibility that outcomes will be different from what we expect. It is the effort to manage both the known-unknowns and unknown-unknowns.

The event-focused view of risk found in the first definition and held in the technology and economics fields is too restrictive during the decision-making process. This is because the largest risks are inherent in the uncertainty of information and the knowledge and models on which decisions are based. This decision **risk** includes:

- The potential for making a less-than-satisfactory decision based on the uncertainty of the requirements
- The accuracy of estimates about parameter values and models
- The completeness of the understanding of the situation and its physics
- The consistency of the team's parameter and model interpretation
- The team's differences in viewpoints about what is important

Planning and management, the second and third definitions of risk, are the result of what is uncertain and unknown—decision risk. Decision risk has little to do with events (as in traditional risk analysis) and much to do with what is known and the decisions based on this knowledge. Further, this type of risk cannot be well modeled using standard probabilities (often called frequentist probabilities, the stuff you may have studied in school) and must use Bayesian methods. This is not to say that traditional methods are unimportant, only that decision risk has not been well addressed and is key in early-systems development.

Worded another way, risk traditionally amounts to answering:

1 What can go wrong? A system fails.
2 How likely is it to happen? Probability depends on past statistics and modeling results.
3 What are the consequences? Money, time, and possibly even lives are wasted.

During decision making, risks are inherent in uncertain knowledge, information, and models. Uncertainty creates risk that a poor decision will be made; the questions are then answered this way:

1 What can go wrong? A poor choice is made.
2 How likely is it to happen? Probability depends on uncertain

knowledge and the team's interpretation of information and models.

3   What are the consequences? Money, time, and possibly lives are wasted.

All of this is good background, but managers are really only interested in answering three questions that support answering the second of the five key questions: "What is the risk that our decision will not turn out as we expect?"

- What can go wrong if I choose option X?
- How likely is it?
- What is the impact?[29]

The first question raises the issue of how we know if our choice was poor. In *Why Decisions Fail*, the definition of a poor decision is one that had no positive impact after two years. There are other measures of a failed decision. For example, our time is up and no satisfactory alternative has been developed. Or not everyone on the team agrees with the choice made and some team members feel disenfranchised. More often, the result of a poor choice is not known until much later. For example, if we choose a bad restaurant, we will not know until we have eaten there. Or if an engineer makes a poor decision on what material to use for a product, this may not be evident until the customers have used the product for a number of years.

One thing is consistent in this discussion:

Without uncertainty there is no risk.

A corollary is that the more uncertainty, the higher the risk of making a poor decision. Thus, a major goal in decision making is to manage the uncertainty.

The methods in this book help you manage four types of risk:

1   *Envisioning Risk*: The risk of solving the wrong problem
2   *Ideation Risk:* The risk of not developing good alternatives
3   *Evaluation Risk:* The risk of choosing a poor alternative
4   *Strategic Risk:* The risk of not following a beneficial strategy

There is a fifth type not addressed here:

5 *Execution Risk:* The risk of not being able to implement the decision

I do not directly address risk again until chapter 9. However, as you read the material in the intervening chapters, be aware of how your knowledge— or lack thereof—creates the different types of risk and how the material I present helps you minimize your risk of a non-robust decision.

Guidelines for Best Estimates

Our discussion leads to a list of guidelines that will help you get the best possible estimates. These guidelines are integrated into the methodology developed in this book and they are the foundation of a robust decision-making process. Remember, decisions can only be as good as the estimates on which they are based.

1 Realize that all estimates are uncertain, and that uncertainty can be managed but not eliminated. Collect both the estimate and its uncertainty. For objective or quantitative estimates, try to obtain high, low, and most-likely values. For qualitative estimates, note the surety of the estimate (from not very sure to very sure) or level of expertise (from unknowledgeable to expert). Other methods for collecting certainty information are described in chapter 8.

2 Don't anchor your estimates. The best estimates come without anchors. Of course, if the budget or time required to get something done is known, then these act as anchors. Nonetheless, employ effective cost and time interview techniques that do not anchor estimates any more than is necessary.

3 Ask for 90% estimates. If the estimates are for time or cost, realize that the average will be about half this value. This implies that half the time the actual value will be greater than one half the estimate and half the time less than this value.

4 Collect the reasons (causes) behind any special-cause uncertainties and your planning based on these. Put no effort into overcoming common-cause uncertainty.

5 Peers or experts should review your estimates, uncertainties, and reasoning.

6 Base your estimates on documented historical information whenever possible. Documentation should include scope, initial estimates, actual results, and what caused any deviation. Very few organizations do this in any formal way.

7 Estimation methods need to become part of the organization's culture and be considered a core competency. All levels of the organization should support estimation training and performance evaluations should reflect the importance of estimation accuracy.

8 While it is true that uncertainty implies low knowledge, this is not bad; it is a signal that work needs to be done or relationships need to be built. Don't kill the messenger who alerts you to uncertainty.

9 Don't bury a research project inside a new process or product development project. If it is warranted, base your uncertainty management on Technology Readiness Level (TRL), volatility of funding, project management, and requirements. Be aware of the TRL level of all technologies on which the current effort is dependent.

10 Be aware of the scope-versus-cost "W" in your organization and how project uncertainty drives it. Either admit that your organization's "W" is the way it does business or develop methods to change it. Note that the ideal "W" would be a single point on the cost-versus-scope plot, achieved within the planned time and resources.

11 Recognize that reserves and buffers are compensations for unmanaged uncertainty.

12 Be aware of how decision risks affect the potential success of decisions.

Before tackling a decision-making methodology, you need one other foundation. Estimates and decisions are made by people. In the next chapter, we will explore how people and teams of people affect the decision-making process.

Teams Don't Make Decisions, But....

Building Effective Decision Teams

Teams don't make decisions... or do they? It depends on whether you consider a decision to be an event or a process. If it is an event—signing off on a purchase order, a design drawing, or another item that commits resources—then a single person makes the decision. But if you consider that decision making is more than an event, that instead it is a process of combining many people's knowledge and expertise to frame a problem, evaluate the alternatives, fuse the results, and decide what-to-do-next (as shown in figure 1.2 on page 32), then the truth is that teams make most decisions. Hence, we devote this chapter to issues that arise within decision-making teams.

There are many good books on teams. Probably the best is *The Team Handbook*, which is now in its third edition and has sold over 1.3 million copies since its introduction in 1988.[1] Although a team's main product is the decisions it makes, the topic of the decision-making process is only found on ten of the 301 pages in the *Handbook*. This isn't to say the information in the *Handbook* and in other team building and management books is not good; it is. But to complete the picture, this chapter covers what is left out of those books—specifically, the practical considerations of the team decision-making process.

The fundamental difference between the discussion of teamwork in this book and what is found in typical books on teamwork is that teamwork books tend to describe *what* a team should do; this book offers tools to help them do it.

This chapter is organized according to the diagram in figure 4.1, which illustrates the elements necessary for decision team success. In order to make the most robust decisions possible, all of these elements at the tails of the arrows must be addressed. The following

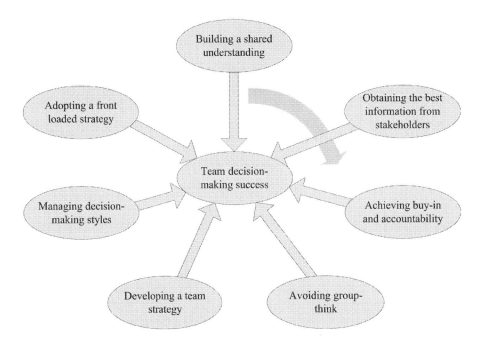

Figure 4.1: Elements for decision team success.

sections tackle them one at a time, beginning at the 12 o'clock position. The resulting discussions are summarized at the end of the chapter and are used to set goals for the rest of the book.

Building a shared understanding

One of the most difficult challenges a team faces is developing a shared understanding of the information available to describe the issue, the possible alternatives, the criteria with which to evaluate the alternatives, the evaluations themselves, and the ultimate resolution. This "understanding" does not mean that the team members agree on anything; instead it means that *when one member uses a term to describe something, all team members essentially understand it to mean the same thing.*

Further, a shared understanding does not mean that everybody on the team knows about all the available alternatives, evaluations, or criteria. This is simply not possible when teams address complex problems. Most complex decisions are based on information from many people, none of whom have all the information, and all of whom have part of the information. And some of the information they have conflicts.

Finally, a shared understanding is not the same as "groupthink," the 5 o'clock item, which I'll discuss later in this chapter.

There is a primary obstacle to reaching a shared understanding, and it is a function of how we understand what others say to us. Basically, our understanding comes when we compare new information to our existing knowledge and past experiences; through these perspectives, we each form our own understanding. This means that when you hear a new idea or a new term, your concept of it is necessarily different from that of the person describing it to you. So in order for you and a colleague to develop a shared understanding, you need to ensure that critical features that are important to both of you are sufficiently understood the same way. This does not mean that you must agree on anything, only that if you explain something to him and he processes it and explains it back to you, it will still make sense to you. The last sentence is the key measure of a shared understanding: If I can explain your concept to you and it makes sense to you, then we are on the same page. The bottom line here is that it takes dialogue—time and effort—for a group of people to develop a similar understanding of any problem or concept.

This leads to the second key point, one that flows directly from the first one. A shared understanding can only be developed through effective communication. But teams often do not communicate effectively. Here's one example: A company that produced consumer products held frequent team meetings to discuss and select new concepts to develop. In the interest of good teamwork, management polled everyone during the meetings to get their opinions. But it didn't ensure that everyone had sufficient understanding of the concepts under discussion so they could make informed comments and decisions. When a consultant observed their meetings, he found that many of the participants did not share an understanding of the concepts, and simply went along with the crowd when it was their turn to vote. One of the strong points of robust decision management is that it supports—actually, compels—effective communication at each step along the way by giving structure to all the decision-making elements: issues, criteria, alternatives, evaluation results, risks, and what-to-do-next.

Obtaining the best information from stakeholders

Teams are responsible for collecting, generating, evaluating, deliberating, fusing, choosing, and acting on information in order to resolve issues. From a decision-management viewpoint, all of these activities are decision-making activities. Thus, the terms "team" and "decision-makers" are used interchangeably in this book.

All decision-making teams are part of a larger group of stakeholders, as shown in figure 4.2. Stakeholders are *everyone* whom a deliberation or decision will affect. For example, the stakeholders for a product design decision usually include:

- The end-use customers for the product
- The people who buy the product (may be different from the end-use customers)
- The manufacturers of the product
- The team members, as they may have to rework a poor decision and their reputations will be affected by the quality of their decisions
- The clerks, who may have to keep track of part numbers and ordering information
- The person who will have to clean the product
- The decision manager who has to sign off on the choices made
- And others

A challenge you face with so many stakeholders involved is that you want to get the best information possible from all of them. For example, it is one thing to have a person from purchasing on the team, and it is another to ensure that her voice is heard and her input utilized. Even if you don't buy in to everything this book has to offer, it is important to take away enough of the methodology to help you manage stakeholder information.

Note that outside experts are shown outside the stakeholder region in figure 4.2. Outside experts might be consultants or vendor representatives. They may not necessarily have an interest in the decisions you make. Your goal is to include their valuable information in the decision-making process while simultaneously managing their objectivity.

Achieving Buy-in and Accountability

People feel accountable for a decision if they play an active role in the process leading up to it. The choice that was made may not have been their first choice, but they contributed to its selection. Accountability is born from collaboration. You know you have collaboration when:

- Everyone can paraphrase the issue to show that he or she understands it.

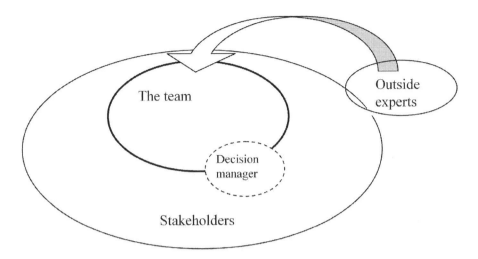

Figure 4.2: Team terminology.

- Everyone has a chance to contribute to solving the problem. This can be accomplished by participating in refining the issue, developing alternative solutions, building criteria, or contributing evaluation information.
- Everyone has a chance to describe what is important to him or her.

Those who do not agree with the final decision will still be likely to support the team because they have been included in the decision-making process and appreciate the work required to reach a decision.

The terms "collaboration," "consensus," and "compromise" are often confused. Collaboration implies sharing information, consensus indicates general agreement, and compromise entails giving up a position. Compromise is like averaging, or mixing too many colors of paint—the result is always brown. Consensus, British Prime Minister Margaret Thatcher once said, is "the process of abandoning all beliefs, principles, values, and policies in search of something in which no one believes, but to which no one objects."

Collaboration, on the other hand, attempts to build a shared vision, accountability, and buy-in, while some on the team may compromise their positions. Big boys and girls realize that their ideas will not always prevail, but that through their contribution to the team, they are in fact an important part of the choices made.

Avoiding Groupthink

Irving Janis coined and popularized the term "Groupthink."[2] He identified the following three symptoms of groupthink:

1 Extreme overestimation of the worth of the group.

2 Abundance of rationalization rather than sound reasoning, starting with a conclusion rather than evidence and then trying to justify that conclusion. Note the similarity to the second blunder listed in *Why Decisions Fail*: jumping on the first idea that comes up and working to justify it.

3 Self-imposed censorship within the group to ward off challenges to the assumptions and beliefs that support the first two assumptions. This is an example of the first *Why Decisions Fail* blunder, using a failure-prone practice.

Groupthink has been blamed for many bad political decisions. The model was developed in response to John Kennedy's ill-fated Bay of Pigs invasion of Cuba in 1961 and decisions about the Vietnam war. More recently, groupthink has been used to describe decisions about the existence of weapons of mass destruction in Iraq.

One way to eliminate groupthink is to have only individuals make decisions. But this is not practical, as I touched on earlier this chapter, since most important corporate and government decisions are so complex that they preclude a single decision maker.

As a rule, preventing a team from adopting groupthink is easier than curing a team of it. By its very nature, groupthink is not obvious to the group, and it is difficult to point it out to a team because all members have set up walls to keep naysayers' voices silent. Some preventative techniques are:

- Ensure that the process honors a diversity of views. (This is the subject of chapter 7.)
- Be evidence driven rather than verdict driven; form your teams to select from among alternative options rather than to justify one option. (See chapter 5.)
- Be goal driven; develop criteria that are a team vision of the ideal solution to which you compare your concepts. (See chapter 6.)
- Be information driven; develop information that helps the team evaluate the alternatives relative to the criteria. (See chapter 9.)

•Be risk focused; try to understand what can go wrong with the alternatives being considered and the decision being made. (See chapter 9).

Developing a Team Decision Strategy

Organizations use many different strategies to make decisions. The following is a list of strategies I have seen in practice. None are very robust, and all represent what the methods in this book work to overcome.

•**Decision by Running Out of Time:** This is the most common form of decision making. There may be some effort made to develop criteria and alternatives, but often time runs out before any effort is made to ensure that the decision is robust. When time runs out, somebody's favorite alternative is selected, while the others are dropped. And you should worry about who that "somebody" is. Some people make running out of time work in their favor—so their favorite idea will be accepted.

A variant of this is **Decision by Chaos**. The president of the company suddenly says, "I want our new product at the Atlanta trade show," which is coming up in two weeks. Now there is no rational way to prepare for the show and still make robust decisions. The decisions made in the chaos of carrying out this impossible task may need revisiting after the show, and work will need to be redone. Some people prefer to work in chaos, and when in positions of power they will manufacture chaos as the everyday working environment.

•**Decision by Fiat:** This is a very common style in autocratic organizations where a manager or someone else in authority decrees that a certain alternative is his or her favorite. This could also be called "Decision by Authority." It is often seen when people choose the boss's idea in order to preserve a relationship with him. But this is more justification than decision making.

•**Decision by Coercion:** A champion for one alternative pressures her colleagues into submission. Often the loudest voice wins, the others having given up. One colleague refers to this style as "hijacking the process."

•**Decision by Competition:** Here concern for who wins is most important. This is often a win-lose situation, and the relationship among individual team members is not considered important.

- **Decision by Voting:** Democracy works, but does not often lead to the best possible choice. This decision-making process is a weak form of compromise. Think how most products would operate if they were designed the way we elect a president.
- **Decision by Inertia:** This style is based on the "We did it that way before" argument. It may result in a robust decision, if the previous one was robust. But using this style doesn't lead to much progress or innovation. Sometimes the tough decision is knowing when to leave cruise control on and when to innovate.

To improve on these non-robust strategies, researchers have studied the *approaches that people use* to solve problems (descriptive studies), and have developed theories about *how people should* solve problems (prescriptive studies). Let's briefly look at the results of these studies.

Descriptive studies[3] have shown that in selecting a strategy, people unconsciously weigh the effort or cost needed to reach a decision versus the accuracy or quality of the needed result. Exactly how they make this trade-off between cost and accuracy is still unknown and is being explored. A majority of these studies have been on simple, static problems, which often have predefined, known alternatives, as well as stated criteria for choosing among them. Researchers in psychology and marketing have thoroughly studied static problems with small sets of discrete choices.

However, most real problems—dynamic problems—are characterized by uncertain, incomplete, inconsistent, and evolving information. Although they are not well studied, they are the norm in portfolio management, purchasing situations, product design, and everyday technical, business, and personal decision making. Strategies used by people solving dynamic problems are very complex and not well understood.

Recently, researchers have begun to study how individuals attempt to solve dynamic problems. Many of these descriptive studies have been of designers.[4] Some of the results show that designers who use an effective strategy:

- Spend time understanding the issues and developing criteria
- Consider multiple alternatives during the process

- Keep options open for as long as possible
- Gather sufficient information to learn as they go
- Iterate through the decision-making process
- Are skeptical of information
- Are aware of what they know and don't know
- Focus on uncertainty as part of their evaluation processes

While descriptive studies try to discover how people make decisions, prescriptive theories have been developed on how people *should* make decisions.[5] For the most part, these theories are analytical; they use sets of equations to evaluate the alternatives and identify the "best" one. But these theories are little used because:

- They do not match well with what people actually do
- They can only be used by experts
- The information about the alternatives and criteria must be quantitative
- The information must be complete
- They are inflexible
- They are weak in their ability to support teams

These two lists set the goals for the robust decision strategy outlined in this book. Specifically, the methods attempt to support the effective strategy in the first list with a structured method that does not fall into the traps of the second list. At a minimum, these lists help set the requirements for such a strategy. In the final section of this chapter, they will be combined with other points to formulate a list of goals.

Managing Decision-Making Styles

Regardless of the strategy adopted by the team, every individual on it has a unique decision-making style or problem-solving behavior. Our decision-making styles affect how we solve problems when we work individually, and the mix of styles on a team has a significant effect on its effectiveness and results.

As a simple example to help underscore the point, consider Molly, Joe, and Vince, a team trying to specify a new computer for their company. Molly, from the accounting department, has a copy of a magazine with some computers marked as potential alternatives. Joe has one specific computer in mind and Vince has thought a lot about the problem. Their dialogue goes like this:

Molly: *Let's get this problem under control. What exactly do we want out of this computer? Can we itemize the criteria for selecting it? It seems to me that we need at least 2.8 GHz speed, 256 MB RAM, and a 60 GB hard disk. These are minimum features to support accounting. What else does it need?*

Joe: *Okay! I agree with you about those numbers for accounting, but what if we want to use it for other things?*

Molly: *(Raising her voice) That again! We'd better agree on who is going to use this computer and for what! Let's start again. Who is going to be the primary user of the computer? The bookkeeper, right?*

Vince: *Calm down. I agree that the goal is to find a computer for the bookkeeper. I hope we can all agree on that. I'd sure like to try some of these computers out. I can't make sense out of these lists of things like RAM, GHz, and other three-letter acronyms.*

Joe: *Okay, the bookkeeper is the primary user, but others may want to use it, too. I still like the one for $3,500 with the really fast processor. Here's one in this catalog that fits the criteria you stated earlier. Let's get this one.*

Molly: *Hold on now, let's not make a hasty decision. It says that it has 128 KB of cache. I don't know much about cache; is that good or what?*

This simple example helps demonstrate five personal problem-solving dimensions and how they apply to teams. These dimensions are based on the Five-Factor Model,[6] the Myers-Briggs Type Indicator,[7] and learning theory. But rather than attempting to describe an individual's personality (the goal of the Five-Factor and Myers-Briggs methods), it simply identifies how personality dimensions affect decision-making. In simple equation form:

Decision-Making Style =
Energy Source +
Information Management Style +
Information Language +
Deliberation Style +
Decision Closure Style

These decision-making dimensions are useful because they help us describe an individual's information management and decision-making preferences.

In the paragraphs below, each of the five dimensions is briefly introduced, after which there are five questions. (The author is not a psychologist and the results of these tests should not be used for anything beyond their intended illustrative purpose.)

Responses to these questions will place you or a colleague on a continuum between two extremes. It is important to note that there are no right answers. In fact, it isn't necessary to take the test for any other reason than to internalize the fact that you and all your colleagues have styles, that your styles are different, and that you need know how to recognize and manage them. So humor yourself, relax, and take these simple tests.

The first personality dimension describes an individual's decision-making **energy source** or **extraversion.** It is a measure of whether you are an **internal** or **external** problem solver. For a rough estimate of your, or a colleague's, decision-making energy source, answer these five questions. If scoring a colleague, pretend you are that person.

1 In a group, do you generally
   a) wait to be introduced?
   b) introduce yourself to others?
2 Does interacting with others
   a) take real effort?
   b) energize you?
3 Do you tend to
   a) listen and reflect?
   b) say what is on your mind?
4 Do you think of yourself as
   a) private?
   b) outgoing?
5 At work do you tend to
   a) keep more to yourself?
   b) be sociable with your colleagues?

Add up the number of "b" values you selected. Match the result to the scale along the bottom of the arrow. This places you or your colleague on the continuum between an internal and external decision-making energy source.

If a person is reflective, is a good listener, thinks and then speaks, and enjoys solving problems alone, then she is an internal problem solver. If the

INTERNAL ENERGY SOURCE EXTERNAL

0   1   2   3   4   5

person's energy comes from outside through interactions with others (i.e., the person is sociable and tends to speak and then think) she is an external problem solver. About 75% of all Americans and 48% of engineering students and top executives are external problem solvers.

In our example, Molly verbalizes a lot, so she is probably an external decision maker. Vince, on the other hand, clearly prefers to operate as an internal problem solver. Joe is probably somewhere in between (sometimes referred to as an "ambivert") and can swing either way as the situation dictates. Again, there is no right or wrong style among them; this is merely the way they operate in this kind of situation. They may show slightly different styles in different situations, but will generally not deviate very far from type.

Awareness of energy sources is a major factor in team interactions where the external types dominate the internal types. Some guidelines on how to manage the two types of energy sources in team situations are:

1. •Help team members who get their energy from within to share more than their final response. Provide them with a strategy that encourages partial solutions and a discussion of them.

2. •Give internal decision makers a more equal say in deliberations.

3. •Encourage external decision makers to hear the contributions of others. This is accomplished through a structure that documents the evolution of information during the decision-making process.

As you will see, the tools presented in this book are intended to help "level the playing field," toning down the external decision makers and allowing the internal types to have their voices heard.

The second dimension reflects your preference for an **information management style** or **originality**. It is a measure of whether you like working with **facts** or **possibilities**. For an estimate of your or a colleague's information management style, answer the following questions.

1 Which word best describes you:
   a) practical?
   b) ingenious?

2 Which interests you more:
   a) the actual?
   b) the possible?

3 In problem solving, do you prefer to
   a) iron out the details?
   b) develop the ideas?

4 Are you inclined to take what is said
   a) literally?
   b) figuratively?

5 Do you generally feel
   a) down-to-earth?
   b) somewhat removed?

Add up the number of "b" values you selected. This sum places you or a colleague on the continuum between facts and possibilities on information management style.

FACTS   INFORMATION MANAGEMENT STYLE   POSSIBILITIES

0   1   2   3   4   5

People who prefer facts and details are literal, practical, and realistic; they appreciate the here and now. Those who think in terms of possibilities, patterns, concepts, and theories are looking for relationships between pieces of information and the meaning of the information. About 75% of Americans are fact-oriented, as are 66% of top executives; yet only 34% of all engineering students are fact-oriented. This is interesting in light of the heavy emphasis on math and science that is the focus of an engineering education. Other labels that could be placed on the scale are Preserver and Explorer. Where the Preservers maintain the system, the Explorers are the boat rockers.

To solve most problems it is important to have a balance between the two extremes. When solving a problem alone, the fact-oriented person must gather firm information to process, whereas the possibility-oriented person probably has trouble balancing his checkbook.

In our example, Molly has gathered facts to use as criteria for selecting a computer, so she will probably score 1 or 2 on the test. Joe seems more interested in possibilities, so he will probably score near 4. There is not enough information to guess where Vince might be on the continuum.

Awareness of information management styles is another factor that can help prevent team interactions from disintegrating. Some guidelines on how to manage the two types are:

- Encourage fact-oriented team members to work on understanding the problem rather than diving right in and analyzing the details of a single, potentially non-robust solution.
- Encourage possibility-oriented team members to be more specific, to deal with details, and to stick to important issues.

The third dimension measures which **information language** a person prefers to use during decision making, **verbal** or **visual**. For a rough idea of your or a colleague's information language style, answer these questions.

1 When you meet someone again, do you remember his or her
   a) face?
   b) name?
2 Do you prefer to
   a) be shown how?
   b) read instructions how?
3 In a book, if there are two descriptions of the same material, which do you look at first:
   a) a diagram?
   b) the text?
4 If they both represented the same thing, would you rather study
   a) a graph?
   b) an equation?
5 If there is a possibility to touch an object, do you
   a) do so eagerly?
   b) hold back?

Add up the number of "b" values you selected. Match this sum with the numbers on the diagram below in order to place you or a colleague on the continuum between visual and verbal information language style.

VISUAL — INFORMATION LANGUAGE → VERBAL

0   1   2   3   4   5

Visual information includes pictures, diagrams, graphs, and hardware. Verbal information includes written or spoken words and mathematical formulas. It is interesting to note that most people favor visual information, yet most classes in school are presented in a verbal language. This mismatch is especially striking in science and engineering classes. In our example, Vince would rather try out the real computer than read words describing it. He is probably more visual than verbal.

When you are working alone, the language you use is not an important consideration. In teams, however, the preferred languages greatly affect the development of a shared vision of the problem and alternative solutions.

Most best practices combine the verbal and the visual. On one project I used the Quality Function Deployment (QFD) method, also called "the house of quality," to help my team understand the requirements of a large, complex project. The QFD method results in a large, very visual matrix that shows an evolution from the voice of the customer to product requirements. I presented the results to a large group at the end of the three-month planning exercise, complete with slides and posters taped to the wall showing all the graphical details. Then, at the end of my presentation, I was introduced to the representative from the funding agency—who was blind. But the verbal/visual structure of the methodology was strong enough to support me and I was able to successfully describe what had been done.

Some guidelines on how to manage the two types of communication language in team situations are:

- Help identify information that needs to be communicated, regardless of language.
- Help identify differences in team members' mental models, encouraging extra effort by both visual and verbal people to communicate clearly with other members to develop a shared understanding.
- If words aren't working, try a diagram or picture. If the picture isn't working, try words.

The fourth dimension reflects the **deliberation style** or **accommodation**, the **objectivity** or **subjectivity** with which decisions are made. To get an estimate of your or a colleague's deliberation style, answer the following five questions.

1. Do you more often let
   a) your heart rule your head?
   b) your head rule your heart?
2. Which is the worse fault:
   a) to be unsympathetic?
   b) to show too much concern?
3. Which do you most value in yourself:
   a) your compassion?
   b) your reason?
4. Which appeals to you more:
   a) harmonious relationships?
   b) getting the job done?
5. In a heated discussion, do you
   a) look for common ground?
   b) stick to your guns?

Add up the number of "b" values you selected. This sum places you or a colleague on the continuum between subjective and objective deliberation styles.

SUBJECTIVE   DELIBERATION STYLE   OBJECTIVE

0   1   2   3   4   5

Some people take a subjective approach, others an objective one. People who make decisions based on an interpersonal involvement, circumstances, and the "right thing to do," take a subjective approach to decision making. These people can be referred to as "adaptors." Conversely, people who are logical, detached, and analytical take an objective approach to making decisions. They challenge others when their logic tells them that they are right. About 51% of Americans are objective decision makers, as are 68% of engineering students and 95% of top executives.

In our example, Vince wants to keep peace in the team and is probably more subjective than objective. Molly may be more objective (this is not yet clear).

Subjective decision makers value team harmony, while objective decision makers value the decision even at the cost of personal relationships. Some guidelines on how to manage these deliberation styles are:

- Help subjective team members discuss differences of opinion without feeling threatened.
- Help the team reach consensus, thereby reassuring subjective decision makers.
- Help objective team members understand and respect how the team functions.

The fifth and final personality dimension relates to the need to actually come to a conclusion during decision making. **Decision closure style** ranges from **flexible** to **decisive**. For a rough estimate of your or a colleague's decision closure style, answer these questions.

1 Do you prefer to
   a) just let things happen?
   b) plan for things to happen?
2 When a decision is to be made, are you more comfortable
   a) before?
   b) after?
3 Is it harder for you to adapt to
   a) routine?
   b) change?
4 Are you more satisfied with
   a) work in progress?
   b) a finished product?
5 Are you more
   a) impulsive?
   b) careful?

Add up the number of "b" values selected. This sum places you or a colleague on the continuum between flexible and decisive decision closure styles.

Some people are flexible and others are decisive. If a person goes with the flow, is adaptive and spontaneous, and finds it difficult to make and stick with decisions, he is considered flexible. If, on the other hand, he

FLEXIBLE  DECISIVE

0   1   2   3   4   5

makes decisions with a minimum of stress and likes an environment that is ordered, scheduled, controlled, and deliberate, then he is decisive. About half of all Americans are decisive, as are 64% of engineering students and 88% of top executives. One characteristic of flexible decision makers is that they have a tendency to procrastinate because they want to remain adaptive. This can make working with them difficult.

In the example, Joe appears spontaneous and may be a very flexible decision-maker. In other words, he may not be content with any decision reached. Some guidelines on how to manage closure styles are:

- Give both flexible and decisive team members a strategy so they can see that problems are solved one step at a time.
- Encourage feedback from other team members so that flexible decision makers can reflect on the decision-making process.
- Discourage flexible decision makers from changing their minds.
- Discourage decisive decision makers from jumping to conclusions without considering the details or other team members.
- Encourage decisive team members to be part of the data collection and review process.
- Remind decisive team members that they are not always right.

As I said at the beginning of this discussion, these behaviors are defined here because it is important to be aware of your own personal style and reflect on how if affects your behavior when making decisions. This awareness is even more important in team situations, where understanding the five dimensions of decision-making style can help you troubleshoot the decision-making process.

I will refer to these five styles often throughout the rest of this book. The methods I have developed strive to be as insensitive to them as possible. Ideally, a robust decision support method should work well regardless of energy source, information management style, information language, deliberation style, or decision closure style. In fact, it should help team members with conflicting styles collaborate. You can be the judge of whether or not the methods attain this goal.

Adopting a front-loaded strategy

One key to team success is support from the organization with adequate resources for a front-loaded strategy, that is, doing more work at first so that less is needed later. Consider figure 4.3, which shows the distribution of project time and investment made over time by an automobile company.[8] The data are actual, and the dashed line is ideal. The actual data indicate that the company put little manpower into the early decisions (in the oval on the diagram) and revisited earlier decisions after the design had been launched (to the right of the "launch" line). In fact, 35% of the total engineering investment was unplanned and occurred after launch. In essence, the company was still designing the automobile and revisiting poorly made decisions as it was selling the product. This caused tooling and assembly line changes during production and the possibility of recalling cars for retrofit, all of which are very expensive endeavors. On the other hand, the ideal curve (the dashed line) shows time spent to make many robust decisions early in the design process and finishing the design of the car before it goes into production. Front-loaded design decisions require more time and effort, but if they are robust, they can lessen the number of changes later, both in hardware and documentation. The actual data include seventy major changes before launch and thirty-six afterward. A decision that costs $1,000 to change early in the design process may cost $10,000 later during product refinement and $1,000,000 or more in tooling, sales, and goodwill expenses if made after production has begun. By the way, the engineering investment curve does not include the costs for scrap and retooling.

Although the example is for automobile design, the pattern is a common one, and the key point to take away from the example is this: **The robustness of the decision-making process is inversely proportional to the time and money it may take downstream to fix the results. You either spend the necessary time, money, and other resources making robust decisions early on or risk spending even more time and money fixing the non-robust results.**

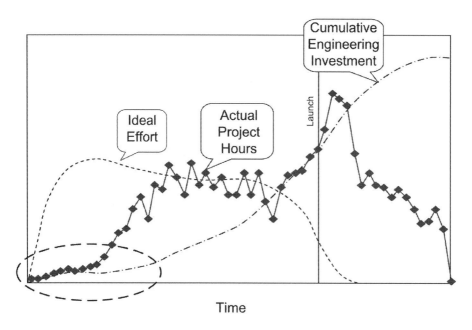

Figure 4.3: Design decisions made during automobile development.

Goals for Robust Decision Support

The concepts introduced in this chapter help set some goals for methods that support robust decisions. Namely, robust decision support methods must:

1   Help the team build a shared understanding, obtaining the best information from stakeholders.
2   Help ensure that the stakeholders buy in to the process and resolution.
3   Help the team avoid groupthink.
4   Give the team a strategy that, while prescriptive, is close enough to natural processes that it is both useful and usable.
5   Level the playing field for decision-making styles. To do this, robust decision support methods must:

    Help internal decision makers share information and get more say in the deliberation while helping external decision makers hear the contribution of others.

    Prevent fact-oriented team members from diving into the details too fast while encouraging possibility-oriented team members to deal with details.

Provide both graphical and textual tools to support the team.

Provide a safe environment for disagreement and building consensus.

Supply a strategy that helps teams come to a resolution one step at a time.

6   Help front-load the process.

The remainder of the book strives to meet these goals.

Everyone Hears Only What He Understands

5

Introduction

The title of this chapter is a quote from the early nineteenth century German poet-philosopher Johann Wolfgang von Goethe. Understanding a problem that needs a decision means developing an initial issue statement, an initial set of alternatives for resolving the issue, and initial criteria by which the alternatives are to be judged. Although in an ideal world you would know the issue, the alternatives, and the criteria from the beginning and they would remain unchanged, for most real-world problems, your understanding evolves as you learn more. Part of the robust decision-making process is to guide this evolution as needed.

An alternative title for this chapter might be "What You Frame Is What You Get." Here the term "frame" is used as in "frame a problem" and it implies how you structure or understand the problem you're addressing. The term has recently taken on a political meaning similar to "spin."[1] And this makes sense because the way you frame the problem—your team's understanding of it—can greatly color the results you get.

Take another look at figure 1.2 on page 32, which illustrates the decision-making process.

You begin at the upper left with "Understand the Problem." In order to do this, you must clarify the issue, generate alternatives, and develop criteria by which to evaluate the alternatives. Note that in the diagram, understanding may be revisited: There is an arrow back to "Understand the Problem" from "Decide what-to-do-next." It is also important to recognize that your understanding is based on uncertain, incomplete, inconsistent, and evolving information. To ignore this is to assume away the most dominant feature of most issues. Managing uncertainty and iteration is key to making robust decisions.

Understanding, or framing, is so central to robust decision making that

I address it in three chapters. This chapter focuses on defining the issue and developing alternatives. The following two chapters address generating criteria.

What Is the Issue?

Defining the Issue

It's amazing how often team members think they're working together when in fact they're not even discussing the same problem. Even if you're working alone, you will generate ideas and evaluate them while developing a clear statement of the issue you're addressing. The only way to ensure that your effort is focused is to explicitly state the issue being addressed. So what is an issue?

> An issue is a **call for action** directed at some **feature** of an **object or process.**

An issue has three required components: a **call for action** on some **feature** of an **object or process.** Let's explore these three component parts through some examples. Note that an issue can be stated as a goal, a question, a task, a problem statement, or an area of concern. Here are some typical issues:

1 Find a fix for a switch that customers complain is hard to turn off.
2 Develop a new concept for our tax service that will attract middle-income customers
3 Which of the new products should we develop first?
4 Should we put a cost reserve in the budget for this project?
5 Choose a vendor from the proposals submitted by Alpha, Beta, and Gamma.
6 Figure out why the customers don't like the new feature.
7 Which government building is most likely to be attacked by a terrorist cell?
8 Should we put our money into product development or marketing?
9 Choose a design for a mobility-aide securement system for use on buses.

Before you read on, write down one or two issues you are currently trying to resolve or a couple you have recently addressed and reached decisions about.

In the first example in my list, the **object** of interest is the switch. However, it is not yet clear what **feature** (i.e., attribute or characteristic) of the switch needs to be addressed. Is it the force needed to turn it off, the switch's position, or some other feature of it? If the force is really the problem, then I'll commit future resources to redesigning the switch (the **action**) to lower the force. If the position is the problem, then any future **action** should reposition the switch. These features may seem to be similar, but they are quite different. Often the first issue in decision making is to refine the issue. Sometimes you have to develop some alternatives and criteria, and maybe even do some evaluation, before you can finalize the issue.

An issue always revolves around a specific object or process represented by a noun or noun phrase. For the above example, this noun is "switch"— a physical object. Besides physical objects, other common issues concern specific tasks or phases in business, manufacturing, or other technological/ business processes. These too can be represented by a noun or noun phrase.

Usually, an issue focuses on some specific **feature** of the object or process. A team may end up working on the "position" of the switch, or the "force." In fact, the real issue here may be to discover what is causing the problem, rather than find a solution to the problem. Aside from these important features, there could be many other features about the switch to address, such as its color, shape, or surface texture.

An issue is a **call for action** by the decision maker(s) on the object or process. Thus, an issue must have an action verb or a verb phrase. Sometimes it is desirable to "fix" an object; at other times it is best to "develop" a new one. The action verb or verb phrase gives a primary indication of the desired action to be taken. Typical action verbs used in issues are "choose," "design," "change," "fix," "develop," "refine," "make," "find," or "generate." There are many other action verbs that could be used. One way to determine an action verb is to ask, "What do I want to do to the object or process?" If the answer is not clear, neither will be the effort to resolve it.

This may all sound trivial, but it is not. Often, the most critical issue is to figure out what the issue is. If you can't clearly identify the object on which the issue is focused and the action called for, then any further work may serve only to waste resources.

A famous decision story centers on the *Mariner 4* Mars probe project. The spacecraft was to fit in a rocket, its solar panels folded against its sides. After launch it was to spin so that the solar panels would unfold by centrifugal force and then lock in a straight-out position. Because these panels were quite large and very fragile, there was concern that they would be damaged when they hit the stops that determined their final position. To address this problem, the major aerospace firm that had the *Mariner* contract initiated a design project to *develop a retarder (dampener) to gently slow the motion of the panels as they reached their final position.* (Note the call to action, object, and feature.)

The constraints on the retarders were quite demanding: They would have to work in the vacuum and cold of space, work with great reliability, and not leak, since any foreign substance on the panels would harm their capability of capturing the sun's energy during the spacecraft's nine-month mission to Mars. The engineers spent millions of dollars and thousands of hours designing the retarders, yet after extensive design work, testing, and simulation, no acceptable devices evolved. With time running out, the design team ran a computer simulation of what would happen if the retarders failed completely; to their amazement, the simulation showed that the panels would safely deploy without any dampening at all. In the end, they realized that there was no need for retarders, and *Mariner 4* successfully went to Mars without them.

The point of this story is not to say that the *Mariner* engineers were poor at their craft, but that they focused on the wrong issue. They spent millions of dollars to learn this. They should have found it out sooner, but they didn't. The issue should have been, *develop a method to ensure that the panels deploy safely.* It is often hard to frame the right issue. Revisit the issues you wrote down and identify the object, features, and call for action in each of them. If they aren't clear, try to refine them. Did they address the right issue? One useful trick is to ask "why" you are addressing the issue, and keep asking "why" until you get to the most basic issue statement. If the *Mariner* engineers had done this they may have run the damperless simulation earlier.

Even more challenging is when team members are unwittingly working on different issues. If everyone isn't working on the same object or process, the results won't have any better focus than the effort. I once videotaped three engineers trying to design a rack to carry a backpack on a mountain bike. The tape showed that two of them were working on one problem while the third was working on a closely related but different problem. This disconnect didn't become obvious until after extensive discussion. The work they performed during this period was not only wasted but confusing. And unfortunately, this kind of experience is not rare.

Often, issues are described with words that express what is wrong with, or what to change about, the object. These provide some information about the criteria that will be used to judge potential solutions. In the switch example, the problem is that the switch is **hard to turn off,** implying a criterion for switch force. Or, issues can be described with words that express what is desired. When buying a car, for example, you might say something like, "I need a new car. I want one that is **fast, comfortable,** and **good-looking.**" All the elements in the second sentence are seeds of criteria that will need later refinement.

Potential alternative solutions will arise during the effort to refine the issue. On the one hand, this natural occurrence is necessary, while on the other, it is a problem. Generally, when we try to understand something, we compare the information at hand to memories of previous experiences. These memories may be of objects or processes that we have seen, read about, or developed in the past. For some issues, we have memories of the same issue or a similar one and this can help us readily make sense of the situation. However, that doesn't mean that we will use the same solution, only that we understand the current issue based on our past experience.

If the issue is new to us, then using our natural cognitive process in order to understand it, we implement a three-step approach:

1   Decompose the issue into sub-issues
2   Try to find partial matches to the sub-issues in our memories
3   Recombine the partial information to fashion a total understanding of the issue

An important point to note is that in order to understand a problem we must recall previous issues and their resolutions. The problem with this is that these recalled solutions give us a predisposition to use them as at least partial solutions to the problem at hand. It is easy to get stuck on these solutions from memory and never seriously consider other alternatives. If this occurs, we are making the second of Nutt's blunders from chapter 1: trying to justify our only idea when we would be better served by generating multiple ideas.

To get around being stuck on the first idea, some decision-making methodologies say that it is best to wait until the problem is fully understood before generating potential alternative solutions. But since initial solutions naturally arise from understanding the problem, and also help us refine the issue, early alternatives naturally occur. Also, issues sometimes come with alternatives already attached: for example, "Choose a vendor from the proposals submitted by Alpha, Beta, and Gamma."

Here's a final point about defining issues before we move on: If you and your team can't write the issue as a single sentence, the issue is not clearly identified. If you're working alone, write the issue out. If you're working with a team, have each individual write his or her sentence alone and then share the sentences for all to see and discuss. Sometimes it takes effort to reduce the description to a single sentence. If someone is struggling with this, have him or her write a paragraph and work on reducing the paragraph to a single sentence. It may be necessary to pare away the initial alternatives, criteria, and other peripheral information to get to the issue.

Issue Stakeholders

Part of defining issues is identifying the issue stakeholders. Consider the following example. I was once on a team of engineers that was awarded a contract to design a system to secure wheelchairs on public transportation buses. This task became necessary because the Americans with Disabilities Act (ADA) of 1990 requires that all public facilities be accessible to all members of society.[2] To conform to this law, public transportation buses need to be able to load and secure wheelchairs and other mobility aids (such as powered scooters and powered chairs). Most bus manufacturers and transit agencies partially complied with the ADA by installing lifts on their vehicles that were able to move mobility aids from street to bus-floor level. But one problem remained: how to secure the wheeled mobility aid once on board the bus. In the case of an accident or extreme movements of the bus, a mobility aid that was not properly secured could become dangerous to the mobility aid user and/or the other passengers on the bus.

Prior to this project, methods used to secure mobility aids included clamps on the wheels and straps (originally designed to secure aircraft cargo) that were wrapped around the passenger and chair. Clamping the wheels presented two problems: First, there is a wide range of wheel diameters and widths, so a single clamp does not fit all wheels. Second, wheels are not particularly strong when gripped at a single point, and are susceptible to damage. Using straps has its own drawbacks; it requires the driver or another passenger to wrap the straps around the mobility aid and passenger—a time-consuming and uncomfortable experience for all concerned.

Our team realized that this was a complex issue and spent significant amounts of time identifying the stakeholders for the issue: "Design a securement system to hold mobility aids on buses."

In this example and for all issues, stakeholders (i.e., customers) for the decision can be identified by consciously and repeatedly asking:

Who will this decision affect?

There is almost always more than one person or group of people who will be affected by the resolution of an issue. By making a list of these people, you can begin to define the stakeholders.

One way to answer the question posed above is to consider everyone who is part of making the decision or who will be affected by the results of the decision. For example, think about any buttons or knobs in your car that you may find hard to reach. The position of these buttons or knobs is the result of decisions that were made without considering you—a stakeholder—either deliberately or accidentally. You were not a member of the team that made these decisions, yet you will be forced to live with the results of them. Every man-made object or process that you touch, smell, see, or use is the result of many decisions; in reaching them, the decision makers may or may not have considered all the stakeholders.

To ensure that you have identified all the stakeholders for an issue, try the following:

1   Itemize everyone who is included in the description of the issue.

In the example, the following stakeholders appeared in the problem description:

- A team of engineers
- Mobility aid users
- Other passengers
- Drivers
- Bus manufacturers
- Transit agencies

Because this may not be a complete list of the problem's stakeholders, a second activity will help us find the unforeseen ones.

2   Itemize everyone downstream.

In the mobility aid example, many other people beyond those already identified may be affected by the development of a mobility aid securement system. One way to find these people is to imagine everyone who might come into contact with the mobility aid from its inception until it is retired. In product development, this means throughout the product's entire life cycle. In business, it means from the time the business issue is initiated until its resolution is no longer evident in the organization or beyond. For most products, the life cycle includes the phases shown in figure 5.1 and for most business decisions the diagram in figure 5.2 itemizes the phases.[3]

Using these or similar diagrams to help refine the stakeholder list, ask this question of each block:

Who will be affected by the decision during this phase in the life cycle?

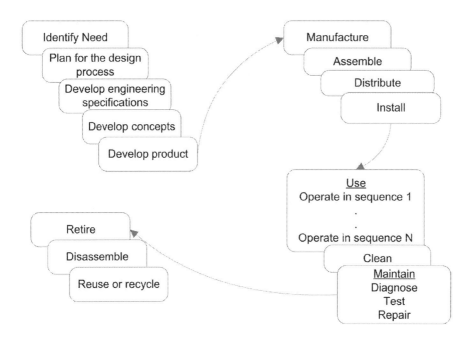

Figure 5.1: The Product Life Cycle.

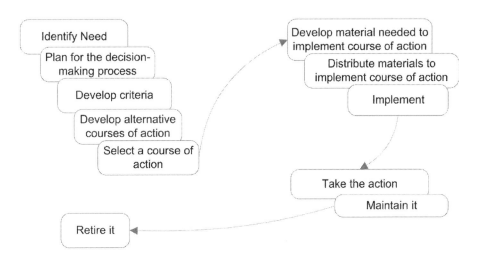

Figure 5.2: Phases of the Business Process Life Cycle.

In our example, following this suggestion, the list of mobility aid stakeholders was amended to include:

- Manufacturing engineers
- Assembly personnel
- Distribution representatives
- Installers
- Cleaners
- Mobility aid maintainer
- Disposal personnel

The resulting list of thirteen stakeholders is fairly extensive. In fact, as the mobility aid project developed, the list got larger. For example, six different classes of mobility aid passengers were identified. The development of this extensive list is not meant to imply that representatives from each type of stakeholder group should be on the decision-making team. It does imply that the team needs to ensure that it has heard each stakeholder's voice. It does not mean they are all important, or that every stakeholder's desire needs to be met.

This stakeholder step is simple, but it is amazing how often decisions can have unintended consequences because the decision makers didn't think about all the people who would be affected. Identifying the stakeholders early in the decision-making process will help minimize later surprises. Go back to the issues you wrote down in the previous section and see if you can make an extensive list of stakeholders. Note how many are obvious—the ones you write down right away—then try to add that many more to the list.

Issue sources

It is important to understand the source of an issue: "Why are we working on this?" Often, people use resources to address issues that are either not important or have lost their importance since first brought up. The only way to know "why we are working on this" is to know the source of the issue.

Sometimes the source is obvious, and the issue addresses some task or activity that has been planned or assigned as part of a project. However, complex issues generate many sub-issues; the source of these may not be so evident.

Most projects begin with a single issue that is something like "Change object X." This issue is then decomposed into many sub-issues that need to be resolved. Typically, project decomposition can be viewed at many different levels of granularity. On a coarse level there are the tasks normally seen in a project plan. These range in time from days to months to complete. The most detailed level is the cognitive problem-solving level that lasts but a minute.[4] All issues, regardless of granular size, have the same structure and evolve in the same manner.

An issue can be directly decomposed when its sub-issues can be resolved independently for the most part. For example, the issue "Develop a system that will signal that an elevator is about to arrive" has two sub-issues: "Develop a system that senses that an elevator is about to arrive" and "Design a system that will signal that it is about to arrive." These two sub-issues can be solved somewhat independently of each other.

In some cases an alternative is proposed for the solution that generates a new issue. This alternative spawns a sub-issue when some feature of the alternative is explored by developing both criteria and alternatives (i.e., sub-alternatives) for it. For example, a proposed new business process requires the purchase of new computers—a new issue is to select the best computer for the process. Unfortunately, many people bore right down into the details of one alternative and work on that to the exclusion of trying to develop information to help them choose a robust solution at a more abstract, less time-consuming, level.

Criteria often become issues themselves. This occurs when criteria are developed for a criterion. For example, one criterion for a new bicycle seat is that it must be comfortable. However, one issue that needs to be resolved is to measure comfort. There are many alternative ways to measure this and there are many criteria used to evaluate these alternatives. Thus, "measure bike seat comfort" becomes a new issue.

The important point about these issue sources is not that any of them are good or bad, only that it is important to be aware of why you are addressing the current issue. If in identifying the source of the issue you find yourself at some very detailed level, you can question whether this is the best use of your limited resources, or ask yourself if you can decide at a higher level.

Your Choice Is Only As Good As the Alternatives You Consider

Alternatives are potential solutions for an issue, and are often called "options," "ideas," "proposals," "hypotheses," or "positions." In an ideal world all the reasonable alternatives would be developed early in the decision-making process. But in practice, they are discovered throughout the process and often beyond it—sometimes too late to be considered, or forcing changes in schedule and budget.

Since a decision is a commitment to use resources, it is imperative that you spend time generating alternatives before you make a decision, not after. That said, as you develop new alternatives, issue understanding also evolves. Many times, important features of solutions are not evident until you propose and evaluate alternatives. These evolving features and their targets refine your understanding of the problem. In decision management, you need to make an effort to be aware of and manage these new features as they occur.

There is strong evidence that the more alternatives are developed, the better the quality of the solution. Most of this evidence is anecdotal, but at least one study has been done.[5] Six mechanical engineers were videotaped as they worked independently on a mechanical design problem. The researchers analyzed the tapes to find out the size of the entire space of possible decisions each engineer explored. (The term "decision space" is refined in the next section.) They found that there were a total of 18 different configurations possible for this device, and that these 18 configurations defined the decision space.

Next, the researchers examined the videotapes to see how many of the 18 possible alternative solutions each subject considered. They then

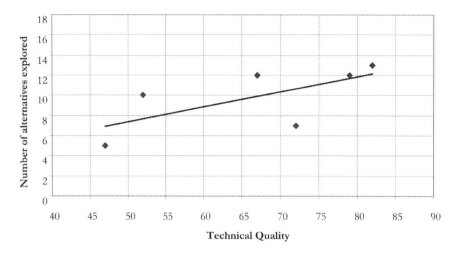

Figure 5.3: The correlation between the number of alternatives developed and product quality.

compared this number to the technical quality of each design. To find this, a team of professional engineers compared the resulting configurations to the design criteria and then added in a subjective rating. Figure 5.3 shows the correlation between the number of alternatives developed and the technical quality of the final configuration. You can see that there is a strong relationship.

The engineer who considered just 5 alternatives only explored 28% of the decision space. The engineer who considered 13 of the alternatives explored 72% of the decision space, and his technical quality was nearly double that of the first engineer. Granted, there were a small number of data points in this study, but this type of experiment is very time consuming to analyze. (For this reason, these are the only such experimental results I know of.) Additionally, we already know that limiting ourselves to a single alternative is one of the three blunders described in *Why Decisions Fail*.

Based on this study, Nutt's findings, and overwhelming anecdotal data, we can conclude that the greater the number of alternatives explored during the solution of a problem, the better the results.

The decision space

Let's further explore the concept of *decision space*—the set of all possible alternatives for the issue under consideration. In the experiment we just discussed, there were three primary functions that the device had to achieve. These resulted in three independent features of the proposed alternatives. Researchers reviewed the tapes to find the total number of ways the six subjects proposed to satisfy these functions. For example, for the first feature, the total number of different alternatives considered among all the subjects was three. This doesn't mean that each subject considered all three of the alternatives, but that the union of all the subjects' ideas was these three alternatives. The second feature had two alternatives and the third had three, as shown in the table below.

Feature 1	Alternative 1-1	Alternative 1-2	Alternative 1-3
Feature 2	Alternative 2-1	Alternative 2-2	
Feature 3	Alternative 3-1	Alternative 3-2	Alternative 3-3

The table shows that there are 3 x 2 x 3 = 18 possible combinations of feature alternatives. This assumes that all the features are independent of one another and that all the feature combinations could physically work together. The three features define a three-dimensional decision space. The eighteen combinations are alternative solutions in this space.

The size of the decision space can range from one to infinity. In most cases, not all the alternatives are known; nor, for that matter, are they even knowable. Figure 5.4 breaks the alternatives in the decision space into three major types.

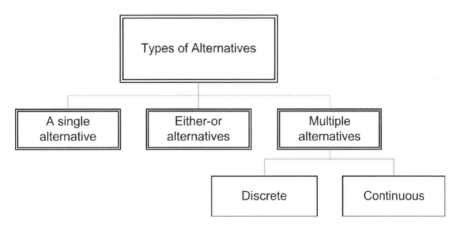

Figure 5.4: Types of alternatives.

A single alternative

In the words of Emile Chartier, "Nothing is more dangerous than an idea when it is the only one you have." Considering just one alternative is not decision making; it's justifying a known conclusion. A manager may have dictated this conclusion—and you're playing the role of "yes man"—or it may just be that your thinking hasn't gone beyond the most obvious idea. Most of the time, we base decisions on a hazy understanding of the issues and use logic to defend our favorite choice. As I pointed out earlier, in order to understand a problem we naturally develop the first solution to it. So our goal is to avoid getting stuck on that solution and instead develop multiple alternatives.

Either-or decisions

Often, problems present themselves as either-or options: "Should we put our money into product development or marketing?" "Do we hire Bob or not?" "Should we take the bid or not?" Both Franklin's method described in chapter 2 and the Evaporating Cloud method I will develop later in this chapter focus on these types of decisions. For some real-life problems, either-or is the reality (you are either pregnant or not), but for most industrial problems, there are many more options to be discovered. The Evaporating Cloud method is very good at refining either-or options into multiple-alternative decisions.

Multiple-alternative decisions

Most types of problems have multiple-alternative solutions. There are two broad types of multiple-alternative decision spaces: discrete and continuous. A **discrete** space has a countable number of distinct alternatives: which person to hire, which restaurant to eat in, and which vendor to choose. In the earlier example, in which there were 18 different alternatives, the decision space is clearly discrete.

In a **continuous** decision space, the alternatives can be represented as any point on a curve or surface represented by a set of equations. For example, deciding on the sales price for a new product or its weight, the takeoff distance for a new airplane, or the span of its wings. Each of these can be represented by an equation or set of equations with the variables taking on any reasonable value. You could just consider specific values of the variables and treat them as discrete.

In robust decision making, we focus on discrete alternatives for two reasons: Most problems have discrete solutions, and you can consider discrete alternatives in a continuous space using methods to sample the space.

The working environment to encourage creative alternatives

Sometimes it's not enough to consider multiple alternatives; some of those alternatives need to be creative, especially in competitive situations. A creative solution to a problem must meet two criteria: It must solve the problem in question, and it must be original. Solving a problem involves understanding it, generating solutions for it, evaluating the solutions, choosing one, and being able to implement the results—the decision-making process. Thus, creativity is more than just coming up with good ideas.

Originality depends on the knowledge of the individual, of the team, and of society as a whole. What is fresh and original to one person may be old news to another. If your customers have never experienced a wheel, for them a wheel is original. Companies and societies can either encourage or discourage creative solutions. If a company relies heavily on the sentiment, "We've always done it this way," then the environment is not conducive to new, creative ideas. If there is not time to explore what might excite customers, it will be difficult to develop creative alternatives. One of the beautiful aspects of a new company is that there is no legacy of how things have always been done; thus, there is a supportive atmosphere for new ideas to flourish.

In a talk I gave before engineering managers at a major corporation, I told the audience that they needed to encourage multiple-alternative generations. One manager responded to this by stating that his engineers always had at least three alternatives. When asked why, he responded that he would not approve a drawing for a new part unless at least two other solutions for the problem were presented at the same time. Although this is a good management idea, it can be tempting to generate other, weaker concepts to get your favorite one approved. Take care to ensure that there are both distinctness and variability in multiple concepts.

Structured Methods to Aid in Generating Alternatives

Although this is not a book about generating ideas, a decision is only as good as the concepts considered. Thus, a brief introduction to idea generation methods is in order. I will introduce four methods: Morphology, TRIZ, Evaporating Cloud, and omphaloskepsis.

Morphology: Organizing to Help Generation

On page 127, I used a table to describe all the combinations of alternatives that the subjects in an experiment could have considered. This type of table is called a morphology. Morphology means "study of forms," from the Greek root word *(morphe)* meaning "form" or "shape." It is commonly used in mechanical engineering design to move from function to form—hence, the name "study of forms."[6] In mechanical engineering the features are mechanical functions and the forms are alternatives that provide the function. This morphological technique can be used during decision making to develop potential alternatives regardless of whether they have to do with form, process, or anything else.

There are three steps in this technique. In the first step, you itemize the features: any attribute of the object or process being studied. In the second, you find as many ideas as possible that can provide each feature. Third, you combine these individual ideas into overall alternatives that hopefully have all of your desired features. Let's use a simple example from an accounting firm to refine each of these steps. Their issue is to choose a method to communicate their quarterly financial statements to the media:[7]

1   Itemize the features

The alternatives you propose to resolve an issue must have certain features.

Features	Ideas			
Medium	Paper	Email attachment	FAX	Browser
Content	Summary only	Summary and details	Summary, details, and comment	
Format	Text only	Text and tables	Text and plots	Text, plots, and narration

These are generally identified in the criteria; however, the criteria may only be measures of the actualization of the feature, not a description of the feature itself. Therefore, if you haven't done it already, your first step in this methodology is to identify the features a solution must have. For example, any communiqué must have three features: medium, content, and format. These are entered in the first column of the table.

2   Develop ideas for each feature

The goal of the second step in developing morphology is to generate as many ideas as possible for each of the features you have identified. If there is a feature for which there is only one alternative idea, it should be reexamined, as few features can be fulfilled by only one alternative. Some ideas for each of the features in the example are shown in the table.

There are a couple of reasons you might have a small number of alternatives for a feature:

- You have made a fundamental assumption without realizing it; you have assumed an alternative, and the feature only describes it. It may be appropriate to make such an assumption, provided that you are aware that you've made it.
- If domain knowledge is limited, then there may be few alternatives. You may need help to develop more ideas. (See TRIZ, below.)

3   Combine to form alternatives

From the second step in developing a morphology, you have a list of ideas generated for each of the features. Now the individual ideas need to be combined into complete alternatives. In this method, you select one idea for each feature and combine those selected into a single potential solution. Some results from our example are:

1 Medium = Paper, Content = Summary only, Format = Text and tables
2 Medium = Paper, Content = Summary and details, Format = Text and plots
3 Medium = Fax, Content = Summary only, Format = Text, plots and narration
4 and many others

But there are pitfalls to this method.

The first problem with it, if it is followed literally, is that it generates too many alternatives. For our simple example there are potentially 48 alternatives (4 x 3 x 4) and this isn't even a complete itemization of all the options.

The second problem is that if the features are not independent, some of the alternatives for one feature may preclude certain alternatives for another feature. Often, this can't be helped, and it isn't fatal—the idea is to develop alternatives, not build a perfect model of the decision space.

The third problem is that the results may not make any sense. In the example, the third alternative isn't possible, as narration isn't faxable. Although the method is a technique for generating alternatives, it also encourages a coarse ongoing evaluation of ideas. Still, you must take care not to eliminate alternatives too readily; a good idea could conceivably be prematurely lost in a cursory evaluation. The goal at this stage is to do only a coarse evaluation and generate all the ideas that are reasonably possible. Faxing narration should clearly be eliminated, but not all poor solutions are that obvious.

In spite of these limitations, morphological thinking is a very useful method for generating multiple alternatives, whether applied formally as described above, or informally. It forces you to recognize unrealized features and generate new ideas.

The TRIZ Method

TRIZ was developed to help engineers develop innovative alternatives. This concept has recently been expanded to aid in the development of business concepts.[8]

TRIZ (pronounced "trees") is the acronym for the Russian phrase "The Theory of Inventive Machines." TRIZ is based on the idea that many of the problems that engineers face contain elements that have already been solved, often in a completely different industry, for a totally unrelated situation, that uses an *entirely different technology* to solve the problem. The theory is that with TRIZ we can systematically innovate; we don't have to wait for an "inspiration" or use trial and error as with other methods. Practitioners of TRIZ have a very high rate of developing new, patentable ideas. To best understand TRIZ, let's look at its history.

TRIZ was developed by Genrikh (or Henry) Altshuller, a mechanical engineer, inventor, and Soviet Navy patent investigator.[9] After World War II, Altshuller was tasked by the Soviet government to study worldwide patents to look for strategic technologies it should know about. He noticed that some of the same principles were used over and over again by completely different industries to solve similar problems, often many years apart.

Altshuller conceived of the idea that inventions could be organized and generalized by function rather than the traditional indexing system. From his findings, he began to develop an extensive knowledge base, which included numerous physical, chemical, and geometric effects as well as many engineering principles, phenomena, and patterns of evolution. At one point, Altshuller wrote a letter to Stalin describing his new approach to improve the rail system, along with products the Soviet Union produced. But the communist system at the time didn't value creative or free thinking. His ideas were scorned as insulting, individualistic, and elitist, and as a result of this letter, he was imprisoned in 1948 for his capitalist and "insulting" ideas. He was not released until 1954, after Stalin's death. Since the 1950s, he published numerous books and technical articles, and taught TRIZ to thousands of students in the former Soviet Union.

Altshuller conducted his initial research in the late 1940s on 400,000 patents. Today the database has been extended to include over 2.5 million patents. This wealth of data has led to many TRIZ methods. I will describe part of the most basic method here; it makes use of Contradictions and Inventive Principles.

Contradictions are "trade-offs" that occur when something gets better and something else gets worse. This means that the ability to fulfill the target for one alternative adversely affects the ability to fulfill another. (This concept of a contradiction plays a major role in the Evaporating Cloud method described in the next section.) Some examples are:

- The suspension absorbs big bumps (good) but is too stiff to absorb the small bumps caused by road roughness (bad).
- Money we put into marketing (good) is money we can't put into product development (bad).
- The product gets stronger (good) but the weight increases (bad).

When using the TRIZ method, your goal is to find the major contradiction that makes the problem hard to solve. Then you use TRIZ's Forty Inventive Principles to generate ideas for overcoming the contradiction.[10] Altshuller discovered the Inventive Principles when he researched patents from many different fields of engineering and reduced each to the basic principle used. He found that forty Inventive Principles underly all patents.[11] These are proposed "solution pathways," or methods of dealing with or eliminating engineering contradictions between parameters.

To see how this works, consider the first contradiction in the list above, "The suspension absorbs big bumps (good) but is too stiff to absorb the small bumps caused by road roughness (bad)." Reviewing the list of Forty Inventive Principles generated the following three ideas. I list each Inventive Principle as a title and follow it with clarifying statements and the idea generated.

Principle #1. **Segmentation:**
   a Divide an object into independent parts.
   b Make an object sectional.
   c Increase the degree of an object's segmentation.

This leads to the idea of having two shock absorbers in series; the soft one takes small bumps and when it is fully compressed, the stiffer one takes the big bumps. In fact, this two-stage action is used in many shock absorbers.

Principle #10. **Prior action:**
   a Carry out the required action in advance in full, or at least in part.
   b Arrange objects so they can go into action without time loss waiting for action.

This leads to the idea of an active suspension, one where the motion is sensed and some form of control system anticipates what is going to happen next to control the suspension's stiffness and damping. Active suspensions have been used for years and even began to appear on bicycles in the late 1990s.

Principle #17. **Moving to a new dimension:**
   a Remove problems in moving an object in a line by two-dimensional movement in a plane.

This leads to the idea of using a linkage to get a more complex motion than can be obtained with a simple swing arm. Linkages are used on most high-end mountain bikes.

For the second contradiction in the list above, "Money we put into marketing (good) is money we can't put into product development (bad)," the Inventive Principles translated into the business domain by Mann and Domb can be used. Rather than explore this contradiction further with TRIZ, we will use the Evaporating Cloud to resolve it.

Evaporating Cloud

The Evaporating Cloud (EC) can help you understand the issue and develop new, non-obvious alternatives to resolve it. It is similar to TRIZ in that it starts with a conflict and grows from there. Eli Goldratt, the father of the

Theory of Constraints and Critical Chain Project Management, developed the Evaporating Cloud.[12]

The most important benefits of the EC are:

- It identifies the issue, starting with an initial conflict.
- It begins with an initial pair of unfavorable alternatives.
- It identifies the two most important and conflicting criteria that may later be traded off against each other.
- It helps identify the assumptions that lead to other criteria and alternatives, and possibly even new issues.

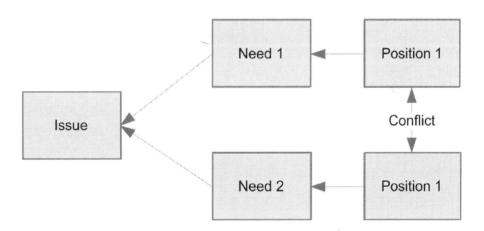

Figure 5.5: Basic structure of the Evaporating Cloud.

Figure 5.5 shows the basic EC. The steps to build this diagram are:

1 Articulate the conflicting positions.
2 Identify the needs forcing the two positions.
3 Identify the issue, the objective of the needs.
4 Generate the assumptions that underlie all of the above.
5 Articulate interjections that can relieve the conflict while meeting the objective.

In Goldratt's view, these steps help take the amorphous mess of a problem (the cloud), structure it, and then evaporate it by developing better alternative solutions and increasing understanding of the issue.

Let's look at the EC steps through the following example.[13] A company's flagship product was once the market leader but now the competition has caught up. The company can either market it more aggressively or put money into updating the design. It doesn't have sufficient resources to do both.

1 Articulate the conflicting positions

The two positions—initial alternatives—are "put money into marketing" versus "put money into product development." These are shown in the EC in figure 5.6. They represent the basic conflict or dilemma. It is assumed here that many issues start with a basic conflict—the problem that brings the issue to light. These two initial positions are alternative, and mutually exclusive, solutions to the problem. You can't have them both. Another way of formulating the initial positions is to state what you want to improve. This is the first position. Then, identify something else that is preventing you from improving the first position or something that becomes compromised if you do improve it.

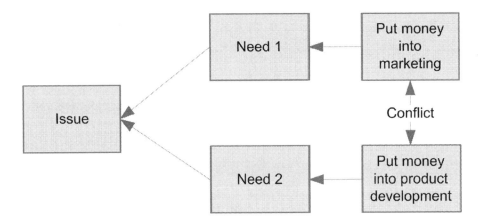

Figure 5.6: The initial positions that cause the conflict.

The conflict between these two positions is what this method is trying to resolve. Don't get too concerned that there are only two alternative positions; they are merely the starting point, and will evaporate as we progress.

2 Identify the needs forcing the two positions

Once the initial positions are identified, the primary "need" or requirement for the position—the "why"—must be discovered. It is the most critical criterion that requires us to choose the position. In this example, we are going to put more money into marketing because we need to make the customer more aware of the product. Similarly, we need to put money into product

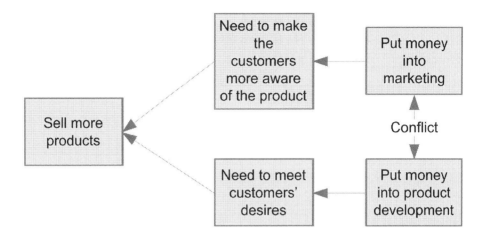

Figure 5.7: The completed initial Evaporating Cloud.

development to make the product itself more competitive. These needs are shown in the diagram in figure 5.7. Ideally, we would like to satisfy both of these needs. They are two initial criteria for a good solution to the problem.

3 Identify the issue, the objective of the needs

Based on the needs, you can identify the issue or objective. The issue answers the question, "Why is all this important?" Here, the reason all this is important is that we want to sell more products. Now we can read the entire diagram, figure 5.7. Across the top—if we put more money into marketing, we will make the customers more aware of the product and sell more products. Across the bottom—if we put more money into product development, we will meet the customer's desires and sell more products. However, although both lead to the same objective, we have a conflict because we assume we can't do both with our limited resources. Often it is useful to develop the issue first and work back to the needs that have created the positions.

4 Generate the assumptions that underlie all of the above

Now comes the fun part. All of the items in this diagram were predicated on assumptions. These assumptions need to be teased out, as each leads to more criteria and alternatives, and maybe even new issues. To do this, consider each arrow and ask "why"; the "because" answers are the assumptions. As there are usually many assumptions for each arrow, if you find only one per arrow, then stretch harder or consider reformulating the cloud.

In figure 5.8, a total of thirteen assumptions have been identified. Some

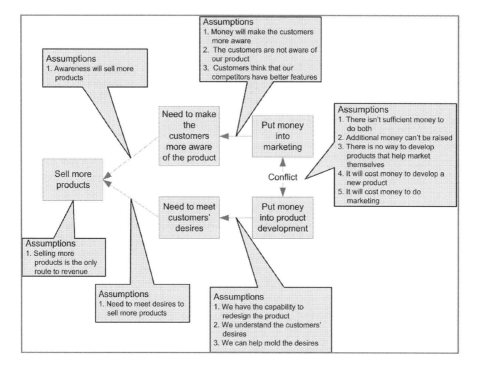

Figure 5.8: The assumptions

of them may seem obvious, and in some cases trivial. But by noting these assumptions you can:

1   Question the diagram for its validity. Some of the assumptions may demand more information (e.g., whether it is true that "the customers are not aware of our product" or "we understand the customers' desires"). The diagram may need reformulating based on what you now know.

2   Note new criteria. Explore how each assumption adds a requirement or constraint to the problem.

3   Identify new alternatives. These are called injections and are the focus of the final step.

5   Articulate injections that can relieve the conflict while meeting the objective

The final step to evaporate the cloud is to add injections. An injection is a new idea that may help break the conflict. Since virtually all assumptions center on why you can't do something, ask the question, "What can eliminate this assumption?" Answers to this question can help develop directions for further study and new alternatives to consider. In this example, some additional research that might help clarify the situation would be:

- Find the customers' awareness of the product
- Find the customers' desires
- Identify the features the customers like better about the competition

Some new ideas that are evident from the EC figure 5.8 include:

- Mold the customers' desires with minor changes to existing product
- Use online marketing to cut costs
- Identify self-marketing products

Although the diagram helps tease out much information, the EC mind-set is even more important:

- The two alternative views, which seem to conflict, do not conflict in reality if they both support the goal. To meet both needs, we need to fix something that is wrong with our perception (recall the story of the six blind men and the elephant).
- The process brings two sides together to focus on developing a new win-win solution that better meets both needs, thus evaporating the apparent conflict, in which each side defends its position. The win-win solution is not a compromise, which is lose-lose.[14]

EC's advantage over most other methods is that it includes a strategy that can help refine the problem and significantly aid in determining what-to-do-next. Let's examine it in terms of problem characteristics:

- **Time available:** Although the initial diagram can be built in minutes, it may take days to realize the assumptions and injections (as is the case with Franklin's method). Thus, decisions needed in minutes or hours are not candidates for this method.
- **Issue size:** This is best suited for problems with two initial alternatives that are in conflict relative to two initial critical

criteria. However, the method can help tease out additional alternatives and criteria.

• **Information distribution**: Although this is a method an individual can use, it is an excellent communication tool that others can build on; thus, you can draw in information from team members when facilitating with this method.

Omphaloskepsis

The last method for developing new ideas that I'd like to introduce you to is a long word, but a short-and-sweet concept: omphaloskepsis, from the Greek *omphalos* (navel) and *skepsis* (examination). You can employ this method while in the shower, riding a bike, walking, or gazing at the clouds. In a large and very important government publication on aircraft stability and control published in the 1970s, the very thin section on analyzing transonic stability recommended omphaloskepsis where no good analytical methods existed. Never underestimate the power of a daydream.

Measuring the Ideal

6

The Importance of Criteria

You have encountered the terms "criteria" and "criterion" many times in this book. I have used these words without introduction to help describe decision making in general and explore the details of issues and alternatives. The fact that I had to use these terms before I could define them clearly for you speaks to the complexity of decision making. But now we can concentrate specifically on criteria and exactly how they lead us to a robust decision.

Merriam-Webster defines criteria as "standards on which a judgment or decision may be based"—a good definition. As I use it, the term "criteria" is also synonymous with "requirements," "goals," "objectives," "constraints," and "specifications," as all limit the acceptable solutions for resolving an issue.

Let's begin with some "truths" about criteria. First:

Criteria define and clarify issues.

One of the issues we started with, "Choose a new car," has little substance without the criteria that the best car must be fast and red, get good mileage, and so forth. Criteria about speed, color, and efficiency define and clarify the issue. Without establishing "standards on which a judgment or decision can be based," an issue is just the statement of a problem, and there is no way to know when you have resolved it.

Our second "truth" is an extended definition of "criteria":

Criteria are the standards against which you evaluate the various features or attributes of alternatives.

This isn't to say that all criteria must be reduced to time, dollars, or some physical attribute, since some criteria are hard to measure and evaluation relative to them will be more "gut feel" than actual measurement. This chapter and the one following concentrate on developing criteria that not only meet this definition, but are discriminatory, measurable, external, independent, and universal, as we will discover. Criteria that have these features are *robust criteria*.

My experience with decision-making teams has demonstrated further criteria "truths":

- Criteria that are not documented early on will change during problem solving. In product development this is commonly called "**feature creep.**"
- If you don't define a satisfactory solution at the beginning, the only way to know you're done is when you **run out of time.**
- **Criteria co-evolve with alternatives.** Note that this point contradicts the first two "truths" in this list. The robust decision-making process requires balancing and managing criteria evolution against both feature creep and running out of time.
- If you haven't articulated your criteria, team members will work toward different goals (trying to meet different criteria) while **believing they are working together on the same issue.** Sometimes the use of unarticulated criteria is a management/negotiation strategy. If criteria are knowingly withheld until the "right" time, the decision-making process is being "gamed" and there is little hope for a robust decision.
- It is possible to make good use of the fact that decision makers may not agree about which criteria are important.

If you infer from this list of truths that it takes both time and trust to develop criteria, you're right. When working on a typical decision problem, you may spend a sizable percentage of your total decision-making time developing a robust set of criteria. That's why I wrote two chapters on the topic—to help ensure that your time spent developing criteria yields good results. Your decision can only be as good as your criteria. To demonstrate this, let's revisit the experiment I introduced in chapter 5.

The experiment made the point that more alternatives are better than fewer. It also yielded some compelling information on criteria. In this

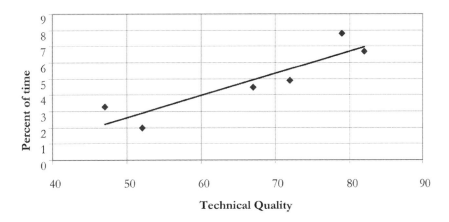

Figure 6.1: The correlation between time spent on criteria development and quality.

experiment six engineers tackled a simple mechanical design problem. In addition to information on alternatives, the experimenters measured the amount of time each of the six engineers spent developing criteria. This included reading the given criteria, rereading them, and refining them. Then a team of professional engineers evaluated the technical quality of each design. Part of the evaluation concerned how well the final designs met the criteria, and part was more subjective—evaluating the elegance of the solution. The evaluation team scored each of the six designs on a Technical Quality scale of 0 to 100.

As figure 6.1 shows, there is a significant relationship between the percentage of time spent analyzing criteria and the technical quality of the result. The engineers who spent around 7% of their time understanding and developing criteria had a 60% better solution than those who spent 2 to 3% of their time developing criteria. I don't mean to imply that 7% is an adequate time for working on the criteria; this particular experiment involved a simple, crafted problem and individuals, not teams.

The engineers didn't spend all their criteria time at the beginning of the task. In fact, the successful engineers worked hard to refine the criteria at the beginning and then revisited and refined them many times during the course of the experiment. This result should come as no surprise: a prime measure of the success of a decision is how well the results meet the criteria. In general, the time you spend up front to clarify the problem (understand the criteria) saves time and many headaches later.

In summary, *where the issue describes the problem, criteria describe a vision of an ideal solution.* A clear vision of the ideal increases the potential for a robust solution to the issue. The following material goes into great depth on the sources of criteria, how to structure them, their types, and how to develop targets for them. I begin each section with the basics and then develop more details. Thus, to get a grasp of the basics, read at least the beginning of each section; then read on according to your interests and needs.

The Structure of Criteria

The first step in developing good criteria is to understand their basic structure and organization. Each criterion has three basic parts: feature, target, and importance. Further, multiple criteria can be organized into simple trees; in doing so, you can gain great clarity on the resolution of an issue. These two topics, criterion structure and organization, are the focus of this section.

The Structure of a Criterion

Consider a simple criterion: "It is critical that the process take less than 30 minutes to complete." There are really three different pieces of information contained in this statement: 1) What **feature** of the proposed processes is being measured—the time it takes; 2) the **target** for the feature—less than 30 minutes; and 3) its **importance**—it is critical. In general, a simple structure for communicating criteria is:

Criterion = Feature + Target + Importance

To briefly define these three:

- A **feature** (also called an "attribute" or "parameter") is a characteristic of the alternatives that may be important to consider.
- A **target** is the stated or unstated goal for the feature. The target determines how you "measure" how well the alternatives resolve the issue.
- **Importance** is the significance of the criterion in resolving the issue from a specific viewpoint. Importance may vary with viewpoint.

We will spend the rest of this chapter and the next refining these definitions.

Consider these examples of issues and the criteria initially identified to support them:

- Design a front suspension system for a new mountain bike.
  - It must absorb road roughness
  - It should have at least 50 millimeters of travel
  - It must fit in the head tube
  - It must cost half as much as the Stone Shock R-5
- What new product should our company develop next?
  - It must have good company fit
  - It must fill a market need
  - It should have a high five-year cash flow
  - It should be simple—with low program complexity
  - It must be a platform for growth
- Where is the best place for our new plant?
  - It should be near a major highway
  - It must have at least 15,000 square feet of light manufacturing space
  - It must have interior decor that is better than the current plant

Each example describes a feature of the potential solutions (as a simple exercise, you can underline the feature in each of the examples) and targets. Some of these targets are quantitative (e.g. 50 millimeters, 15,000 square feet); for some others we can develop quantitative targets without much work; and others are qualitative (e.g., decor *better than* the current plant, *good* company fit). We will worry more about the targets later in the chapter. For now, let's look at features more closely.

The **features** in the examples listed above (as distinct from their **targets**) are:

- A front suspension must have these features:
  - Energy absorption
  - Axial travel (move in an axial direction)
  - Physical fit (dimensional interference)
  - Cost
- A new product must have these features:
  - A company fit

- Potential to fill a need
- Cash flow
- Complexity measure
- Growth platform
- A new plant must have these features:
  - Measurable distance from a major highway
  - Light manufacturing space
  - Decor

Many of these features are obvious: A product must have distribution channels, and a plant needs to be near a major highway. Those that are not clear are probably in need of refinement. It is important to identify the feature in each criterion for two reasons: to reinforce the fact that the problem being solved is the one you think you are solving, and to build shared understanding.

After you have identified criteria features, it's important to take the following steps:

Ensure that the features are independent

Each feature should identify a unique attribute of the alternatives. There should be no overlapping between features: They should be exclusive. This is often difficult to accomplish, because it's so hard to identify dependence. To demonstrate this, let's say that in the initial list of criteria for choosing a new product, a company proposes two criteria:

- The product is consistent with the company's focus/story
- The product contributes to the company's image

Although both of these features may seem important, in many ways they are not independent; image and story overlap. So the team will need to refine these two features, either eliminating one or defining both of them in such a way that they describe independent features of the alternatives they're considering. This may seem like extra work, but refining these ill-formed features will help to build a shared understanding of the issue.

There is a simple way to detect dependence between two measures, and that is to ask the following: Regardless of the alternatives you are considering, does increased team satisfaction relative to criterion A *always* imply either increased or decreased satisfaction relative to criterion B? If the answer is no, then they are independent. A single, reasonable counterexample to the question (an alternative that increases satisfaction in A while decreasing it in B) is sufficient to show independence.

2. Ensure that the features are complete

This is an oft-stated criterion for criteria. The problem is that it is virtually impossible to know what a "complete" set of criteria features is for all but the simplest problems. There are many methods sprinkled throughout this book designed to help you develop sets of criteria, but there is no measure that they are complete. Further, since features are not of equal importance, the features that go undiscovered are, hopefully, the least important. If you follow the methods suggested here, you should be able to develop a sufficiently complete set of features, but there are no guarantees.

These first two qualities of features—independence and completeness—are so important and prevalent that they have earned the acronym "MECE," Mutually Exclusive and Collectively Exhaustive, pronounced "Me-C." You should consciously ask yourself if your criteria are MECE.

3. Ensure that features measure only one thing

Features must measure only one thing; that is, have a single degree of freedom. I can explain this best with an example. An inkjet printer manufacturer was developing a new print head architecture. One criterion was "the ink should travel at between 98 and 102 meters per second with a standard deviation of less than 1 meter per second." There are actually two features being measured here: the average speed and the variation on that speed. In statistical terms, the average and the variance represent two degrees of freedom. It is easy to imagine alternative inkjet configurations that have the same average speed, but are affected differently by other conditions; or alternatively, an ink delivery system that is on the average slower than the 98 to 102 meter-per-second goal, but has smaller variation than other alternatives that meet the speed goal.

4. Ensure that features are universal

A universal feature characterizes an important attribute of *all* the proposed alternatives. If only some of the alternatives possess a feature, then that criterion is not universal, and either the issue is not well defined or some of the alternatives have features that aren't consistent with the issue being addressed. To remedy this, abstract the issue up a level. For example, if you have a criterion about the wait time for elevators when selecting a new building, and some of the buildings you're considering are single-story, then that criterion is not universal. The criterion should instead be written to describe the time it takes to get from one office to another. Then it will apply to buildings of any number of stories.

5 Ensure that the features are external

Let's say that you're a senior-level manager of a large organization, and a middle-level manager who reports to you has presented you with three different options for managing the work in her section. In deciding among the options, you are interested in things like how much each will cost, the through-put of each, system stability, and other features. The middle-level manager, on the other hand, is concerned with decisions she needs to make to provide the through-put, stability, etc. that you want to see: how to meet your criterion. Those kinds of decisions are too detailed for you to worry about.

The way to look at this, whether considering a physical device, a process, or a business system, is that every system or object has a boundary. Senior-level decision makers are often outside this boundary: i.e., external to the system or object. Thus the only sense they can have about the performance of the system or object is what they discern through the boundary. They cannot observe everything that happens inside it: the internal workings of the system or object. They can't influence or measure the internal features. In the world of computer science, this is called "information hiding." The internal information is hidden from external eyes.

For example, let's say I want to buy a car. Some of my criteria will be about its performance. For instance, I want a car that can go 0 to 60 miles per hour (100 kph) in under 5 seconds. Now let's say that, to ensure that I get the performance I want, I add another criterion: It must have a 6-cylinder engine. The number of cylinders is an *internal* feature and may not be important to the selection of a car. It may be irrelevant. Cars with 4, 6, or 8 cylinders may be able to meet any target I set for the acceleration feature. So itemizing the number of cylinders doesn't help, unless it affects some other criterion I have chosen.

The differentiation between internal and external features plays an even more important role in business situations in which it is more difficult to discern both the boundary and what is externally measurable. Trying to measure and control internal features of subgroups in order to manage the larger organization is such a pervasive phenomenon that it has a name—"micromanaging." Take care not to micromanage your decisions.

State criteria positively

There is some evidence that all criteria should be worded so that targets (either stated or implied) are positive—all glasses are half full, with none half empty, "the car should be red or white" not "the car should not be black," or "the process should be efficient" not "the process should create no waste." This is tied to some of the same arguments I made when discussing framing and psychological effects. Negatively worded criteria are just looked at differently than those worded positively. So it is best to be consistently positive.

Criteria Organization

Most issues have a simple organization with a single level of criteria. For example, the issue of choosing a new plant site might look like figure 6.2. Here the features are a single level in a simple tree with the issue as the trunk (rectangle) and the criterion features as the branches (rounded-corner rectangles).

On the other hand, the portfolio management issue "select the best products to develop," abbreviated here as "choose best from portfolio," is more complex. On the surface, it can be drawn like the plant site tree with all criteria at a single level as shown in figure 6.3, but none of these features is easy to measure. When you read the title of each feature, your immediate tendency is to decompose it into a finer hierarchy of features to be measured. And that's exactly what we will do to develop a feature hierarchy.

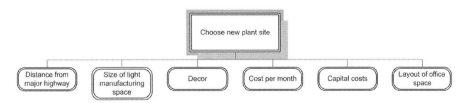

Figure 6.2: Criteria for a new plant site.

Feature Hierarchies

A much more detailed list of features that may be important for portfolio decisions is shown in figure 6.4: a criteria or feature hierarchy.[1] In total, there are nineteen second-level features that can be used to manage the portfolio.

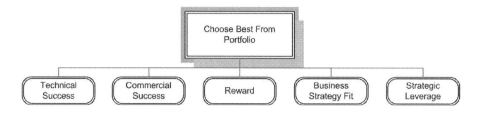

Figure 6.3: Top-level features for portfolio management.

Trees like this one don't come easily. Certainly, not all can be built top-down as this example implies. The templates in chapter 12 can help you get this process started, but if they don't fit your issue, I recommend the following sequence of activities:[2]

1   Write an initial set of criteria on sticky notes, one per sheet. Each should describe at least the feature to be measured and, optionally, the target if it is known. Targets may be represented by specific values or by terms like "maximize," "minimize," "better than," "similar to," or other imprecise terms. These will be refined later.

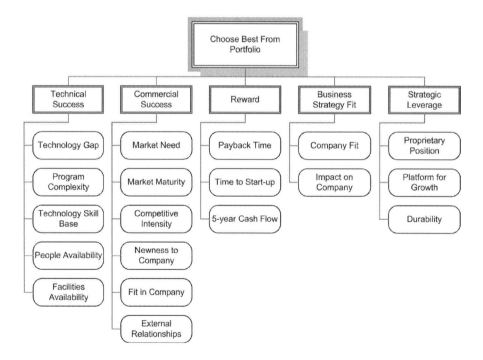

Figure 6.4: Detailed list of criteria features for portfolio management.

2 With the sticky notes spread on a table or wall, arrange them so that those that are related, or have an affinity for each other, are together. This can be done by the team and can be facilitated with programs like MindManager.[3]

3 For each grouping that evolves, develop an overall term for the feature that is measured. The overall or system features are the top-level criteria for the issue.

4 Reading down a branch should answer the question, "How do we measure the system feature?" In figure 6.4, it measures "Reward" by considering the "Payback Time" and "Time to Start-up" and "5-year Cash Flow" ("and" is used between all three terms to reinforce the thought that these three are all necessary, as discussed in item 6 of this list).

5 Reading up a branch should tell you why the criterion is needed. For example, "Program Complexity" is one feature that is needed to measure "Technical Success."

6 For any system feature, each of the features (the leaves on the branch) should be necessary, sufficient, and independent. Asking the following can help ensure these:

- To ensure **necessity,** ask, "Must I measure Feature X to ensure System Feature Y?"
- To ensure **sufficiency,** ask, "Are there any other ways to measure System Feature Y?"
- To ensure **independence,** ask, "If I have an alternative and change a feature of it, do I affect more than one criterion?" If the answer is yes, the criteria may be dependent.

This type of criteria structure is often called a hierarchy.[4] A good resource for discovering criteria and organizing them in hierarchies is Ralph Keeney's book, *Value-Focused Thinking*.[5] This book refers to the top level in the hierarchy as the "fundamental objective," which I refer to as the "issue." "Value" is what is important to the decision maker, a decomposition of the fundamental objective. Values are "features" in our lexicon, but this name, "value," can help us focus on discovering what is important.

Shared Criteria

In complex systems, it is common for criteria to be shared among sub-issues, or "systems of systems." Consider an example in the development

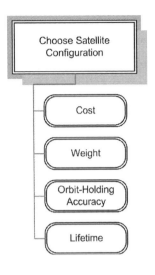

Figure 6.5: Shared feature example.

of a satellite, shown in figure 6.5. For the issue "Choose satellite configuration," the features are as shown organized vertically rather than horizontally as in earlier examples. This makes no difference; either way works. Three of the many subsystems of the satellite are shown in figure 6.6. In it, the issue is in the rectangular box; the features are in rounded boxes.

Each of the three subsystems presents a sub-issue that needs a decision: the selection of a system for the satellite. Each has a set of criteria, as shown by the feature lists. What is different here is that there are now three classes of criteria:

1 Those that are shared among sub-issues like weight and cost. In satellite systems shared criteria are usually weight, cost, and power. Usually, shared criteria for the subsystems sum to the value specified in the system, e.g., $weight_{satellite} = weight_{control\ system} + weight_{communication\ system} + weight_{structure}$. The shared criteria need not be shared across all the subsystems.

2 Some system criteria are only inherited by some of the subsystems. For example, orbit-holding accuracy in figure 6.5 is a feature of only the control system in figure 6.6.

3 Each subsystem has features that are important to it but not important to the others, or to the system directly. For example, assembly complexity is only important to the structure. These are called local, or subsystem, features or criteria.

Why go into all this detail? There are three reasons:

- Each sub-issue could be addressed independently to find the best alternative. For example, we can find the best control system, but it may not yield the best satellite. Still, there are decisions to be made about each of these subsystems.
- Managing shared criteria is a great challenge. One method is to allocate initial targets for cost, for example, to each subsystem

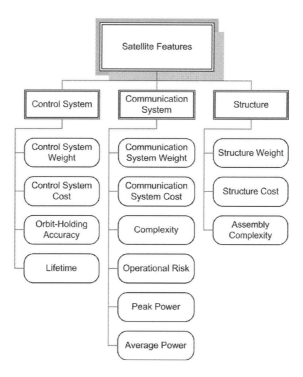

Figure 6.6: Satellite example features.

and then monitor the costs determined for the alternatives considered.

- If the system decision makers concern themselves with subsystem criteria, they are micromanaging. System-level decision makers have enough problems with the criteria for system issues without worrying about features of the subsystems. These are internal features as far as the system decision makers are concerned.

Managing the criteria in systems of systems is not easy, and beyond the suggestions I describe in this section, there are no formalized methods for doing so. One approach that can make this daunting task easier is to reduce the number of criteria to a minimum by focusing on those that are discriminating, as you will see in the following section.

Criteria Discrimination and Trade-off

Criteria must help reveal the differences between the alternatives. This may seem simple, but often it is not. Let's look at this with a simple example. If I go to a store to buy a bicycle, I do not tell the clerk that one of my criteria for choosing is that it should have two wheels. All bikes have two wheels, so a criterion built on this feature doesn't help me discriminate between the different models. If I tell him that I want one that I can use on trails, however, he can use that feature to discriminate among the bikes in his store.

Two examples from my consulting work will help illustrate the concept of discrimination. In the first one, a company that required a custom piece of electronic equipment sent an RFP to its vendors. In it were listed 60-plus criteria for physical size, power required, signal conditioning, etc. When the company received the proposals, they were filtered based on the criteria. Those that didn't meet the criteria were eliminated from consideration. Then came the hard part: figuring out how to discriminate among the remaining acceptable proposals. Unfortunately, the true "discriminating criteria," those that could help in selecting the best from among the remaining proposals, had not been well articulated in the initial set of requirements.

A second company, one that develops inkjet printers, formed a team to select the ink chemistry for a new delivery system. The team was composed of eighteen people from six different functions in the organization, e.g., ink chemistry, manufacturing, and image quality. Altogether, they too had over 60 criteria that had to be met before they could approve a new ink chemistry. Most of these criteria filtered out inks that couldn't meet their basic needs. Only a few were used to discriminate between the strongest candidates. Developing the discriminating features based on the initial list took team effort, but helped the team develop a shared understanding of the problem and, ultimately, make a robust decision.

Figure 6.7 shows criteria classified into two main types: filters and discriminators. Discriminators are further subclassified as trade-off or critical. To better understand the discriminator/filter classification, consider the Kano model, which was developed by Dr. Noriaki Kano in the early 1980s as a way to describe customer satisfaction. The model was introduced in the United States in the early 1990s. In figure 6.8, customer satisfaction is plotted against product or process function. On the plot, customer satisfaction ranges from disgust to delight. On the function axis there are actually two pieces of information. The first relates to the level of discrimination of the feature and the second relates to how well the target for the feature

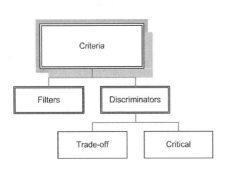

Figure 6.7: Classification of criteria.

is met. This will become clearer in the discussion ahead. Function ranges from "the function is absent" to "the function is fully implemented." On the plot, there are three different types of product features: **basic features, performance features,** and **excitement features.**

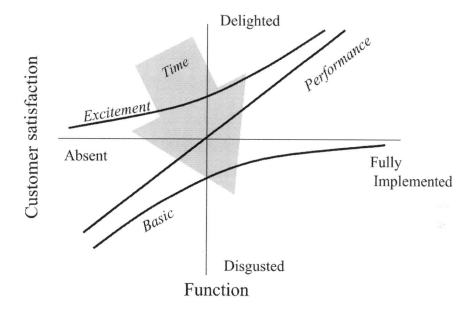

Figure 6.8: Kano's model of customer satisfaction.

Basic features, represented by the lowest curve on the figure, refer to product attributes that are not verbalized; they are assumed to exist. The only time they are mentioned is if they are missing. If a basic feature is not fully implemented in the final product, the customer will be disgusted with it. If it is included, the customer will be neutral. A bicycle should have two wheels; no customer will mention the number of wheels as a basic feature of a bicycle with two wheels as the target. But if the bicycle they buy doesn't have two wheels, they will not be very happy. Many of the criteria listed in RFPs only measure basic features. They only filter; they do not discriminate.

Performance features refer to customers' requirements that can be verbalized as: the better the performance, the better the product. These key features are generally not hard to identify. The targets for them, however, may be difficult. Continuing with the bicycle example, the better the brakes are, the happier the customer will be. One feature that measures the quality of brakes is their stopping distance. In general, the shorter the stopping distance without losing control, the better. Performance features are sometimes filters, sometimes discriminators. If all brakes proposed have similar stopping distances, then that performance feature is not a discriminator.

Excitement features are the prime goal in determining the voice of the customer. These are often unspoken, because customers do not expect them to be met. If they are absent the customers are neutral. But if the customer's reaction to the design decision is surprise and delight at the additional functions, the chance of the product's success is high. Excitement features are often called "wow" features. For example, no one actually expects that a bicycle will be comfortable to sit on. When BikeE Corporation first introduced its bicycle with very comfortable seats, the typical customer reaction was "Wow!" Excitement features are always discriminators. One reason that criteria evolve along with issue resolution is that it is difficult to itemize excitement features at the beginning of a project.

Over time, excitement-level criteria become performance-level criteria and, ultimately, basic criteria. This is true for most features of home entertainment systems, car gadgets, and other consumer products. When first introduced, a new feature is special to one brand and consumers are surprised and delighted. The next year, every brand has that feature, with some performing it better than others. After a few years, the feature is not even mentioned in advertising because it is an expected feature of the product. This migration with time is shown as an arrow in figure 6.8.

Although Kano's model is product-oriented, the philosophy relates to all decision making. The features that measure performance and excitement criteria are important to find, as these give the discriminatory criteria.

Within the discriminatory criteria, some features can be **traded off**, while others are **critical**. Usually, most discriminatory criteria can be traded off against each other. What this means is that weakness in one measure is compensated for, or traded off by, strength in another (hence these criteria are sometimes referred to as "compensatory" criteria). For example, in portfolio management, an alternative that is weak in "business strategy fit" may be strong in "commercial success." Further, other alternatives may be developed that trade off commercial success for business strategy fit, giving up one to get the other.

Where trade-off criteria can compensate for each other—that is, poor performance in one criterion can be made up for by good performance in others—this is not the case with critical criteria. Like a filter criterion, a critical criterion defines features that cannot be done without. But there are subtle and important differences. Consider two examples to help differentiate between filter and critical criteria.

In the "reward" criterion in the "choose the best portfolio" example, say that "5-year cash flow" and "payback time" can be traded off, but we think that there is a minimum "start-up time" above which we can't consider any alternative. This means that "start-up time" is a filter criterion; i.e., any alternative worth considering should have a start-up time of less than six months.

But let's say that we're designing a satellite and one of the criteria is that needs to be in orbit 300 kilometers above the earth and it needs an orbital velocity of 7.73 km/sec to achieve this orbit. Say that there is some uncertainty about the ability of the rocket/satellite combinations being considered to achieve this velocity, and we want to integrate this uncertainty into our decision. This criterion could be a filter (any alternative not achieving orbital velocity should be eliminated from consideration), but due to uncertainty we don't want to eliminate alternatives that might be able to achieve the velocity and do everything else well. Thus, where the other criteria can be traded off, the velocity can't; yet it isn't a filter.

The difference between trade-off and critical criteria can be explained using "or" and "and." For example, say there are three criteria: A, B, and C, and one alternative satisfies all three criteria fairly well. A second alternative is weak in meeting A, but is really great relative to C. Overall, the second alternative may be better than the first, as high performance in C is traded off for weaker performance in A. This trade-off can be worded as the need to do well relative to criterion A *or* criterion C. Criterion B is very important, but our uncertainty may be so high that using it as a filter would eliminate all alternatives. So, we include it as a critical criterion. Now an acceptable alternative must do well relative to (A *or* C) *and* B.

The reason all of this is so important will become very clear in the next chapter, where you'll see that most decisions are made based on very few discriminating criteria. Thus, it is essential to understand which criteria can help discriminate among the alternatives and which only filter.

Targets Come in Three Styles

So far in this chapter we have worked on criterion features. Now it's time to address the second component of a criterion, its target:

Criterion = Feature + **Target** + Importance

Before we tackle targets, note that in this book I make a big deal about the difference between the target and the importance of a criterion. During team meetings, many conflicts arise because of differences of opinion about what is important, not about targets. This isn't always obvious, but it's generally easier to get agreement on targets than it is on importance. In this chapter, I will refine how to develop targets. The entire next chapter is focused on managing differences of opinion about importance—and making positive use of these differences. By separating these two components, it is possible to manage the process while minimizing disagreement.

A target provides "standards" by which your alternatives will be judged. During evaluation (which we'll discuss in chapters 8 and 9), you will compare features of proposed alternatives to targets, some of which are clearly stated while others are much more vague.

There are three different types of targets. For each criterion, the type you choose determines how you will evaluate alternatives relative to the criterion's feature. The three types are:

- Qualitative (e.g., I want a car that looks good)
- Quantitative (e.g., My car must do at least 50 mph)
- 5-point (e.g., Seating comfort must score at least 4 out of 5)

Each type will be developed in a section below.

Qualitative targets

Good practice says that all targets should be measurable. This is not a new idea. In the late nineteenth century Lord Kelvin said, "When you cannot measure it... your knowledge is of meager and unsatisfactory kind." In 1921, the economist Frank Knight added, "Oh, well, if you cannot measure, measure anyhow." And in a letter to President Roosevelt, Albert Einstein warned, "Not everything that counts can be counted and not everything that can be counted, counts."

What Knight and Einstein realized is that, despite our desire to measure, important decisions still contain many qualitative, non-measurable evaluations. For example, the 60-plus criteria mentioned earlier, which were listed by the company seeking to purchase a custom piece of electronic equipment in its RFP, were all measurable. After using these filter criteria, the company had five acceptable proposals. Note that they didn't realize that all 60-plus were filter criteria but, when it came time to figure out how they were going to discriminate among the remaining five, they had no written plan. When they began to discuss these five proposals, many unstated, qualitative criteria evolved (e.g., "good relationship with vendor," "ability of vendor to deliver," etc.). These were the criteria that helped them discriminate among the vendors and decide which one to purchase from.

Qualitative targets are actually yes/no targets. This is shown in each of the examples in which the criterion features are emphasized.

- Alternative X **looks good**—yes or no
- Alternative X **feels right**—yes or no
- Alternative X **meets the needs of group Y**—yes or no
- Alternative X **is easy to install**—yes or no
- Alternative X **is always delivered on time**—yes or no
- Alternative X **is a good prospect for the future**—yes or no

One limitation of these kinds of qualitative targets is that when we try to decide yes or no, we usually find that things are not that black and white. When people make qualitative evaluations, they compare an alternative solution to a stated or unstated target, i.e., a datum or benchmark. Often, they compare alternatives to some existing object or function (e.g., a current process or product) or to the best alternative developed to date. Criteria of this type call for relative comparisons between alternatives and the datum object or function. For relative criteria, the goal will be dependent on the datum's feature. For example:

- better looking than the Ford
- easier to install than the current widget
- company fit is better than project Gamma's
- impact on the company is less than project Tau's

Note that these are worded as yes/no statements: e.g., yes, alternative X is better looking than the Ford, or no, it's not.

Sometimes a criterion has no stated target; For example:

- Technology gap is small
- Fit with the company is good

In these criteria, there is an implied target. The evaluator will know it when he or she sees it, but doesn't or can't yet articulate it. The problem here is that there is no actual target: There is no way to know when acceptable performance has been reached. But if many people make evaluations relative to such a target-less criteria and their evaluations are fused, the criteria may still be sufficient, as I'll show in chapter 9.

Quantitative targets

Quantitative targets have numerical values: e.g., weight < 50 kg; ROI > $2.3M; or cost < $27. Traditionally, quantitative targets are single valued, as these are. For a portfolio evaluation issue a target might be "The time to start up should be < 11 months." While the single-valued target of 11 months may be based on prior projects, and thus may be achievable, in decision management there are two problems with it. First, what if one alternative project that is evaluated is estimated at 11.1 months and another at 10.9 months? Suppose further that the one estimated at 11.1 months is much better than the other one relative to most other trade-off criteria. Are you necessarily going to eliminate the longer one? Probably not, as you will trade off the failure to meet start-up time with success in the other measures. Now suppose that instead of 11.1 months, the estimate is 11.5 months; would you still trade it off? Maybe. Then what about 12.5 months? The alternative has decreasing utility to you as the estimate increases. What is clear is that the original target of 11 months is not adequate to represent what happens in reality. There is uncertainty about what constitutes meeting the criterion.

Second, the 11-month target may be volatile. Volatility expresses how easy it is to change a target value. Targets can change due to outside pressures or gains in internal knowledge. What if the 11-month target is actually known to be changing? Then filtering out the 11.1-month project from consideration would be an error. The moral of this story:

Single-valued targets do not take into account criterion uncertainty and volatility.

In this section we will explore a simple model that does better at reflecting this reality. This model of setting target values, which compensates for uncertainty and volatility, is based on Kano's model combined with utility theory. Technically, "utility" is a measure of the happiness or satisfaction gained by meeting a target. In Kano's model, customer satisfaction is measured on a scale that ranges from delighted (full utility) to disgusted (no utility). Realizing that the purpose of a target value is to set a goal that will delight customers, Kano's scale seems to be a good basis for setting target values. This leads to the need to set two target values: one that delights the customer and one that disgusts him. Other terms often used for the delighted value are "the target" or "ideal," and for the disgusted value, "threshold" and "disappointment."

Consider the criterion "time to start up" introduced at the beginning of this section. For this criterion, the lower the start-up time the happier you will be; it is a "less-is-better" criterion. So ask the following two questions:

- **What is the delighted value—the value below which you will be delighted regardless of value?**
- **What is the disgusted value—the value above which you will be disgusted, regardless of value?**

These two values characterize a robust target. In the example, you may be delighted if an alternative can reach start-up in 10 months and disgusted if it takes 12 months, as shown on the less-is-better utility curve in figure 6.9.

Here, any value less than 10 months is shown graphically as customer delight, and has full utility (1.0). Any alternative that is estimated to take over 12 months is disgusting, and has no utility (0.0). Any value in between the two targets is a linearly interpolated satisfaction between delighted and disgusted. A project that is estimated to take 11 months has a utility of 0.5. Note that 11.5-month projects (utility = .25) are penalized relative to 10.5-month projects (utility = .75), but *not* eliminated.

There are many more complex utility curves available. Some make a smoothed "S" shape, and some sag in the middle. But these more complex curves are often more detailed than the information upon which they are based. Additionally, it is usually hard enough for a team to set a single target value, and the approach suggested here requires just one additional piece of information: a second target value. Other, more complex methods require more complex models of usually uncertain information, and are not worth the added effort.

In setting the delighted and disgusted target values, it is best to combine the customers' desires with benchmarks from previous and competitive solutions to similar problems. If the current process requires 6 people for its completion and it is known that competitors use 5 to 7 people to do similar processes, then it may be foolish to set a target of 3 people as a delighted

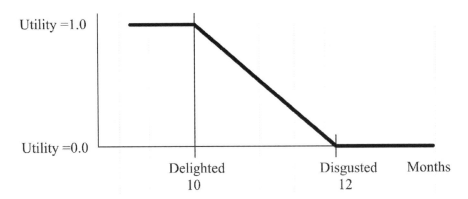

Figure 6.9: Less-is-better utility curve.

value in developing a new system to accomplish the same process. However, if you have ideas for new methods, then maybe 3 is a good delighted value. The important thing about benchmarking is that it forces reflection on the target choices.

Where the time-to-start-up example above and figure 6.9 are for targets where less-is-better (<), similar plots can be made for more-is-better (>) and specific-target-is-best (=), as shown in figure 6.10.

By far the most frequently used curves are less-is-better and more-is-better. Decision makers seldom specify the specific-target-best curve. This seems surprising, since in formal analyses we always work to a specific value; but in practice, people mostly want more or less of a feature. Note that the specific-target-best does not have to be symmetrical as shown, but making it otherwise requires three pieces of information to fully form the target: the mean, high, and low values.

As we conclude this discussion of quantitative targets, keep in mind that that's what these utility curves represent: targets. I've said nothing yet about how well any alternative solution *meets* the targets. That will come later.

5-point scales

In the previous two sections we explored qualitative and quantitative targets. A third way to measure value is to use discrete words such as: very important, important, neutral, unimportant, and very unimportant. These 5 different levels define what I call an N-point scale, where here N = 5. N-point scales are often used when trying to add real "measure" to qualitative criteria. While it's tempting to do this, take care. Many books suggest using these scales without any thought about what they are really measuring. One criticism of popular methods such as the Decision Matrix introduced in chapter 2 is that they lack measurement clarity.

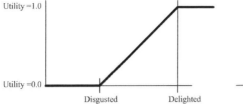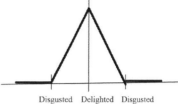

Figure 6.10: Utility curves for more-is-better and specific-target-best.

Discrete scales sometimes have 3 levels, and sometimes 5 or even 9. The range in market research is from 3 to 7. With more than 7 choices people can't do good differentiation between the levels. Five levels seems a good compromise between having too many levels and not enough. Thus, the following discussion focuses on 5-point scales (often called a Likert Scale). Typically on these scales, a score of 5 means that the target is fully met and a score of 1 means that it is not met at all. A goal of our discussion here is to clarify what 5-point scales actually measure.

It is important to realize that these scales are proxies for either qualitative or quantitative measures. As discussed earlier, qualitative scales are binary: yes or no measures. So any words used to assist in describing these must give a probability of yes-ness (it could be no-ness, but it is best practice to always measure the positive attributes of alternatives). The best set of words to do this is:

- Strongly agree = 5
- Agree (or Somewhat Agree) = 4
- Neutral = 3
- Disagree (or Somewhat Disagree) = 2
- Strongly Disagree = 1

For example:

- "I strongly agree that the proposed product looks good." This implies that there is high probability that the product looks good.
- "I agree that this car is comfortable." This implies a moderately high probability that it is comfortable.
- "I am neutral that this is easy to use." This implies that it is a 50-50 guess whether the product being evaluated is easy to use.
- "I disagree that the technology gap is small." This implies

that there is low probability that the technology gap is small (conversely the probability is high that the technology gap is large).

- "I strongly disagree that the fit with the company is better than project Gamma's." This implies that there is very low probability that the project being evaluated has a better company fit than does project Gamma.

Table 6.1 shows other textual scales that can be used to assist in a 5-point measure.[6] If you use any of these, be sure that you are truly measuring yes-ness, the probability of yes. In other words, a criterion like "excellent quality" gives both the feature "quality" and the target "excellent." "Excellent quality" can be measured using the "agreement" words listed above.

Score		Probability	Agreement	Frequency	Importance	Quality
5		Very high	Strongly agree	Always	Very important	Excellent
4		High	Somewhat agree	Frequently	Important	Above average
3		Medium	Undecided	Occasionally	Neutral	Average
2		Low	Somewhat disagree	Rarely	Minor importance	Below average
1		Very low	Strongly disagree	Never	Unimportant	Poor

Table 6.1. 5-point scales.

5-point scales can also measure the degree to which something occurs. In this sense, they're a form of quantitative measure. This may seem trivial—separating out "the probability that something occurs" from the "degree to which it occurs"—but they are fundamentally (and mathematically) different. Consider the measure "Market need," with 5-point responses like:

5 = Proven customer demand
4 = Some customers have mentioned need
3 = Competition thinks market exists
2 = Suspected near-term market
1 = None

Is this qualitative or quantitative? It could be either. For example, reword the feature as "proven customer demand" to make it qualitative. In that case:

5 = Strongly agree (there is a very high probability that there is customer demand)

4 = Agree (some customers have mentioned it; there is high probability that there is customer demand)

3 = Neutral (competition thinks market exists; there is neutral probability that there is customer demand)

2 = Disagree (no current market, but suspect one near-term: there is low probability that there is customer demand)

1 = Strongly disagree (none; there is very low probability that there is customer demand)

Or, moving more toward the quantitative, you can try to assess the values, the degree to which there is proven customer demand. (When you read this example, do not confuse your certainty about the estimate with the target being set. Here, only the target is considered; evaluation certainty will become important later.) Reworded for degree, the 5-point scale is:

5 = Proven customer demand (>$3M in sales in next 3 years)

4 = Some customers have mentioned need ($1M-$3M in sales in next 3 years)

3 = Competition thinks market exists ($0M-$2M in sales in next 3 years)

2 = Suspected near-term market ($0M-$1M in sales in next 3 years)

1 = None (no sales in next 3 years)

As another example, there is danger in rewording the criterion "high quality" as just "quality" and asking for response in terms of "excellent" to "poor," as suggested in the last column of table 6.1. Terms like "excellent" do not indicate either probability or degree very well, although they are an abstraction of degree.

It is important to decide which type of criterion you are developing, for two reasons. First, it brings clarity to the criteria and leads to better communication among the team members and other evaluators. Second, numerical methods to manage qualitative and quantitative information are different because the information content in the two types is different. We will look at this in chapter 9. When using the 5-point method, do take care that you know whether you're using it as a qualitative or quantitative measure.

To keep things simple, you should word all 5-point criteria so that they can measure probability. This implies *putting the target, no matter how abstract, in the criterion statement*. As examples:

- "Importance" should be "More important than Y"
- "Looks" should be "looks good" or "looks better than the current product"
- "Easy to use" is okay as it is, or it could be "easier to use than X"
- "Fast" should be "faster than a speeding bullet"
- "Team experience" is okay, but it can be improved to "team experienced for this project"

Note that all these can be answered in terms from the "Agreement" column in table 6.1 or in terms of the probability of criterion satisfaction being "very high" through "very low," as suggested in the "Generic" column. Also, note that adding a 5-point scale as a qualitative measure allows evaluations to be made more easily relative to some known basis. This was done in the first four examples above.

An Example

Figure 6.11 is figure 6.4 rewritten, with targets added for selected criteria. It shows all the major types of criteria targets.

Making qualitative targets measurable

Although Lord Kelvin and others teach that all criteria should be measurable, it is often best to leave qualitative criterion as they are. If you can show how the team evaluates alternatives relative to unstated qualitative targets (as I'll do in chapter 9) you can reach a decision much more rapidly than if you refine the criteria to be 5-point or qualitative types. In robust decision making, it is often best to leave criteria qualitative at first and refine them as needed. A truly robust process will inform you when you need to refine criteria.

But if you want to refine a qualitative criterion, I suggest the following:

- If the criterion uses adjectives like fast, easy, simple, or other unmeasurable descriptions, ask the question, "How can I tell if this object is [adjective]?" For example, "How can I tell if a project will meet 'market need'?" or "How can I tell if the

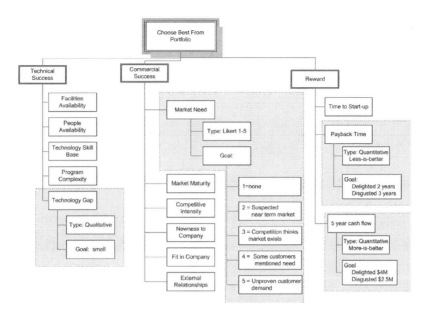

Figure 6.11: Portfolio criteria target examples.

plant has a better interior decor?" This may lead to 5-point or quantitative targets.

- Ask, "What does it mean that [qualitative criterion]?" For example, "What does it mean that the new plant has a better interior decor than the current plant?" The answers to this question might be subjective, but there might also be some objective measures, as itemized in the next guideline.

- Make a list of all the units that might be used to characterize the feature being measured. Standard physics units such as time, distance, and weight can be supplemented with "number of steps (successful, or completed)" or "percent of (customers or time)." To measure the satisfaction of the decor, the criteria might be refined to "the number of employees who find the drawings of the new decor better than the old one will be greater than 75%." Or, it might be measured in terms of the number of colors, number of different shapes, distance traveled between key points, distance between key people, or number of uninterrupted lines of sight.

As a simple exercise, look back at the features itemized for portfolio evaluation in figures 6.4 or 6.11. For each feature, ask yourself whether it is qualitative or quantitative. It is only quantitative if you can 1) identify a measure of the goodness of the feature (the vertical axis on the Kano diagram), 2) associate specific units to the measure, and 3) write instructions so that someone can consistently evaluate alternatives. For example, is "program complexity" qualitative or quantitative? You probably have some gut feel for what is complex in your organization, so you could evaluate this qualitatively. However, you could also make "program complexity" quantitative. Here are some measures you might consider:

- Part or subsystems count, or process steps (Units = number of parts, subsystems, or steps)
- Estimated time to develop and release (Units = weeks or months)
- Current estimated technology readiness level (TRL) (see chapter 8) (Units = a number between 1 and 9)
- Develop a custom 1-5 scale where 1 = not very complex, and 5 = very complex (Units = 1-5) or even better, restate criterion as "low program complexity" and use the agreement scale.

The point here is that you may be able to refine qualitative criteria to 5-point or quantitative, but it may not be worth it. Many portfolio methods try to reduce all the measures to Net Present Value (NPV). However, this purely financial approach to project evaluation leads to poor results because all information is uncertain—namely, financial estimates are often wrong (sometimes by orders of magnitude); estimated financial value generally decreases throughout a project; and there are measures of potential product success that are better modeled if not translated into NPV.[6]

Goals for Criteria That Support Robust Decision Making

Careful definition of criteria is essential to making robust decisions, and concern for targets is key to robust criteria. The effort spent refining criteria directly reduces the risk of solving the wrong problem.

Working to develop criteria can have very positive benefits for the different decision-making styles that were introduced in chapter 4, especially in a team situation. Criteria development work:

- Encourages internal problem solvers to share information
- Focuses flexible decision makers so that they limit the issue; this helps them settle on a resolution

- Encourages possibility-oriented and decisive team members to face the details of developing criteria before they run off and solve the wrong problem

Now let's quickly review the major points of this chapter. In your decision-making efforts you should:

- Force criteria development early in the process while managing criteria evolution and refinement.
- Present a strategy to develop the features that criteria measure.
- Clearly separate targets from importance.
- Ensure the robust formulation of qualitative, 5-point, and quantitative criteria.

Importance Is in the Eye of the Beholder

7

The Importance of Importance

Consider this scenario. My wife and are at a dealership buying a new car. I want a fast, red car. My wife wants one that gets better than thirty miles per gallon. It isn't that I don't care about efficiency or that my wife isn't concerned about speed or color, it's just that I think color and speed are very important and she feels the same way about efficiency. What is important here is that the features (color, top speed, and efficiency) have targets that we can agree on (red, fast, and thirty miles to the gallon). And at the same time the two stakeholders (my wife and I) assign different levels of importance to these criteria.

Where the previous chapter focused on features and targets, the first two elements that make up a criterion, here we will focus on importance, the third element in the equation:

Criterion = Feature + Target + **Importance**

One way my wife and I can begin to work toward a decision is to use a simple equation to formalize what we're doing. For each car, we can each calculate our satisfaction this way:

Car satisfaction = redness x importance of red + speed x importance of speed + mileage x importance of mileage.

Here, importance is accounted for as weightings on criteria (as is done with most decision-support methods). Criteria with higher weightings are more important than those with lower weightings. For me, the first two "importance" values are high, and for my wife the last one is high. How a set of criteria is weighted depends on the stakeholders' values, their job functions, and other difficult-to-manage factors. Note that we do this naturally with every decision we make; we just don't often stop to think about it and formalize it.

More generally:

> ## Overall Satisfaction with Alternative A =
> $\sum$(Importance of Criterion C x
> Belief That Alternative A Satisfies Criterion C)

This equation becomes important in later chapters, but we need to introduce it now. It says that your level of satisfaction with a specific alternative is the sum of how well you believe it satisfies each discriminating criterion times a weight that reflects how important the criteria is to you. Note that this equation doesn't work all the time. If having good mileage doesn't compensate for having poor top speed, I won't be happy with the car. This equation only works if I'm willing to trade off success relative to one criterion for poor performance relative to another criterion. If not, the equation will need modification. We'll look at this more closely in chapter 9.

The equation aside, it is vital to separate importance from targets, to capture importance from the different stakeholders, and to manage the differences between them. This is what we will explore in this chapter.

When we make simple decisions, it is common for us to choose the most important criterion and use only it to evaluate our alternatives. This is the most cognitively economic thing we can do. Alternatives that meet the criterion remain for further evaluation; those that do not are eliminated. Then the next most important criterion is used to evaluate the remaining alternatives, and so on, until one alternative is left.[1]

You can see this type of strategy in car dealerships every day: My wife and I want a fast, red car that gets at least thirty miles to the gallon. Let's assume that my most important criterion is "the car should be red." The first thing I'll do is look to see if there are any red cars on the lot and then I eliminate all non-red ones. Next, I'll consider my second most important criterion: top speed. If I find a red, fast car, I may ignore the other less important criteria, such as mileage, and go for the car that is in front of me at that moment. There are many other "filter" criteria that limit which cars I will even consider. If there are multiple red, fast cars, I will focus most on the ones that get thirty miles per gallon or better to help discriminate among them. Certainly, this strategy won't work if there is more than one decision maker and the decision makers disagree about what is most important, as is the case with my wife and me.

This simple example is a microcosm of decision situations in business and technology. What is significant here is that there are usually a few very important criteria that help us discriminate among the options that we have not filtered out. Further, this list of criteria differs from person to person—from viewpoint to viewpoint. We will explore both of these points, taking the differences in viewpoint first.

Honor different viewpoints

Inconsistency among stakeholders about what is important is a source of disagreement, richness, and frustration in decision making. A primary consideration in robust decision making is that each of these differing voices is valid and needs to be heard and honored. A robust decision comes as close as possible to satisfying all of the viewpoints, and the methods here are designed to help this occur.

There are three ways to work with differences of opinion about what is important: Ignore the differences, negotiate them, or honor them. Let's examine each of these options.

Have you ever been in a meeting that seemed endless? Perhaps everyone was talking about the same issue, but the discussion just kept circling around and around. One possible cause of this painful situation is a failure to manage the differences in what people think is important. If the differences are ignored, the meeting ends only when people are out of time or patience, or the most powerful person in the room makes the decision. In any case, the resulting decision will have poor buy-in and will likely not be very robust. Thus, the first approach for dealing with importance differences—ignoring them—is an option, but a poor one.

A second approach, which many decision-support consultants follow, is to come to an agreement on a single company viewpoint about what is important. This can be achieved either through negotiation or averaging.

The goal of negotiation is to try to make winners of all the critical stakeholders. Finding the intersection of criteria that they all consider important (i.e., a win-win situation) ensures agreement. If there is no intersection, the goal is to find a relaxed set of weightings that still addresses the issue and leads to a win-compromise situation.

If negotiating doesn't work, averaging might. But when you average viewpoints, you lose the richness of team members' responsibilities and opinions. In fact, these differences are a form of uncertainty, and even nego-tiation is an effort to average out the uncertainty. Remember, it's like mixing paint. If you take all the colors of the rainbow and stir them together, you get brown—always!

A third approach to working with importance differences is to recognize and appreciate them as a richness factor, and then discover alternatives that are satisfactory regardless of the varying viewpoints people have. This may or may not be possible, but it is a good goal and it avoids the pitfalls of ig-noring and negotiating or averaging. If you honor importance differences, you get a more robust result. You will find a methodology for doing just that in chapter 9.

Give me the few and the strong

The second point about importance is that only a few key criteria drive most decisions. Consider the following. Suppose that there are ten discriminat-ing criteria and they are all equally important. In this case, any one of them can only have a 10% effect on a decision. So changing the importance of one criterion from, say, 50% to 100% can only have a 5% effect—not very large.

It's more likely that some of the criteria are more important than others. In fact, if you merely rank the criteria with the most important first and the second most important next, etc., and then figure out the weights as if each criterion is just 33% more important than the one just lower than it in the ranking, you get weighting that looks like figure 7.1. The top four criteria

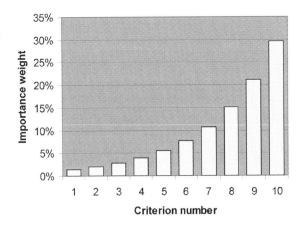

Figure 7.1: Importance weighting example.

account for 78% of the total importance. One of the methods I'll explain shortly uses an algorithm similar to this as a simple way to assign importance weights.

Regardless of what method you use to assign importance weights, you must keep this in mind:

> In most cases, only a small number of criteria has an influence on the alternative chosen

It is important to realize this for at least two reasons. First, you and every other stakeholder only have a few criteria that you consider worth fighting for—those that are most important to you. The others are either filter criteria or, if they discriminate, they won't sway the decision. It is important that you know which are your top four or five criteria and are prepared to back down on the others.

Second, be aware that knowledge of this fact can be used to "game" the deliberation. Consider the following. Let's say that you can see that a decision is not going your way. You've already decided on your favorite alternative, but it doesn't look like it will be chosen. What can you do? You can micromanage the situation by finding a criterion that your favorite alternative satisfies very well and exaggerating its importance. You win! If two people use this technique, you wind up with dueling dishonest micromanagers. A fistfight would work just as well and be quicker! Clearly, skewing importance in this way will not result in a robust decision. I describe it here so you can recognize it as a technique that you should try to thwart. Read on for methods that will help you with this.

Importance Weighting Methods

Now we'll examine four methods for capturing importance weightings. Note that I only recommend two of them; I discuss the others because they are widely used and you should be aware of their drawbacks. All four methods apply to trade-off criteria. As we saw in the previous chapter, trade-off criteria imply that when evaluating an alternative, weakness relative to one criterion can be compensated for by strength relative to others. Critical criteria require a different method. You'll find an approach for managing them in the next section.

The example of portfolio management I introduced in the previous chapter appears again here to demonstrate each method. But this time, let's put some people on the case. A team composed of Mark, Fred, and Sue needs to choose which product in their portfolio to develop. The team has decided to use the set of criteria developed in the previous chapter. Refer to figure 6.3 on page 150, showing each criterion's feature.

For the moment, the team is only focused on the top level of features (Technical Success, Commercial Success, Reward, Business Strategy Fit, and Strategic Leverage) and is trying to determine the relative importance of each.

The Independent Importance weighting method

The Independent Method is the one most commonly used for determining importance. Although it has problems that are easily overcome by some of the other methods and it is not one I recommend, it's the best starting point.

As I mentioned, Mark, Fred, and Sue are using the five top-level criteria to evaluate the alternative products. They have decided to use the independent weighting strategy to model each of their viewpoints about what is important. The independent weighting strategy is this:

> Give each of the criteria a score between 1 and N that reflects how important it is. A score of 1 means that it has no importance and a score of N means that it is very important.

Using these instructions the team members have each filled in table 7.1 with N = 100. The scores are shown and then normalized (in parentheses) to add up to 100 for comparison with the other methods.

	Mark	Fred	Sue
Technical Success	95 (22)	60 (20)	90 (46)
Commercial Success	80 (18)	58 (19)	10 (5)
Reward	85 (19)	62 (21)	0 (0)
Business Strategy Fit	85 (19)	55 (18)	95 (49)
Strategic Leverage	92 (21)	65 (22)	0 (0)

Table 7.1 Independent weightings

To Mark, everything is important; all his weights are greater than 80. Sue has used most of the 0–100 range to express her ratings of the importance of the criteria; she thinks two of the criteria are vital and the others have little or no importance. Fred thinks everything is of nearly equal importance.

This scheme results in a number of potential problems:

1 *The total scores are not the same.* Mark's score totals to a higher value than the others' do. If the team isn't careful, Mark may have a louder voice in the decision because his total score is higher. Of course, using the normalized scores, as shown in the parentheses, resolves them. But then all of Fred's weights are around 20, lower than he may think accurately reflects his opinion.

2 *Mark thinks everything is important.* That's a problem with this method: It's too easy to say that everything is important. This is also true of the commonly used system of using 5 terms to describe importance, such as, "Check the one that best indicates criterion importance:"

- Very important
- Important
- Neutral
- Not too important
- Unimportant

Most people will select the top two most of the time. In fact, I was recently involved in a large survey of nearly a hundred people about what topics were important to teach in engineering education. For each of about seventy topics, each evaluator had to use the 5-item scale above to rate its importance. Not surprisingly, everything turned out to be "important" or "very important." As a result, the survey team learned very little.

3 *Fred doesn't differentiate.* Fred scores everything about the same and does not differentiate what is really important. Of course, if this scoring is a true reflection of his assessment, then there is no problem; maybe he really thinks that every feature is of equal importance.

One technique that may help Fred differentiate is to mentally translate all of the criteria into equivalent dollars, or to some other common scale. To do this, Fred should ask the question: "How much will it cost the company if there is not <criterion>?" For example, it may be easier to compare the question "How much will it cost the company if there is not *commercial success?"* to "How much will it cost the company is there is not *technical success?"* But the limitations of translating measures to cost have already been discussed. It would be more useful to use the fixed sum and the ranking strategies I will explain shortly.

4 *Sue is extreme.* She has scored all the criteria either very high or very low. She may really think that the Reward has no importance, but this is unlikely. If all the decision makers think that a specific criterion is unimportant, then it should be eliminated, since it doesn't help discriminate between alternatives.

Even though it is used very often, I can't recommend the Independent Method. It's too easy to manipulate and it doesn't result in good differentiation about what is really important. The Fixed Sum method I'll introduce next gets around these significant problems with no more additional work.

The Fixed Sum importance weighting method

The Fixed Sum method is the same as Independent importance weighting except for one key distinction: The sum of all the weights must equal a fixed number. This forces users to think about relative importance instead of absolute importance, as is the case with the Independent Importance weighting method. If you want to rank one criterion as very important, then it forces you to realize that the others must be relatively unimportant. I highly recommend this method because of these features.

The strategy is:

> Give each of the criteria a score that reflects how important it is. The sum of the all scores must equal N, where N is 1.0, 100, or 3 to 5 times the number of criteria being weighted.

The team decides to use the Fixed Sum method to revisit their importance weightings. You can see the results are shown in table 7.2, which uses a fixed sum of 100 points.

This method has normalized the weights and forced the decision makers to question their weightings. Mark has had to admit that not every criterion is essential. Fred has held fast with his opinion that everything has about the same importance; but now we can readily see that he has compared the trade-offs between the criteria.

Sue has also kept her view that two of the criteria are very important and

	Mark	Fred	Sue
Technical Success	8	20	40
Commercial Success	36	20	8
Reward	16	24	0
Business Strategy Fit	24	16	52
Strategic Leverage	16	20	0
Total	100	100	100

Table 7.2: Fixed sum weightings.

the others much less so. As a result of forced normalization, the team can be more confident that this is an accurate reflection of her opinion.

This method also has an interesting self-checking feature. When people are having a hard time trading off the importance of some of the criteria, this is often evidence of poorly defined features. If they are thinking, "Well, criterion A is important, but if X occurred, it would not be as important as criterion B," it may be time to revisit the criteria, as they may not be MECE: Mutually Exclusive and Collectively Exhaustive.

This method is no harder to do than the Independent Weighting, has none of its weaknesses, and can point out flaws in the initial formulation. I can highly recommend it.

The Ranking Importance weighting method

Some researchers claim that asking decision makers to weigh criteria is so fraught with error that it is easier, and no less accurate, just to ask them to rank the criteria and then automatically set the weights according to the ranking.[2] Although this may sound flaky, I will show that it works quite well. The strategy works as follows:

First, ask the question, "If a fictional alternative did not meet any of the criteria (it is the worst possible alternative) and you could improve just one of its features, which feature would you choose to improve in order to make this alternative as good as possible?" Answering this question helps identify the selection of the most important criterion. Label this as criterion number 1. Next, excluding the chosen feature in the first round, ask the same question again to find criterion number 2. Continue through all criteria until they are in rank order.

Alternatively, write each criterion on a sticky note and arrange them on a wall or desk, with the most important on top. This is best done in a Pair-wise fashion by selecting the criteria two at a time and asking, "If an alternative could meet only one of these, which criteria would I choose?" Then, move the chosen one to the top and the other to the bottom of the arrangement.

Regardless of which of these two you use, you can convert the final ranking to a weighting by using table 7.3. This table shows the Rank Order Centroid (ROC) method. The mathematics for deriving this table are shown in an endnote.[3] Table 7.3 shows the weights for up to 12 criteria. If you have more, you can use the equation in the endnote to easily extend the table.

To demonstrate how to use table 7.3, let's go back to Mark, Fred, and Sue. They have each rank-ordered their criteria as shown in the table 7.4. They're working with five criteria, so they have also added (in brackets) the values in the shaded column in table 7.3. The criterion ranked the highest, 1, is given a weight of 45.7; the second highest is weighted at 25.6, and so on.

	# of criteria	3	4	5	6	7	8	9	10	11	12
R	1st	61.1	52.1	45.7	40.8	37.0	34.0	31.4	29.3	27.4	25.9
A	2nd	27.8	27.1	25.6	24.2	22.8	21.5	20.3	19.3	18.4	17.5
N	3rd	11.1	14.6	15.7	15.8	15.6	15.2	14.8	14.3	13.8	13.4
K	4th		6.2	9.0	10.3	10.8	11.1	11.1	11.0	10.8	10.6
I	5th			4.0	6.1	7.3	7.9	8.3	8.5	8.5	8.5
N	6th				2.8	4.5	5.4	6.1	6.5	6.7	6.8
G	7th					2.0	3.3	4.2	4.8	5.2	5.4
	8th						1.6	2.6	3.4	3.9	4.2
	9th							1.2	2.1	2.8	3.2
	10th								1.0	1.7	2.3
	11th									.8	1.5
	12th										.7
	Sum	100.0	100.0	100.0	100.0	100.0	100.0	100.0	100.0	100.0	100.0

Table 7.3: Weights based on ROC method.

Some likely questions about this method are, "What if two criteria are of equal importance?" (as Fred believes), and "What if some things are very important and others are not at all?" (as Sue thinks). Also, "How can simple ranking give a good model of weighting?" There are a number of responses:

- If the entire team agreed with Fred—all the criteria are of equal importance—then this method will fail. But, most people are like Mark, and see some features as more important than others do.
- If the entire team agreed with Sue, those criteria that are not highly weighted should be eliminated because they do not help

to discriminate among the alternatives. If the team disagrees on which ones to eliminate, the method will fail.

- Although there are extreme cases in which this method does fail, for most situations the results are good, are easy to acquire, and if used by a team with multiple viewpoints, probably give results that are as good as those of more laborious methods.

If you have more than six criteria, this method's results usually agree with the results of other methods, but this one requires less work. Note the comparison of Mark's results for the Sum, the ROC, and the Pair-wise comparison methods shown in table 7.5, as well as my comments on the Pair-wise comparison method in the paragraph following this list.

	Mark	Fred	Sue
Technical Success	5 (4.0)	1 (45.7)	2 (25.6)
Commercial Success	1 (45.7)	2 (25.6)	3 (15.8)
Reward	4 (9.0)	4 (9.0)	4 (9.0)
Business Strategy Fit	2 (25.6)	3 (15.8)	1 (45.7)
Strategic Leverage	3 (15.8)	5 (4.0)	5 (4.0)
Total	(100)	(100)	(100)

Table 7.4: Rank-ordered weightings.

In fact, Ranking Importance weighting has been compared to the results of other, more laborious methods, like the Pair-wise comparison that I'll discuss in the next section; it's been shown to give virtually identical results with much less work. I recommend it as a starting point for teams, since it's so easy to do. But if some stakeholders feel this it doesn't represent their feelings well, the weightings are fairly equal like Fred's, or the distribution is extreme like Sue's, the Fixed Sum importance weighting method may be more appropriate.

Rating (a_{ij})	Relative Importance
1	Same importance
3	Slightly more important
5	Moderately more important
7	Much more important
9	Extremely more important

Table 7.5. Pair-wise comparison terminology

Pair-wise comparison importance weighting

I'll present one final method here: Pair-wise comparison, the cornerstone of the Analytical Hierarchy Process (AHP). It is widely used, but not recommended. I include it here both for completeness and to show why it is inferior to the methods I've already presented. Due to its laborious nature, we will only follow Sue as she uses it.

The AHP was introduced by Dr. Tom Saaty in the 1970s.[4] It is a theoretically founded approach based on Pair-wise comparison. It can be used to help find relative importance weightings and to compare multiple alternatives relative to each other, one criterion at a time. AHP has gained some popularity, but it is time consuming because the number of comparisons explode geometrically with the number of criteria. And there is no proof that the added work improves the results.

There are four steps to the Pair-wise comparison method. I'll describe them, and then we'll apply them to Sue's weightings.

Step 1: Generate a comparison matrix.

The technique consists of taking all pairs of criteria C_i, C_j and asking two questions: Which criterion is more important, C_i or C_j? and, How much more important is it relative to the criterion of lesser importance? The answer to the second question is a value a_{ij} ranging from 1 to 9, as assigned in table 7.5.

The value of a_{ij} is used to generate the elements in a matrix where i is a row and j is a column. Since each criterion is of the same importance as itself, the diagonal in the matrix is filled with 1s. If C_i is more important than C_j the score from table 7.5 is entered in the ith row and jth column and the reciprocal of the importance score (i.e., 1/score) in the jth row and ith column. The structure of the matrix looks as like table 7.6.

In order to build the matrix you must do a Pair-wise comparison of $\frac{n(n-1)}{2}$ pairs of criteria. For our portfolio example of 5 top-level criteria, this is 10 comparisons. However, if you wanted to compare all nineteen criteria at a detailed level, there

Table 7.6: Pair-wise comparison matrix.

would be 171 comparisons. This number can be reduced to 42, as I will show later, but that's still a hefty number.

For our example of comparing the five top-level portfolio criteria, Sue's ten Step 1 comparisons yield:

- Technical Success is slightly more important than Commercial Success (3)
- Technical Success is moderately more important than Reward (5)
- Business Strategy Fit is slightly more important than Technical Success (3)
- Technical Success is much more important than Strategic Leverage (7)
- Commercial Success has the same importance as Reward (1)
- Business Strategy Fit is slightly more important than Commercial Success (3)
- Commercial Success is moderately more important than Strategic Leverage (5)
- Business Strategy Fit is moderately more important than Reward (5)
- Strategic Leverage is slightly more important than Reward (3)
- Business Strategy Fit is extremely more important than Strategic Leverage (9)

Step 2: Normalize the matrix by dividing each entry in a column by the column's sum.

Step 3. Compute the arithmetic average of each row in the normalized matrix. This value gives an estimate of the relative weights of the criteria being compared. The averages should sum to 1.0 as a check.

Step 4. Compute the Consistency Ratio. Because judgments will never agree perfectly, the degree of consistency achieved is measured by a Consistency Ratio (CR) indicating the probability that the matrix was randomly generated. I won't go into detail about computing the consistency ratio here. This and other details about Pair-wise comparison can be found in Dr. Saaty's book on AHP.[5]

Here's what the matrix looks like:

	Technical Success	Commercial Success	Reward	Business Strategy Fit	Strategic Leverage
Technical Success	1	3	5	1/3	7
Commercial Success	1/3	1	1	1/3	5
Reward	1/5	1	1	1/5	3
Business Strategy Fit	3	3	5	1	9
Strategic Leverage	1/7	1/3	1/3	1/9	1

Table 7.7: Raw data in Pair-wise comparison matrix.

Normalizing, as called for in Step 2, and computing the weights, Step 3, are shown in table 7.8.

	Technical Success	Commercial Success	Reward	Business Strategy Fit	Strategic Leverage	Average x 100
Technical Success	.21	.36	.40	.17	.28	28
Commercial Success	.07	.12	.08	.17	.20	13
Reward	.04	.12	.08	.07	.12	9
Business Strategy Fit	.64	.36	.40	.51	.36	45
Strategic Leverage	.03	.04	.03	05	.04	4
					Sum	99

Table 7.8: Final Pair-wise comparison matrix.

Pair-wise comparison has a solid theoretical foundation based on judgments about pairs of criteria and the properties of the reciprocal matrix of

Pair-wise comparisons. The advantage of this technique is that it can use information from handbooks or regression output, or decision makers/experts can be asked to rank-order individual factors. The disadvantages of Pair-wise comparisons are:

- The number of judgments that must be made increases geometrically with the number of criteria. But, as I stated earlier, this can be managed to some degree in some cases. Regardless, it is laborious compared to other methods.
- If one criterion is changed or another added, the whole process must virtually be begun again.
- It usually compares closely with the Ranking method, which is much easier, more robust to changes, and faster to do. This is not only true for the portfolio example, but in every case I've examined.
- Although it has a firm mathematical background and can be used to ensure consistency, its added work isn't warranted because there simply is no right answer. And if you honor multiple team members' viewpoints, variation is accounted for.

For all these reasons, but primarily because of the extra work involved without evidence that it does any better than the simpler methods, I don't recommend the AHP method.

Comparison of methods and conclusions

All of the results I have covered in this chapter are listed in table 7.9. For Mark, the Sum method and Rank method agree fairly well, differing by an average of 5%. For Fred, the comparison is not as good—12%—because the Rank method will not let him claim that all are of near equal importance. In Sue's case, the Sum and Rank methods only differ by 8%—not

	Mark			Fred			Sue			
	Ind.	Sum	Rank	Ind.	Sum	Rank	Ind.	Sum	Rank	Pair
Technical Success	22	8	4	20	20	46	46	40	26	28
Commercial Success	18	36	46	19	20	26	5	8	16	13
Reward	19	16	9	21	24	9	0	0	9	9
Business Strategy Fit	19	24	26	18	16	16	49	52	46	45
Strategic Leverage	21	16	16	22	20	4	0	0	4	4

Table 7.9: Comparison of methods.

bad considering how extreme her weightings are. Comparing the Rank and the Pair-wise methods yields only a 1% difference. This is typical of comparisons of these two methods.

Additionally, for the Sum and Rank methods, and with the exception of Fred's Sum results, the top two criteria have at least 60% of the importance and the top three have at least 78%. This is generally the case, and supports the earlier assertion that in most cases only a small number of criteria have an influence on the chosen alternative.

The results provoke the question, "Which method is correct?" It is hard to know, since there is no "correct" answer. So this leads to another question: "If there is no correct answer, what do I do to get the best possible results?" Getting the best possible results implies using as little time as possible while ensuring that the importance weightings reflect the stakeholders' opinions about what is important. The following meets these criteria and is a summary of all we have discussed so far in this chapter.

1   Above all, identify what is important to whom.

2   Separate importance from criterion targets.

3   Honor the importance weightings from multiple stakeholders. This eliminates the need for one "correct" result by allowing results to be seen through multiple eyes.

4   Don't use the Independent weighting strategy. Although it's popular and easy to use, it has the potential to produce poor results.

5   Use a Fixed Sum strategy, since it produces better results than Independent weighting and takes very little extra effort.

6   If there are more than six criteria, alternatively use the Ranking strategy. This requires less work than the Fixed Sum and affords good results.

7   Don't use Pair-wise comparisons, as the additional work involved is not worth the effort. The Ranking method generally gives similar results, and is easier to do modify.

8   If you want a single combined team importance rating (which I do not recommend, and will address again in chapter 10), use the Ranking strategy. It is best with teams who can communally order the criteria by moving sticky notes on a wall or table.

9 If the majority of the team gives a criterion a very low importance, then eliminate it. It will not help discriminate among the alternatives.

10 If many on the team cannot determine the difference between two criteria, the criteria may be poor. Ensure that the criteria are MECE.

I could end this chapter here, but many problems are more complex (e.g., the multiple levels in the Portfolio feature tree) and not all criteria can be traded off. So I'll address these issues in the next two sections.

Managing Hierarchies

In our portfolio example, there are five top-level criteria with nineteen second-level criteria. Before I show you a method to manage all nineteen, I need to note that, in most cases, not all of these criteria are discriminators. If we only consider the criteria that discriminate, the total may be less than nineteen. The following is the best methodology to follow in managing a hierarchy of criteria. It works with any of the methods in the previous section.

Step 1: At the top level, determine the importance weightings.

Step 2: For each sub-group, determine the importance within the group.

Step 3: The total importance for each criteria in the sub-group is the product of its importance weighting in the group, times that of its parent.

For example: Suppose Sue uses the weights found by the Ranking method for the top level (See table 7.4):

•Technical Success	25.6
•Commercial Success	15.8
•Reward	9.0
•Business Strategy Fit	45.7
•Strategic Leverage	4.0
Total	100.0

Now she uses the Sum method to determine the importance weights within the Technology Success group, which gives these values:

- Technology Gap   35.0
- Program Complexity   27.0
- Technology Skill Base   8.0
- People Availability   8.0
- Facilities Available   22.0
- Total   100.0

Finally, multiplying these by the importance of Technology Success (25.6), and remembering that these numbers are all percentages, yields the results below. For example, Technology Gap importance is .256 x .350 = .090 or 9.0%.

- Technology Gap   9.0
- Program Complexity   6.9
- Technology Skill Base   2.1
- People Availability   2.0
- Facilities Available   5.6
- Total   25.6

The total for Technology Success is as it should be: 25.6%. A similar approach applies to all the other detailed criteria. The sum total over the entire hierarchy will be 100%. Note that all the sub-criteria will have importance weights of less than 10%. This implies that nothing is very important when there are nineteen criteria. This isn't generally true, as only a few criteria actually drive most decisions.

Using the Sum or Rank methods, this decomposition requires six separate comparisons, one at the top level and one for each of the detail set of criteria. For the Pair-wise comparison method, decomposition is what allows 42 Pair-wise comparisons rather than 171.

Hierarchies are intellectually satisfying. The challenge is to determine which of the criteria in them filter and which discriminate. As you can see above, if the entire tree is used to make a decision, nothing is important and decisions will be difficult to make.

Critical Criteria

Where all the methods in this chapter support trade-off criteria by using a weighted sum (the formula shown at the beginning of this chapter), critical criteria can't managed in this way. Critical criteria cannot be traded off; an alternative that doesn't meet a critical criterion is unacceptable and must be eliminated.

Decision researchers have tried for years to find a good method to handle critical criteria, but there is no easy way to do this. Most methods revolve around using multiplication rather than addition in the formula shown at the beginning of this chapter. The problem with this approach is that when just a few criteria are not fully met, satisfaction drops to near zero. There are two fixes for this. First, question every critical criterion and see if it can be used as a filter. Second, there are robust methods introduced in chapter 10 to manage critical criteria (these cannot be done by hand). But for now, use the methods for trade-off criteria to weight all criteria and note which ones are critical.

Goals for Importance That Support Robust Decision Making

In this chapter, I have emphasized the need to:

1   Identify what is important to whom
2   Separate importance from criterion targets
3   Honor the importance weightings from multiple stakeholders

If there are two or more people involved in making a decision, it is impossible to control differences in opinion about what is important. Thus, one goal of robust decision making is to honor the differences, use them to guide deliberation, and develop decisions that are satisfactory to all parties. In the following chapters, you will see how this is done.

Decisions Are Based on Your Belief About an Uncertain Future

8

All the material you've read in previous chapters leads here, where the fun begins. I may have depressed you in chapter 3 when I described how poor most estimates are because of uncertainty. I may have made matters even worse when I delved into the basic cognitive factors that affect our ability to make robust decisions. Then in chapter 5 we began to learn how we go about understanding, or framing, problems. Now we are at the point where we can evaluate, fuse, and decide what-to-do-next. In the next few chapters I will bring together everything we have explored to date, introducing you to a methodology that:

- Helps you to manage uncertainty
- Supports building a shared understanding
- Supports multiple cognitive styles to help ensure buy-in and accountability
- Helps avoid groupthink
- Supports a mix of qualitative, quantitative, and 5-point evaluations
- Supports incomplete evaluations
- Supports multiple viewpoints about what is important
- Answers the five key questions:
  1 Which is the best alternative?
  2 What is the risk that our decision will not turn out as we expect?
  3 Do we know enough to make a good decision yet?
  4 Is there buy-in for the decision?
  5 What do we need to do next to feel confident about our decision, within the scope of our limited resources?

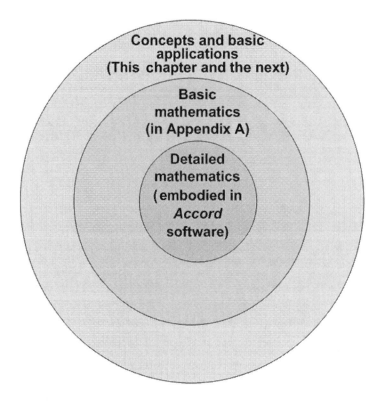

Figure 8.1: The hierarchy of detail.

This chapter will get us just partway there; achieving everything on the list will require the methods I will develop in the next chapter. Here our focus is on a major factor in decision making: belief. **It is your belief in estimates about an uncertain future that drives all of your decisions.** No matter how firm your data may seem, it still comes down to belief in how well they prophesy the future that determines what you do next.

The methods I discuss here are based on Artificial Intelligence mathematics. This underlying mathematics is quite complex, but you don't need to understand it or even read about it to make use of the methods. You will find virtually no mathematics in this chapter or the next. I only assume that you have a very basic knowledge of probabilities.

The hierarchy of detail available to you is shown in figure 8.1. If you would like more detail on the math, you can find it in appendix A. Even more complex math is programmed into *Accord*, the robust decision-support tool. It is easy to use and requires no mathematical skill. You can download *Accord* and use it as you work through this chapter; for details, see appendix B.

It's Only Your Beliefs That Count

The title of this chapter, "Decisions Are Based on Your Belief About an Uncertain Future," emphasizes the importance of beliefs in evaluation results, in estimations, in your own knowledge, in what you are told, etc. Your beliefs are based on your core values, your role in the organization, and your estimates about past events and the current state of things—and most importantly, about events, actions, and objects yet to come.

Consider our example team from chapter 1. John, Anne, Bob, and Lisa are working on choosing a proposal from three that passed their filtering criteria: Grex, Swale, and Able Industries. One criterion they think is important is that the system must be "easy to use"—a qualitative criterion. We learned that in the past, Grex's products have not been easy to use, but as Lisa informed the team, there have been changes at Grex. It also came to light that there had been very little training allotted to using the last Grex system. Thus, a second criterion is "training time"—a less-the-better criterion. Based on past experience, the team will be delighted if the training time is 4 hours or less and disgusted if it is greater than 8 hours. A third criterion is the cost of the system. They were given a budget of $20,000, but know that there is some "wiggle room" (read as "uncertainty").

After reading the three proposals, the team members held a meeting to recap their situation:

- They have all had experience with Grex. Some of it was good, some bad. Some on the team have knowledge about Swale, and Able Industries is new to everyone.
- The vendors were not given a specific cost target to hit, but all are in a reasonable range. There is some difference of opinion about what is included in the cost in the Grex proposal, and there is some uncertainty about exactly what each of the proposals would really wind up costing.
- No one is very certain about the training proposals. Lisa's interpretation of Swale's training time seems much different from John's and Bob's.
- There isn't strong agreement about the experience level of the vendors' teams.
- The team needs to reach a decision as soon as possible and doesn't have time to go through the process of requesting more

information from the vendors. In other words, they are under
pressure to make a decision based on the material at hand.

The situation I just described is very common. Many decision-making teams
find themselves in situations where:

1   Evaluations of the alternatives relative to the criteria are a mix
    of qualitative and quantitative.
2   Knowledge about the evaluations is unevenly distributed among
    the team members.
3   Members don't agree on some evaluations.
4   There is even uncertainty about the quantitative evaluations.
5   There is not sufficient time to learn what is needed.

If a decision needs to be made right now, it will be based on the current
level of team evaluation. And as we can see, this is uncertain, incomplete,
inconsistent, and evolving. Reducing the team members' uncertainty would
require time and other resources that just don't exist. Peter L. Bernstein
sums up this problem nicely in a great quote from *Against the Gods: The
Remarkable Story of Risk*:[1]

> The information you have is not the information you
>   want.
> The information you want is not the information you
>   need.
> The information you need is not the information you
>   can obtain.
> The information you can obtain costs more than you
>   want to pay.

So how do we manage this situation? The methods we have already
covered—Franklin's method, the Decision Matrix, and the Evaporating
Cloud—may help the team, but before we reconsider any of them let's gen-
eralize the problem and then tear it apart.

All decision-support methods rely on the evaluation of alternatives relative to criteria, as shown in figure 8.2. For any decision problem, M
alternatives are evaluated relative to N criteria for a total of N x M possible
evaluations. Further, there may be K evaluators, each contributing some or

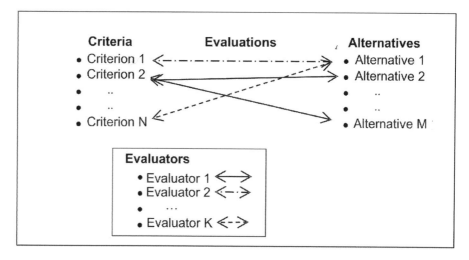

Figure 8.2: The role of evaluation.

all of the evaluations and raising the total number of possible evaluations to N x M x K. Be aware that when you are making a decision, the N x M x K pieces of information are swirling about your meetings, hall talk, e-mails, and other deliberations whether or not you choose to itemize, manage, and leverage them. The goal of robust decision making is to harness, manage, and control them.

Each of the N x M x K evaluations is an estimate of how well an alternative meets a criterion. The information for the evaluations can come from many different sources:

- Intuition
- Opinion
- Analytical simulations
- Experimental testing
- Personal knowledge
- Consultants
- The guy next door
- Omphaloskepsis

Regardless of the source, **an evaluation is only an estimate of how well an alternative satisfies a stated or unstated criterion.** Even when good analytical simulations are available, all evaluation results are only estimates of the real situation (remember from chapter 3 how poor our ability to estimate is). Teams must reach decisions based on evaluations that are best estimates of how the alternatives will perform relative to the criteria. In our example, Lisa's estimate of Swales' proposed training time is much different from John's and Bob's. Regardless of the fidelity of the information provided, this kind of difference of opinion is quite common.

Evaluations are uncertain. Evaluations can range from wild guesses to the results of high-fidelity detailed simulations. To most engineers and other technologists, evaluation means performing quantitative simulations, doing experiments, or solving equations, which result in numerical information for estimating criterion satisfaction. Even if high-fidelity analysis is possible, the results are only as good as the initial data, the model used, and the interpretations of the model.

A major point about evaluations (and a key point in this book) can be shown through the team's work on estimates. Swale estimates that its training time will be 5 hours. This value, "5 hours," is John's evaluation of the training time only if he believes it to be true. Based on his knowledge and experience, he may actually believe that the training time may be as good as 3 hours if they eliminate some unneeded material, but he may also believe that it could take as many as 6 hours to be effective. Lisa may believe, based on her own knowledge and experience, that the training time could even be as high as 9 hours and that, in spite of the time proposed, it won't be effective unless it takes at least 7 hours. **The key point is this: It is only the *belief* in evaluations that counts. Team members project their knowledge, values, roles, and experience into an uncertain future and make decisions based on their beliefs in uncertain evaluation estimates.** John Boyd pointed out this kind of filtering in his development of the OODA Loop, which we discussed in chapter 2. There, the second "O"—Orient— is the interpretation of the results of Observations (the first "O") in preparation for decision making. Here, we are formally trying to manage orientation. The more qualitative the evaluations, the more they are nothing other than beliefs in uncertain estimates. But even the results of the most detailed high-fidelity simulation are subject to interpretation by multiple evaluators who each bring their world of knowledge, experience, team role, and culture to the task of interpreting the results.

Because this is the environment in which we make decisions, the remainder of this book focuses on understanding and managing belief. The term "belief" may sound strange when applied to technical decisions, but we need to come to grips with it. **It makes no difference if an evaluation is based on a wild guess or on detailed simulations; it is the decision** maker's *belief* in the alternative's ability to meet the criteria that is the basis for a decision. This isn't a bad thing. It's just something that needs to be recognized, supported, and managed. Most decision-making methods can't do this. But stay tuned—I will introduce you to a simple method that can.

To help manage belief, I divide evaluation into two independent parts: **Level of Criteria Satisfaction** and **Level of Certainty**. You are used to thinking of evaluation as determining the Level of Criterion Satisfaction. This is what you evaluate in a Decision Matrix or when using any other method in which evaluation is a single, deterministic value. This often results in evaluations like "I think that Grex's system will be easy to use" or "Swale proposed a four-hour training time." But a second dimension—Level of Certainty—is added to each evaluation to account for certainty. This can be shown on the two dimensions of a Belief Map.

Belief Maps: Windows on Evaluations

A Belief Map is a simple graphical representation of the Level of Criterion Satisfaction and Level of Certainty for a particular evaluation. Figure 8.3 shows a Belief Map.* The team members have placed dots on it to indicate their evaluations of the "ease of use" criterion for Grex.

The two axes on a Belief Map are the **Level of Criterion Satisfaction** (alternatively, **Level of Evidence**) and **Level of Certainty**. I will cover the methods for determining these levels later in this chapter. But for now, let's gain an understanding of Belief Maps and why they are important.

In figure 8.3 Anne has represented her evaluation with a dot that shows she believes that Grex has a medium (M) to high (H) Level of Criterion Satisfaction relative to the unstated goal of "easy to use." Based on her knowledge

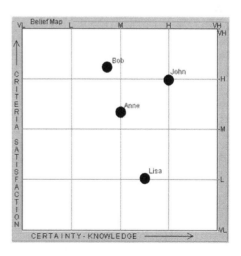

*Note that figure 8.3 and all subsequent Belief Maps in this book are screen shots from *Accord*. Of course, Belief Maps can be made in any medium, but the value of inputting them in *Accord* will become clear in the next chapter.

Figure 8.3: Belief Map.

of Grex and information in its proposal, her Level of Certainty about this evaluation is medium (M). For this qualitative criterion, think of certainty as equivalent to knowledge: Anne's self-assessed knowledge about Grex is medium. John, on the other hand, bases his evaluation on his past work with Grex, so he is more certain and has higher satisfaction with what Grex has proposed. Lisa is not impressed, and has medium to high certainty in her evaluation. Bob thinks there is high to very high probability that Grex's product is easy to use, but is more uncertain than the others in this assessment

Although the prime reason for using Belief Maps is to capture evaluation satisfaction and certainty, they also serve to assist in deliberation. Consider the following:

- Belief Maps foster the building of a shared understanding. As figure 8.3 shows, the points on the Belief Map can communicate each team member's evaluation to all other team members. When there is a low level of consensus (to be explored in chapter 10) team members can discuss it and find out why the disagreement occurred; this will lead to clarification of the alternatives and criteria. Generally, evaluation disagreements occur for one of three reasons:
    1 Different evaluators interpret the alternative being evaluated differently.
    2 Different evaluators understand the criterion being used in different ways.
    3 The evaluators just disagree in their assessments.
    The first two of these may be important to discuss and resolve. It may not be possible to resolve the third, but the reasons for the disagreement are important to recognize.
- Belief Maps can help **avoid groupthink.** Although building consensus would seem to lead to groupthink, this can be avoided by requiring each team member to place his or her points on the map independently. Only after they have been merged onto a single Belief Map does discussion begin.
- Belief Maps help **uncover beliefs that are not robust.** For example, a Belief Map will help expose the salesman who tells Engineering that all printers must print faster based on one conversation with one customer who said her printer was too slow.

Further discussion might show that her printer is five years old. By putting a point on the map and then having to explain it, each team member has to reveal the assumptions and underlying evidence for his or her evaluation.

- Belief Maps can help **map the evolution** of knowledge and criterion satisfaction. I will demonstrate this later in this chapter when I track the Wright Brothers' development of the airplane using Belief Maps.

- Belief Maps help **balance differences in Energy Source.** (This term and others that follow are the measures of decision-making style discussed in chapter 4.) By providing a graphical representation of evaluations, Belief Maps help give internal decision makers a voice that otherwise often gets lost, and help external decision makers to hear the contributions of others.

- Belief Maps help **balance differences in Information Management Style.** They help fact-oriented team members to work on the entire problem rather than diving too deep on a single evaluation. They encourage possibility-oriented team members to be more specific, to deal with details, and to stick to important issues.

- Belief Maps help **balance differences in Deliberation Style.** They help subjective team members discuss differences of opinion without feeling threatened and help the team reach consensus, thereby reassuring them.

- Belief Maps help **balance differences in Decision Closure Style.** They can discourage flexible decision makers from changing their minds while discouraging decisive decision makers from jumping to conclusions without considering the details or the views of other team members. They can help decisive team members be part of the data collection and review process.

Further detail about how to determine the Levels of Criterion Satisfaction and Certainty will help you understand Belief Maps. But first, some general comments:

For qualitative evaluations, Level of Certainty is really a measure of the level of knowledge you bring to an evaluation. If you have high knowledge, you can be more certain about your Level of Criterion Satisfaction (most of the time—read on). If your knowledge is low, you are not very certain.

Bob thinks that there is a high probability that Grex's product is easy to use, but he has medium to low knowledge about Grex—his uncertainty is high. John's knowledge about Grex is high, so there is high certainty in his evaluations. In general, the relationship between knowledge and certainty can be written in equation form as:

Certainty = 1 - uncertainty = knowledge

While this is generally true, it may sometimes be the case that the more you know, the more uncertain you are: It may take knowledge to know what you don't know, or how poor your evaluation really is. In this instance, certainty may not equal knowledge, but may instead be inversely proportional to it. Despite this, for qualitative evaluations the term "knowledge" is descriptive, and it will be used interchangeably with "certainty."

At this point, you may want to experience Belief Maps. If so, download *Accord* software (see appendix B) and work through the examples in parallel with your reading.

Understanding these basics about Belief Maps, we can now detail how they are used for qualitative, quantitative, and 5-point evaluations. I summarize the detailed information on these three types of evaluations at the end of this section.

Qualitative Evaluations

For qualitative evaluations, the **Level of Criterion Satisfaction** (or **Evidence**) is the probability that the alternative meets the often-unstated criterion target, or to put it in the terms we saw in chapter 7, the yes-ness of the alternative. As examples, consider the following three statements: It is likely that Grex's product is easy to use; The Audi TT is the best-looking car on the planet!; or, It is impossible that Swale will deliver this on time. In the first statement, the evaluator is relating that the probability is high that Grex's product is easy to use. In the second, the evaluator is 100% convinced about the looks of the Audi TT. In the third, the probability is very low that Swale will deliver on time. Note that none of these has a target other than Yes or No. This is typical of qualitative criteria.

The Level of Criterion Satisfaction ranges from 100%, implying that Yes, it is a sure thing that the alternative meets the criterion, to 0%, implying that No, the alternative does not meet the target at all. These numerical values are the probabilities of Yes, the alternative fully satisfies the criterion.

A value of 75% communicates a 75% chance of meeting the stated or unstated qualitative target.

More often than not, qualitative evaluations are compared relative to each other. In other words, one evaluation is used as a datum (often informally and unstated) and all the others are then compared to it. This is similar to Stuart Pugh's modification of the Decision Matrix discussed in chapter 2.

Level of Certainty is not commonly measured, yet it is key to understanding belief and decision making. As with Level of Criterion Satisfaction, the Level of Certainty is also measured as a probability. Where the Level of Criterion Satisfaction ranges from 0% to 100%, the Level of Certainty ranges from 50% to 100%. The rationale for this is that a certainty of 50% is no better than the flip of a coin—the probability is 50-50 that the evaluation is correct. At the other end of the scale, a probability of 100% implies that the certainty is very high and the Level of Criterion Satisfaction is a good assessment of the situation. More details on how to get to these probabilities in a minute.

To better understand Belief Maps, consider Bob evaluating the ease of use of Grex's proposed solution. As shown in figure 8.4, if he puts his point in the upper right corner, he is claiming he is an expert (his certainty is very high) and is confident that Grex is easy to use (Level of Criteria Satisfaction = 100%, or VH on the Belief Map, Level of Certainty = 100%). Thus, he 100% believes that Grex is easy to use. If he puts his point in the lower right corner, he is expert and confident that it is not easy to use (Level of Criteria Satisfaction = 0%, Level of Certainty = 100%). Here he believes that Grex has a zero probability of meeting this criterion.

If he puts his evaluation point in the upper left corner, he is hopelessly optimistic: "I don't know anything about this, but I am sure it is easy to use." (Level of Criteria Satisfaction = 100%, Level of Certainty = 50%, or VL on the Belief Map.) This is sometimes referred to this as "the salesman's corner." This is no better than flipping a coin, so belief = 50%.

If he puts his evaluation point in the lower left corner (Level of Criteria Satisfaction = 0%, Level of Certainty = 50%), then he believes that Grex's proposed solution can't meet the criterion, even though he has no knowledge on which to base this belief. This is called the "Eeyore corner," after the character in A.A. Milne's *Winnie the Pooh*, who thinks everything will turn out badly no matter how little he knows. It is also called the "engineer's corner" because engineers are characteristically pessimistic. This evaluation is

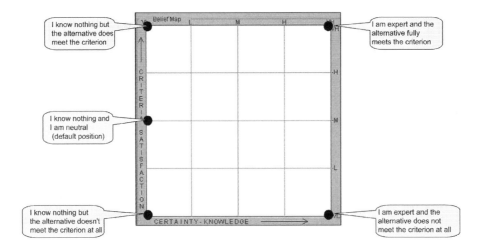

Figure 8.4: The four corners of the Belief Map.

no better than flipping a coin, so belief = 50%. In fact, the entire left border of the belief map has belief = 50%, as any dot placed there is based on no certainty or knowledge at all.

If Bob puts his point anywhere with Level of Criterion Satisfaction = 50%, he is neutral in his evaluation. Grex is neither good nor bad in its ease of use. Consequently, regardless of his knowledge or Level of Certainty, his belief is 50%.

Finally, the default position for evaluation points on the Belief Map is the center left—I know nothing and I am neutral. A point placed here is the same as not offering any evaluation at all (incomplete evaluation).

Now let's look at a more realistic example. Consider the Belief Map in figure 8.5, which shows Bob's ease of use evaluation of the three alternatives. Ignoring the horizontal axis for now, these three evaluations convey two types of information. First, let's examine the relative assessment of the three alternatives. Grex's proposed solution is somewhat easier to use than are Swale's and Able's. Second, there is an implied target relative to which Grex has high to very high probability (about 80%) that it meets this target and the other two have a medium, or 50%, chance. This target is sometimes unstated and differs from evaluator to evaluator. However, representing the separate evaluations on the Belief Map can reveal whether or not these differences are worth resolving.

One obvious question about Belief Maps is how you measure the Level of Certainty probabilities. There are three ways to get at this assessment.

I developed the first qualitative knowledge/certainty assessment method by giving sixty people a list of twenty-five words that indicated some level of

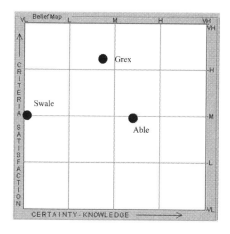

Figure 8.5: Bob's evaluation for ease of use.

knowledge (e.g., guru, amateur, and ignorant). For each word the subjects were asked, "Out of 100 questions, how many will a [one of the words] person get correct?" For example, "Out of 100 questions, how many will an [amateur] get correct?" I reduced the results to find the average percentage as judged by the participants and the standard deviation of their rating. The words with the lowest standard deviation (i.e., the least variation among the subjects) are shown in the adjacent table. For example, on average, most people think that someone who is "informed" will get 80% of the questions correct. However, people are notoriously inconsistent in their use of these and other terms that convey their certainty. The use of Belief Map graphics helps alleviate this limitation.

Term	Probability
Expert	100%
Experienced	90%
Informed	80%
Amateur	70%
Weak	60%
Unknowledgeable	50%

A second scale is based on the simple 5-point measure. Using this scale, someone with high knowledge feels that her knowledge means her Level of Criterion Satisfaction assessment should only be slightly discounted. (The actual implication of the 87% will be refined in the next section.) There is no study to support the distribution of the five terms. They are evenly spread over the range.

A third way to assess certainty is the more formalized method of using technology readiness. The technology-readiness technique was developed in the aerospace industry to assess knowledge about technical systems.[2]

Term	Probability
Very high	100%
High	87%
Medium	75%
Low	62%
Very low	50%

Here the term "technology" in "technology readiness" means any process or science that is used by the features being evaluated. This method does not apply to every situation, but it can give good insight into how much you actually know about something. See more on technology readiness assessment in chapter 12, page 277.

You can use five questions to measure technology readiness for business or technical systems.

1. **Can you use the alternative with known resources?**

   If reliable processes have not been refined for the method or technology, then either the technology should not be used or there must be a separate program to develop this capability. This question directly addresses execution risk. The risk of developing the capability is that the separate program could fail, jeopardizing the entire project.

2. **Do you know the sensitivity of the feature(s) to uncertainties?**

   It is essential to know the sensitivity of the product or process to uncertainties.

3. **Have you identified the failure modes?**

   Every type of system has feature failure modes. Failure modes can be found by answering the question, "What if this feature fails to occur?" This can be extended to read, "What if this feature fails to occur at the right time?"; "What if this feature fails to occur in the right sequence?"; or "What if this feature fails to occur completely?"

4. **Do examples exist that demonstrate positive answers to the first three questions?**

   The most crucial measure of a technology's readiness is its prior use in a laboratory model, other product, or other project. If the technology has not been demonstrated as mature enough for use, the decision maker should be very wary of assurances that it will be ready in time for use. Conversely, if only proven alternatives are considered, then no innovation occurs.

5. **Can you control the feature throughout the life of the product or process?**

   This question addresses the later stages of the process or product's life cycle: manufacture, use, service, and retirement. This also raises other questions. What by-products come from using this technology? Can the by-products be safely disposed of? How will this product be retired? Will it degrade safely? Answering these questions is the responsibility of the decision makers.

The sum of the number of these questions you can answer positively is directly proportional to your knowledge about the system; thus it is an insight into your level of certainty.

NASA has formalized Technology Readiness Levels (TRLs) into nine levels, as shown in figure 8.6. The uncertainty is quite high (knowledge is low) about TRL 1–4 systems, but by the time a system has matured to TRL 8–9, knowledge is high and there will be few surprises.

Regardless of how you assess it, an obvious question arises. Who should assess a decision maker's Level of Knowledge or Certainty? There are only two choices: self-assessment or other-assessment. It is tempting to suggest that another party (e.g. a staff psychologist, the rest of the team, or a manager) should assess team members' knowledge, but this is clearly not a realistic solution. The first hurdle is that knowledge usually varies from feature to feature and from alternative to alternative, so there would be an explosion of assessments. Second, assessment is fraught with personal biases. So the only remaining option is that the Level of Certainty must be self-assessed. Three factors can help keep the decision maker's self-assessment as accurate as possible:

•By articulating the Level of Certainty, it is easier to visualize how much is known. This helps team members align their

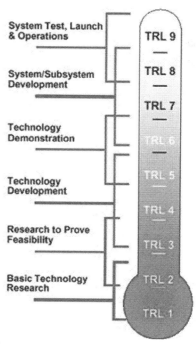

NASA Technology Readiness Levels (TRLs)

TRL 9: Actual system "flight proven" through successful mission operations

TRL 8: Actual system completed and "flight qualified" through test and demonstration (ground or space)

TRL 7: System prototype demonstration in a space environment

TRL 6: System/subsystem model or prototype demonstration in a relevant environment (ground or space)

TRL 5: Component and/or breadboard validation in relevant environment

TRL 4: Component and/or breadboard validation in laboratory environment

TRL 3: Analytical and experimental critical function and/or characteristic proof of concept

TRL 2: Technology concept and/or application formulated

TRL 1: Basic principles observed and reported

Figure 8.6: NASA Technology Readiness Scale.

definitions. This is certainly superior to pretending that the same amount is known about each alternative relative to each criterion.

- Certainty is one of the measures displayed on a Belief Map. This display allows relative comparison of certainty by the team. It also serves as a basis for discussion and developing a more even picture of team knowledge.

- Once the self-assessment is made visual, it is possible to discount a team member's evaluation during decision making in order to see the effect on the results. Therefore, if it is believed that one person has over-estimated his or her knowledge, this can be accounted for.

In Bob's evaluation of "easy to use" (figure 8.5), we see that he has the highest knowledge about Able Industries and has none about Swale. In fact, Bob's point at very low knowledge and medium Level of Criterion Satisfaction is the default point for all assessments. This implies that Bob did not evaluate this alternative/criterion pair, either because his knowledge was so low that he didn't want to bother or because his assessment was so neutral that it wasn't worth his time to do so.

Figure 8.7 shows the evaluation points from figure 8.3 with the addition of curved lines called "isolines." The theory behind isolines is developed in appendix B.

According to the isolines, John's belief in the ease of use of the Grex product is about 69% (his point falls very close to the curved line corresponding to 0.7). Notice that the criterion satisfaction value of 75% (the point projected on the right axis) has been discounted because of his lack of certainty. If he had judged himself an expert with the same level of criterion satisfaction, his belief would instead be 75%.

Bob, whose Level of Criterion Satisfaction is above John's, has a belief of about 63% due to his lack of knowledge. If Bob's point

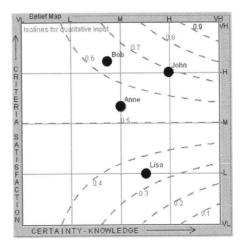

Figure 8.7: The team's evaluation of Grex versus "easy to use."

was all the way to the left side of the Belief Map, then his belief would be only 50%. Lisa's Level of Criterion Satisfaction of 25% results in a belief of 34% due to her uncertainty.

These curves effectively discount the stated criterion satisfaction by the lack of knowledge or certainty factor. This is intuitive. The less certain you are in your evaluation, the more your evaluation should be discounted to 50%, the flip of a coin. Further, in the next chapter we will see how these belief values are fused to give team evaluations.

Quantitative Evaluations

For quantitative or measured criterion, the Level of Criterion Satisfaction is a measure of how an alternative compares to the delighted and disgusted targets developed in chapter 7. For example, the team set its delighted cost target at $20,000 and its disgusted target at $25,000. Back in chapter 7 these two values were used to characterize a utility curve that basically stated: Any cost less than $20,000 meets the ideal and has full utility; any cost greater than $25,000 is poor and has no utility; and any cost in between has proportional utility. Grex proposed a cost of $22,500, halfway between delighted and disgusted; thus, it has 50% utility.

Lisa, however, is uncertain what the actual cost might be. She feels that there is some room for negotiation to get the cost down to $21,000, but that it might also climb to $24,000. These five points—delighted, disgusted, best estimate, high, and low—are shown on a number line in figure 8.8. The delighted point is represented by a thumbs-up icon, the disgusted by a thumbs-down icon, the most likely by a large dot, the high and low by brackets, and the heavy line shows the range from pessimistic to optimistic, i.e., low to high. In this case, Lisa's most-likely evaluation is halfway between delighted and disgusted, and her uncertainty covers a range from $21,000 to $24,000. The figure is a screen shot from *Accord*, where actual numerical values for high, most likely, and low can also be entered on the right.

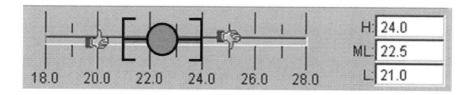

Figure 8.8: Number line for Lisa's evaluation of Grex's proposed cost.

These values can be translated onto the Belief Map. For quantitative evaluations, the Level of Criterion Satisfaction is essentially the mean evaluation value, while the standard deviation of the distribution given by the high, low, and most likely relates to the Level of Certainty. A most-likely value estimated at $20,000 or less implies that Grex has a 100% probability of meeting the target set for the criterion. Thus, the Level of Criterion Satisfaction is very high, or 100%. On the other hand, if evaluation results in a most-likely estimate of $25,000 or more, the evaluator is disgusted, and the Level of Criterion Satisfaction is zero. For Lisa, her most-likely evaluation is halfway between, so Lisa's criterion satisfaction is 50%. An estimate of Level of Criterion Satisfaction is:

$$\text{Level of Criterion Satisfaction} \approx 100 \times (1 - (\text{delighted} - \text{most-likely}) / (\text{delighted} - \text{disgusted}))$$

For this example, the Level of Criterion Satisfaction:

$$100 \times (1 - (20000 - 22500) / (20000 - 25000)) = 50\%.$$

This evaluation will be transferred to a Belief Map later in this section.

In reality, this equation is only correct when the distribution is symmetrical about the most likely. The Level of Criteria Satisfaction is actually the mean value of the distribution defined by the three points: high, most likely, and low. For symmetrical or near-symmetrical distributions, the mean is equal to the most likely. The more precise and much more complicated model is in *Accord* and is detailed further in appendix A.

John believes that the potential for variation in the actual cost is higher than Lisa does, as shown in figure 8.9. Note that his Level of Criterion Satisfaction estimated by the most likely point is the same as Lisa's.

Bob is a little more pessimistic, seeing no opportunity for the cost to go lower than that, as shown in figure 8.10.

Anne sees things differently. On reading the proposal, she notes that some necessary items have been left out and that these will increase the actual cost. Her evaluation in figure 8.11 shows that she believes the cost will most likely be $25,000, but it could be worse. Thus, her Level of Criterion Satisfaction is 0%. At best it is the proposed value of $22,500.

The **Level of Certainty** for quantitative evaluations is a representation of the variation about the most likely value. In the example, John initially

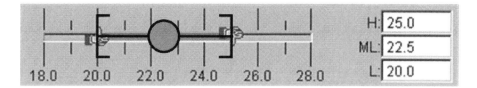

Figure 8.9: John's evaluation of the cost of Grex's proposed cost.

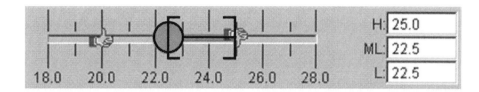

Figure 8.10: Bob's evaluation of the cost of Grex's proposed cost.

estimated that Grex's product would most likely cost $22,500, with a pessimistic estimate of $25,000 and an optimistic one of $20,000, as shown on his number line. John's uncertainty spans the entire range from delighted to disgusted. In a decision-making situation, this Level of Uncertainty adds

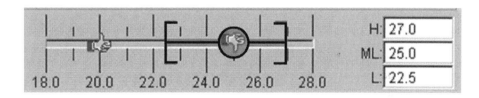

Figure 8.11: Anne's evaluation of the cost of Grex's proposed cost.

little useful information, so his certainty is very low. The Level of Certainty can be estimated by:[3]

Level of Certainty
100 x (1 – .5 (range of estimate between delighted and disgusted) / (delighted – disgusted))

For John's evaluation of Grex this is: 100 – 50 x (5,000/5,000) = 50%.

Lisa and Bob's evaluations are more certain than John's, as the range is smaller. All of these results are shown on a Belief Map in figure 8.12, a screen shot from *Accord*. The values shown may differ from those calculated by hand, as the algorithm in *Accord* is more sophisticated and can better handle asymmetric situations like Bob's evaluation.

If you compare the number lines to the Belief Map, you'll find that the full story is much easier to see on the Belief Map.

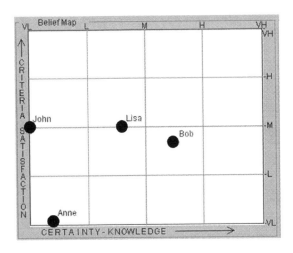

Figure 8.12: Belief Map for team evaluation of Grex's proposed cost.

5-point evaluations

Five-point scales usually result from an effort either to put numerical values on qualitative criterion, or to discretize quantitative criterion. For qualitative criterion there are usually no stated targets, only implied levels of delight or disgust. Typically, 5-point scales are used to measure probability, agreement, frequency, importance, or quality, as shown in chapter 7 on page 164.

The 5-point scale measures the Levels of Criterion Satisfaction. For example, the team decided to use a 5-point Agreement Scale to measure "highly experienced team," where 1 = "Strongly Disagree" and 5 = "Strongly Agree." Let's say that when Anne evaluates Able Industries she gives it a 4 (Somewhat Agree), but her knowledge is weak. She needs a way to convey this Level of Certainty in her evaluation. Even more important to consider: What does John do? He knows virtually nothing about Able. He could evaluate it as 3 (Undecided), but this isn't right, as it confounds the Level of Criterion Satisfaction with Level of Certainty.

The evaluations for the entire team are shown in figure 8.13. Here the evaluations all lie on one of the horizontal lines corresponding to the five levels of agreement. They can be anywhere on these lines to represent Level of Certainty. In this screen shot from *Accord*, the radio button next to "Somewhat Agree" is on, and the slider is positioned at Anne's evaluation.

John's point is shown at the default location, indicating that he knows nothing and is neutral in his assessment. The other two team members know about as much as Anne, but don't agree well with her evaluation.

It will become clear in chapter 10 whether this disagreement is important enough to warrant resolution.

Belief Map Summary

Belief Maps are used to capture evaluations—be they qualitative, quantitative, or 5-point—on a common graphical interface that plots Level of Criterion Satisfaction versus Level of Certainty. The goal of Belief Maps is to help in:

- •Building a shared understanding
- •Avoiding groupthink
- •Uncovering beliefs that are not robust
- •Mapping the evolution of knowledge and criterion satisfaction
- •Balancing differences in energy source
- •Balancing differences in information management style
- •Balancing differences in deliberation style
- •Balancing differences in decision closure style

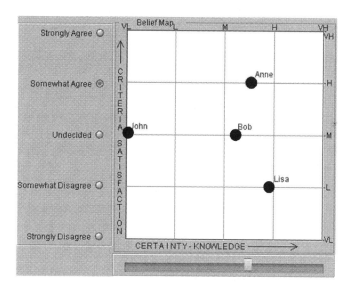

Figure 8.13: Belief Map for 5-point evaluation of Able Industries' team experience.

To get used to using Belief Maps, I suggest that during your next meeting, when the conversation about some feature of an alternative solution to an issue just keeps swirling around, you facilitate by:

1 Clearly identifying the criterion.

2 Determining if it is best measured as qualitative, quantitative, or 5-point.

3 Drawing a Belief Map on something that everyone can see and reach: a white board, transparency, or piece of paper.

4 Explaining the four corners to your colleagues as shown in figure 8.4.

5 Having them put their points on the Belief Map as independently as the situation allows.

6 Using the resulting map to manage your meeting.

Enhancing the Decision Matrix with Belief Maps

What makes Belief Maps so important is not only their ability to help you capture and manage uncertainty, but also their ability to help you compare and contrast different evaluations to help teams build a shared understanding. On a single plot you can display a mix of qualitative, quantitative, and 5-point evaluations on a common display. This basis becomes even more important in the next chapter, when we will fuse the information together. For now, let's reconsider our example problem and see how to use a Decision Matrix to support the team. Note that the following material explains a lot about Belief Maps and extends the capabilities of the Decision Matrix. At the same time, it can get tedious. But if you do it on a computer, tedium turns to insight, as you will see in the next chapter.

Table 8.1 shows the basic Decision Matrix with no data entered. Symbols are shown in the third column to denote the type of evaluation: Q = qualitative, 5 = 5-point scale, and < = less-is-better. The Decision Matrix only supports a single decision maker, so let's focus on Lisa. First, she uses the Decision Matrix without considering uncertainty. For consistency, she uses a percentage scale for her evaluations, where 100% equals: "strongly agree" for the qualitative assessment of "easy to use"; a score of 5 on the 5-point assessment for "highly experienced team"; and the "delighted" target for "cost" and "training time." She enters her evaluation in table 8.2, and using the weighted sum, finds the weighted satisfaction scores in the last row. She clearly favors Able Industries.

As I discussed when I introduced the Decision Matrix, this method is very helpful, but it has its limitations:

			Wt	Alternatives		
				Grex	Able Industries	Swale
Criteria	Training time	<				
	Easy to use	Q				
	Highly experienced team	5				
	Cost	<				
		Satisfaction				

Table 8.1: Basic Decision Matrix.

			Wt	Alternatives		
				Grex	Able Industries	Swale
Criteria	Training time	<	.37	75%	100%	0%
	Easy to use	Q	.20	25%	80%	75%
	Highly experienced team	5	.17	25%	24%	50%
	Cost	<	.26	50%	60%	72%
		Weighted satisfaction		50%	73%	42%

Table 8.2: Lisa's Decision Matrix with no accounting for uncertainty.

1   It can't include uncertainty.
2   It can't manage incomplete information.
3   It's difficult to mix qualitative and quantitative evaluation results.
4   It's difficult to combine different team members' evaluations.
5   It is assumed that all criteria can be traded off.
6   The underlying mathematics can lead to a less-than-best result.

Lisa already managed the third limitation by tying all the evaluations to a 100% scale. This actually violates the last limitation, as there is no real mathematical basis for doing so (see appendix A for more on this). I will address limitations 4 through 6 in the next chapter.

Lisa can manage uncertainty and incompleteness (items 1 and 2) by using the methods introduced in this chapter. The results of her evaluations are shown on the Belief Maps in figure 8.14, one for each of the alternatives. Representing information by alternative is but one way to use Belief Maps. To best explore why the points on Lisa's Belief Maps are where they are, I will address them one criterion at a time.

Lisa's "easy to use" evaluation is summarized on the Belief Map shown in figure 8.15. She believes that Grex's proposed product has a low probability of being easy to use and she has a medium-to-high certainty in her

213

evaluation. She represents this information as a point in the lower right quadrant of the belief map. Her Level of Criterion Satisfaction is low: 25% of total satisfaction. The value of 25% is what she entered in the Decision Matrix we saw earlier. Correcting for uncertainty raises her level of belief to 35%, as can be seen by interpolating between lines of constant belief. If it seems odd that uncertainty raises her belief, remember that the lower your

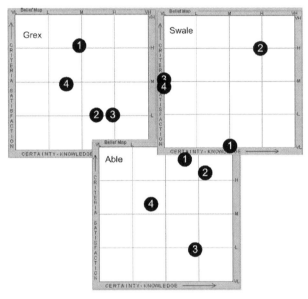

Figure 8.14: Lisa's Belief Maps for the three alternatives where 1 = training time, 2 = easy to use, 3 = highly experienced team, and 4 = cost.

certainty, the closer you are to flipping a coin—50-50.

The Swale and Able evaluations are near each other, and show that she believes both of these company's products have a high probability of being easy to use. In table 8.2, she entered the belief values from her Belief Maps into her Decision Matrix. Compare the values here to those in table 8.3, without certainty considered.

Lisa's "highly experienced team" evaluation is based on a 5-point scale. In figure 8.16 she places her

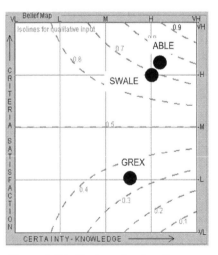

Figure 8.15: Lisa's evaluation for ease of use.

points to show her "low" evaluation of the experience of Grex and Able's teams. In both instances, her certainty is high. She does not evaluate Swale at all, so the corresponding point defaults to neutral Level of Criterion Satisfaction assessment and very low Level of Certainty assessment.

Evaluations for "training time" and "cost" were done using number lines and then transposing the points on them to the Belief Maps. The number lines in figures 8.17 and 8.18 show how Lisa evaluated

Figure 8.16: Lisa's evaluation for highly experienced team.

the three alternatives. For each of these the Level of Criterion Satisfaction and Level of Certainty were calculated and entered on the Belief Map.

For Able's cost, the middle number line in figure 8.17 and 8.18,

$$\text{Level of Criterion Satisfaction} \approx 100 \times (1 - (\text{delighted} - \text{most-likely}) / (\text{delighted} - \text{disgusted})) = 100 \times (1 - (20.0 - 22.0) / (20.0 - 25.0)) = 60\%$$

And

$$\text{Level of Certainty} \approx 100 \times (1 - .5 (\text{range of estimate between delighted and disgusted}) / \text{delighted} - \text{disgusted})) = 100 \times (1 - .5 \times 3.0 / (20.0 - 25.0)) = 70\%$$

This is point 4 on the Able part of figure 8.14. Let me reiterate that these equations are only estimates. Lisa's evaluation of the cost of Swale, for example, is asymmetric and partially outside the delighted–disgusted range. For this situation, the estimates of the Levels of Criterion Satisfaction and Certainty using these simple equations are off by as much as 50%.

Table 8.3 shows the updated values for the Decision Matrix including uncertainty. When compared to table 8.3, which does not take uncertainty into account, we see that the differences are not extreme. Grex is 3% higher,

			Wt	Alternatives		
				Grex	Able Industries	Swale
Criteria	Training time	<	.37	75%	100%	0%
	Easy to use	Q	.20	35%	74%	69%
	Highly experienced team	5	.17	32%	31%	50%
	Cost	<	.26	50%	60%	72%
	Weighted satisfaction			53%	73%	41%

Table 8.3 Lisa's Decision Matrix with uncertainty accounted for.

Swale 1% lower, and Able unchanged. This result is misleading, since the Level of Certainty for the two quantitative measures cannot be accurately calculated nor utilized by hand. In actuality, when calculated using computer code, Lisa's satisfaction with Able is only 68%, which is 5% lower than originally calculated, and her satisfaction with Swale is only 35%, or 7% lower (a 17% change from the original analysis). These differences are significant.

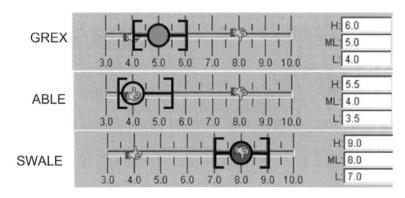

Figure 8.17: Lisa's evaluation of training time.

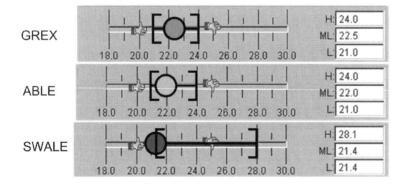

Figure 8.18: Lisa's evaluation of cost.

In this section the Belief Map was shown to support visualization and partially compensate for uncertainty. The next chapter will further refine the use of uncertainty, fuse team evaluations, and show how the use of a readily available computer program can make all of this work virtually automatic.

Putting the Wright Brothers on the Belief Map

To demonstrate another useful aspect of Belief Maps—communicating the evolution of information—I will use them to describe the work of the Wright Brothers from 1899 through December 2003.[4] Of course, Orville and Wilbur did not use Belief Maps, but in reading through their extensive notes and letters, I found that the evolution of their criteria satisfaction and knowledge was evident and can be expressed graphically with Belief Maps. And besides, who knows?

In 1899, the Wrights became interested in manned flight. Until that time Otto Lilienthal had had the greatest success in flying. Unfortunately, he was killed in a glider accident in 1896. He had been the first to attempt a scientific study of flight, recording data on his many gliders and attempting to develop the basic physics upon which he could design an airplane. His goal was to develop a glider and then add propulsion by flapping the glider's wings. He controlled his gliders by shifting his weight, much like hang gliders do today. Lilienthal wrote many papers and books in which he published basic equations for calculating the performance of a glider.[5]

Figure 8.17: Otto Lilienthal.

The Wright Brother's situation in 1899 was typical of most engineering and business problems: There were multiple courses of action and all the information was uncertain, incomplete, inconsistent, and evolving. It was in this environment that they decided to try to develop manned flight. They began by reading all the material they could find, including that by Lilienthal. In May 1900 Wilbur wrote to a mentor, "For some time I have been afflicted with the belief that flight is possible to man. My disease has increased in severity and I feel it will soon cost me an increased amount of money if not my life."

During this early period they realized there were five top-level criteria for a powered airplane:

1   There must be adequate lift to carry the machine,
    the propulsion system, and a man.
2   There must be longitudinal control to make the airplane go up
    and down.
3   There must be lateral control to make the airplane bank
    and turn.
4   There must be sufficient power.
5   There must be a propulsion system to convert the power
    to thrust.

They evolved the airplane by building a new platform each year and testing it each fall at Kitty Hawk, North Carolina during their off-season from the bicycle business in Dayton, Ohio. The discussion here concerns what they learned from their 1900, 1901, and 1902 gliders, which led up to the powered 1903 "Flyer," the first airplane. These four planes are shown in figure 8.18.

Here we see the 1900 glider being flown as a kite, as it didn't have enough lift to support either of the brothers. During design, they had based their airfoil shape and wing size on the equations published by Lilienthal and others. They were still able to test their concept of wing warping—twisting the wings to gain lateral control—and it showed great promise. The 1901 glider is much larger than the 1900 and it was able to carry Orville (shown) and Wilbur as they glided down Kill Devil Hill in Kitty Hawk. However, it still didn't produce the lift they had calculated and, although the wing warping did produce a turn, they couldn't control it and would often end up going the wrong way. Results from the 1901 experiments were so poor that Wilbur said when returning to Dayton on the train, "Nobody will fly for a thousand years."

But in best researcher tradition, Wilbur got over his failure and the brothers spent the next months testing airfoils and wing geometry, refining their ability to analyze lift. The results were embodied in the 1902 glider (shown with Wilbur on board), again much larger than its predecessor.

Figure 8.18: The Wright Brothers' gliders and powered aircraft.

From the beginning, the 1902 glider worked much better than the earlier gliders—when going straight. However, when they tried to turn they still ran into difficulty. Experiments led first to a fixed vertical tail, and then to a movable rudder that was linked to the wing warping system. By the end of their flying season at Kitty Hawk, the Wrights had developed the first controllable glider, had an accurate analytical basis for calculating lift, and had empirically developed methods for longitudinal (moving the horizontal stabilizer) and lateral control.

They returned to Dayton with the expectation that they only needed to add an engine for power and a propeller for propulsion. They believed that they could buy a suitable engine off the shelf and that they could adopt propeller theory from steam turbine and steamship propellers for their needs. On December 3, 1902, Orville sent letters to motor manufacturers asking for a power source with 8–9 brake horsepower (hp) that weighed less than 180 pounds (22 lb/hp). He received ten responses and none could meet the specifications. Thus, on December 25, Orville, his brother, and their shop mechanic, Charlie Taylor, proceeded to design and build an engine that produced 16 hp and weighed 150 lbs (8.4 lb/hp).

In a parallel effort, Wilbur learned that knowledge about propellers was all empirical—there was no underlying theory—and could not be applied to airplanes. On December 29, 1902, Wilbur wrote, "Recently done a little experimenting with screws [propellers] and are trying to get a clear understanding of just how they work and why. It is a very perplexing problem." By spring he had developed basic propeller theory and a propeller design for the Flyer. This propeller was unlike any made before, and Wilbur worried that either he was wrong or that he knew much more than anyone else about propellers. Luckily, the latter proved true.

The evolution of the brothers' evaluation of lift is shown on a Belief Map in figure 8.19. Based on their reading, they thought that lift was a solved problem, even though there was some uncertainty in the literature. Their 1900 and 1901 gliders convinced them that their estimation of their knowledge (and that of the community as a whole) was vastly overrated. Their 1902 experiments and subsequent success with the 1902 glider increased their knowledge so they could design in sufficient lift.

Lateral control evaluation is shown on the Belief Map in figure 8.20. The brothers began with a dislike for the weight shifting used by Lilienthal and others. They had the idea that wing warping would solve the problem, but knew little about it. They tried an early kite and verified its potential with the 1900 glider. Difficulty with the 1901 glider added to their knowledge but lowered their confidence in solving the problem. Finally, work on the 1902 glider provided them with a successful solution.

The engine and propeller evaluations are shown in Figure 8.21 For both of these, the Wrights assumed a communal knowledge and ability to meet their needs. They learned in late 1902 that they were wrong, that what was known was far less than they had assumed, and they subsequently solved the problems themselves. Although their contribution to engine technology is small, this effort led to the first propeller theory—one still used today—and the first successful propellers. In fact, the propellers the Wrights built, based on the theory they developed during this period, are nearly as efficient as modern propellers.

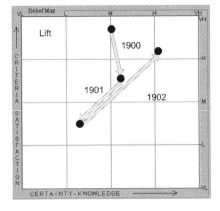

Figure 8.19: Evolution of lift.

This example emphasizes the Belief Map's ability to track and understand the evolution of technologies that result from multiple decisions. I do not mean to imply that if the Wrights had been using Belief Maps they would have realized the lack of maturity of propellers and engines. It would have been interesting, however, to see how Belief Maps might have affected the Orville and Wilbur team. They were often at odds, and struggled to reach important decisions.

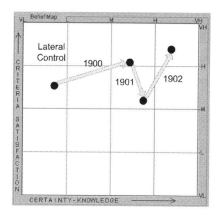

Figure 8.20: Evolution of lateral control.

Summary

Assessing the Levels of Criterion Satisfaction and Certainty on Belief Maps is a major step in making robust decisions. If nothing else, by this time you should be convinced that 1) information on which decisions are based is uncertain, 2) it is your belief in this uncertain information that drives your evaluations, and 3) your belief is part of the team's shared understanding that is necessary for buy-in and accountability. The Belief Maps introduced here offer a simple, graphical way to manage these facts. They will also serve us in the next chapter, where we will use the evaluations to help make decisions.

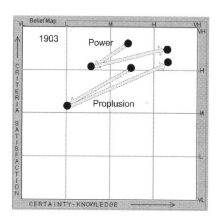

Figure 8.21: Evolution of power and propulsion.

221

Robust Decision Making
—Putting It All Together

9

This is where it all comes together, where everything we've discussed in the previous eight chapters helps you answer the five key questions of robust decision making. Now we get to see how these questions and their answers flow as you work through the decision-making process.

First and foremost, you and your team want to know two things:

1   Which is the best alternative? *and*
2   What is the risk that our decision will not turn out
    as we expect?

Next, once you can identify a best alternative and are satisfied with the risk that comes along with it, you want some assurance that you can affirmatively answer the third and fourth key questions:

3   Do we know enough to make a good decision yet? *and*
4   Is there buy-in for the decision?

If you can't satisfactorily answer the first four questions, then you are faced with the fifth one:

5   What do we need to do next to feel confident about our
    decision, within the scope of our limited resources?

This last question directs you to additional tasks described in this book that are designed to help you find the best alternative that has acceptable levels of risk, knowledge, and buy-in. This what-to-next analysis is the subject of chapter 10.

The best way to explain the concepts that apply to any set of alternatives and criteria is by example. So, to walk you through the process of answering these five not-so-easy questions, we'll check back in with the system selection team we met in chapter 1. We'll look over their shoulders as they work to choose the best from among the proposals they've received, using the following types of analysis to answer their questions; these form the foundation of robust decision making.

- Finding alternative satisfaction and the probability of being best
- Fusing (combining) team evaluations
- Managing the results from multiple viewpoints on importance
- Calculating consensus
- Calculating risk
- Calculating what-to-do-next

In the discussion that follows, *Accord* software screen shots show the team's evaluations and the results of their computations. While it is not essential to use *Accord* software to work through the five questions, the software is a powerful tool that underscores the points I make here, and the screen shots help to illustrate the process. You can read this chapter alone and gain great insight, or you can choose to download the trial version of *Accord*, which contains this example, and work alongside the team.

You may wonder, Why the reliance on *Accord?* Simply put, it allows you to work through complex decisions in a focused and systematic way while juggling numerous pieces of information. Remember, complexity multiplies in a hurry. In the case of the system selection team's work, where just four people need to evaluate three alternatives using four criteria, there are forty-eight pieces of uncertain information to combine. And it is exactly this kind of information that floats around the room during tedious, nonproductive meetings. This level of complexity is simply too much for most of us to manage in our heads without solid support—and this is why so many decisions fail. With *Accord* we can go beyond the paper-and-pencil methods we explored in earlier chapters and let the software do some of the heavy lifting for us.

Another reason to rely on software is that the most robust decision making uses Bayesian probabilities and other Artificial Intelligence methods as its mathematical foundation. The math is difficult for even a trained analyst

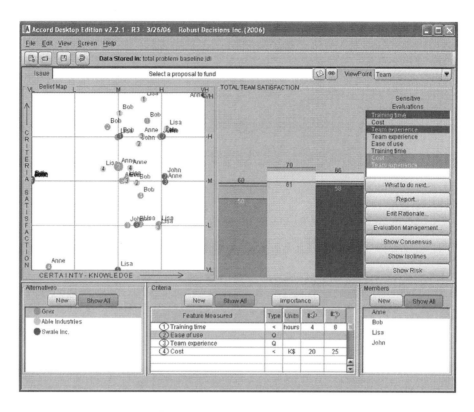

Figure 9.1: Accord *screen shot.*

to do, and it's impossible to do in "real time." But it's done automatically and invisibly in *Accord,* and that frees you up to address those all-important five questions.

Accord is a one-screen decision-management utility with a couple of additional pop-up windows. It is the embodiment of Bayesian Team Support (see appendix A). Figure 9.1 shows a screen shot of the system selection team's problem. Don't worry about the details on the screen for now; I will explain them as we go. Suffice it to say that the bottom third of the screen is used for framing the problem, the upper left is the Belief Map, and the upper right contains analytical results that help you answer the five key questions. Let's see how our team's decision is modeled and analyzed through *Accord.*

When we first met John, Anne, Bob, and Lisa, they were working on selecting a proposal from among three that had passed their filtering criteria. Now we will begin to follow the four decision makers as they work to select one of the three alternatives. The alternatives, criteria, and team members are summarized in figure 9.2, the lower portion of the *Accord* screen. The

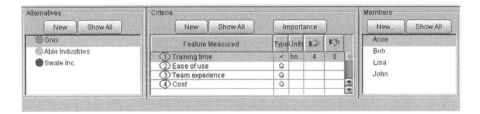

Figure 9.2: Alternatives, criteria, and team members.

three alternatives are listed on the left, the criteria in the center, and the decision makers on the right.

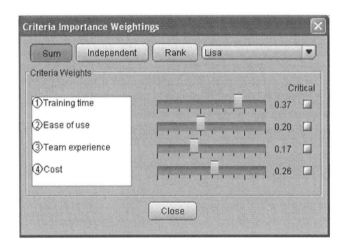

Figure 9.3: Lisa's criteria importance weightings.

Anne, Bob, Lisa, and John all represent different functions within the organization. Thus, they have different opinions about what is important. Lisa from Human Resources has set her importance weightings in the pop-up window shown in figure 9.3. The entire team's importance weightings are shown in table 9.1. Lisa thinks that training time and cost are most

	John	Anne	Bob	Lisa
Training time	0.25	0.12	0.27	0.37
Ease of use	0.31	0.21	0.35	0.20
Team experience	0.25	0.30	0.23	0.17
Cost	0.19	0.37	0.15	0.26
Total	1.00	1.00	1.00	1.00

Table 9.1: The team's importance weightings.

important. Because Anne manages the users, she thinks that cost and team experience are most important. Bob, advocating for the end user, thinks that ease of use is most important, and John from Engineering thinks the criteria are nearly equal in importance, with ease of use dominating.

The team has framed the issue (identified their alternatives and criteria and assigned relative importance to them) and they are ready to take the next step—collecting and fusing the evaluation information.

What Is the Best Alternative?
One Person's Evaluation

Let's follow John's evaluation of Swale's proposal and see how one person evaluates a single alternative. This is a recap of material presented in the previous chapter on the role belief plays in decision making; I stress it again here because it sets the stage for the rest of the process.

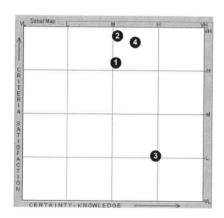

Figure 9.4: Belief Map showing John's evaluation of Swale's proposal.

John uses a Belief Map to evaluate Swale (figure 9.4). The numbers in the dots refer to the criteria listed in figure 9.2. His evaluations are of a mix of qualitative, 5-point, and quantitative evaluations. Point 1 is John's evaluation of the training time criterion. Swale's proposal stated that it would take just 3 hours to train people on the use of the system it proposed. Based on his experience, John believes this is the most optimistic scenario, and he thinks that, in reality, training time would fall in the range shown on the number line in figure 9.5.

John thinks that his knowledge about ease of use (point number 2, a

Figure 9.5: John's evaluation of Swale's training time.

qualitative criterion) is in the mid-range; nonetheless, he is fairly confident that it would be easy to use. He evaluates the Swale team's experience on a 1–5 scale, and is a little pessimistic about it. He "somewhat disagrees" when evaluating the criterion, "The team is well experienced for this project," and his certainty about this is high.

The cost criterion is quantitative, with a delighted target of $20,000, and the team will be disgusted if it costs more than $25,000. Swale quoted $20,000, but John thinks this might creep up (see figure 9.6).

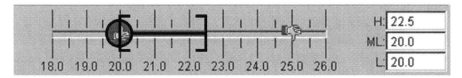

	H:	22.5
	ML:	20.0
18.0 19.0 20.0 21.0 22.0 23.0 24.0 25.0 26.0	L:	20.0

Figure 9.6: John's evaluation of Swale's cost.

John's importance weighting and his beliefs as developed on the Belief Map are shown in table 9.2, where his overall satisfaction with Swale is calculated by hand. I discussed how these calculations are made in the previous chapter, but *Accord* does this automatically, with the results represented graphically in figure 9.7.

	Weights	Belief	Weighted value
Training time	0.25	0.68	.25*.68 = .17
Ease of use	0.31	0.73	.31*.73 = .23
Team experience	0.25	0.27	.25*.27 = .07
Project cost	0.19	0.80	.19*.80 = .15
Total	1.00		Satisfaction = .62

Table 9.2: John's evaluation of Swale.

John's evaluation and what he thinks is important, as calculated by *Accord*, put his satisfaction for Swale at 62%—the rightmost bar on figure 9.7. The figure also shows that Grex is 67% satisfactory to him, and Able Industries comes in at 54%. These results, whether derived by hand or computer, offer the first pieces of evidence that can answer two of the key questions: "Which is the best alternative?" And "What is the risk that our decision will not turn out as we expect?"

If the decision were based solely on John's input, Grex, the first alterna-

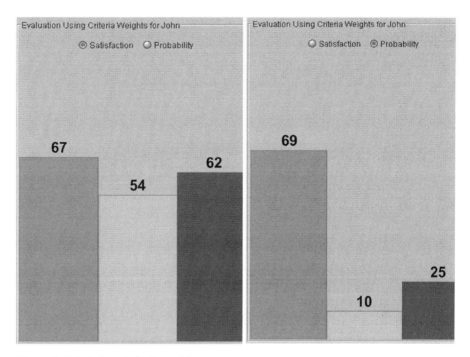

Figure 9.7: John's satisfaction with
the alternatives.

Figure 9.8: Probability of being best.

tive, is considered most satisfactory. However, there is a risk that it will not achieve the stated "delighted values" and/or the unstated qualitative goals. The calculation of this risk at this stage is simple: 100% - 67% = 33%. Based on this simple calculation, there is a 33% probability that Grex will not satisfy all the criteria. (Actually, though, the risk is greater than 33%, as you will see later in the chapter.)

Another indicator of which alternative is best is an analysis of the probability of its being best, based on the evaluation information (see figure 9.8). Note that the probabilities add up to 100%. The figure shows that, based on the current information, Grex has a 69% chance of being the best of the three alternatives, with Able Industries having a 10% chance and Swale having a 21% chance. (Note: This analysis is a feature of *Accord*. It is not possible to do this by hand; see appendix A for details.)

So if John were the only person on the team, he could at least answer the first two of the five key questions. He could conclude that Grex is best (but not by much over Swale) and that there is a 33% expectation that it will not meet all the criteria. But such results are only based on John's evaluation. We haven't yet reached the point where we can answer the other questions—not until we include Anne, Bob, and Lisa in the process.

And what will happen when the other evaluations are added to John's? By his own admission, his knowledge is limited, and others may know much more or may see things differently. The picture can change dramatically when everyone contributes. So let's add the other team members now.

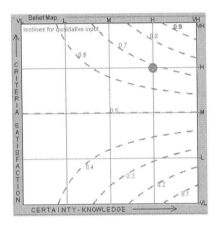

Figure 9.9: John's evaluation of Grex's ease of use.

What Is the Best Alternative? A Team Analysis

The other team members can easily do evaluations similar to John's. But then the team has four separate evaluations to grapple with. Independent of one another, these won't help them build a shared understanding, buy-in, or accountability, and won't help them answer the key questions. So next we'll see how to fuse everybody's evaluations to create better information upon which to support a decision by the group.

To explain how this works, first consider the qualitative criterion, "ease of use." Let's assume that John has evaluated Grex for this particular measure and has concluded that his criterion satisfaction and certainty are both high, or 75%, as shown in figure 9.9. This puts his belief at 68% on the isolines. Now let's say that Anne also evaluates the ease of use of Grex's product and puts her qualitative point at the same location as John's. Now the team has two members, both of whom claim high knowledge and high criterion satisfaction, at the same point on the Belief Map. What do you think the team belief, the fusion of the individual beliefs, should be: 68%—or should it be higher? What if Lisa also evaluates Grex and puts her point in the same place? If you have many people who all claim high knowledge and indicate their belief that Grex's product is easy to use, this is an indication that yes, Grex's product is easy to use, and this is the same as a single expert's evaluation that it is easy to use—a single point in the upper right corner. This is the power of strong agreement in a qualitative assessment. Think about it. If no one on your team is an expert, but all have some knowledge and all agree that Grex's product is going to be easy to use, then you will feel as confident in this

Number of people	Team belief
1	68%
2	82%
3	91%
4	96%
5	98%

Table 9.3: Team belief.

assessment as you would if one expert told you the same information.

A rough estimate of this effect can be found by adding together the beliefs of all the decision makers. Then, from the sum, subtract $(N-1)/2$, where N is the number of decision makers.[1] Limit the result to 100%. Table 9.3 shows this calculation for an increasing number of people who put their points at the same place as John's.

But most evaluations do not net this kind of result. The actual evaluation of the Grex product's ease of use is shown on the Belief Map in figure 9.10. It's not easy to tell exactly what the fused team belief is by looking at the map. *Accord*, however, calculates it to be 70%. This seems right because, while Anne and Bob support John to some degree, which could increase the Team Belief substantially, Lisa believes it will not be so easy to use, and thus reduces it. This example demonstrates the complexity of fusing team information, and it also shows that the results you can visualize by using Belief Maps agree with both your intuition and with *Accord's* analysis.

You might ask, Why introduce this complexity to your evaluation information? Why not just average the evaluations of the team? This approach fails on two fronts. First, it doesn't support the phenomenon of several team members agreeing—if four people have a 68% belief, the average would be 68% belief. This doesn't allow you to see and utilize the power of strong agreement. Second, as I mentioned earlier in the book, averaging is like mixing paint—it always results in brown. You lose important subtleties when you average these kinds of evaluations together.

The situation is different, however, for quantitative evaluations. Consider the evaluation of Grex for "cost." The team agreed that they would be delighted with $20,000 and disgusted with $25,000. Grex's proposal came

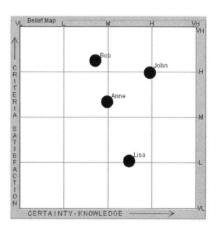

Figure 9.10: The actual team evaluation of Grex's ease of use.

231

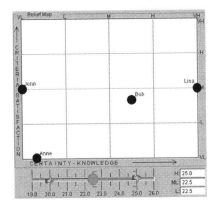

Figure 9.11: The evaluation of the cost of Grex.

in at $22,500. Now here is what the team actually believes about the cost.

Bob has worked on many similar projects. He knows that, even though this is a fixed-cost contract, by the time negotiations are complete and with other contingencies in the contract, there will be some flexibility in the final cost. He estimates that the most likely cost is $22,500; it won't go any lower, and it may go as high as $25,000. This opinion is reflected on the number line under the Belief Map in figure 9.11.

Lisa takes the bid at face value. But the validity of her evaluation should be questioned, as will become evident.

Anne suspects that the fine print will contain a higher cost than the bid. She knows that it will never be lower than $22,500. She thinks it's more than likely that it will be $25,000, and that it may go as high as $27,000.

John, from Engineering, chooses not to evaluate cost, leaving that to the others.

Figure 9.11 shows the four evaluations on a Belief Map. If this information is fused, Lisa's view will dominate, as she claims there is no uncertainty in her evaluation and the team belief is 50% ($22,500, halfway between $20,000 and $25,000). This swamps the evaluations Bob and Anne made. John, on the other hand, has no effect on the results, as he is neutral and claims no knowledge.

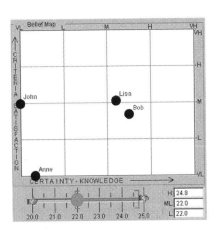

Figure 9.12: Reevaluation of the cost of Grex.

Lisa has treated the bid as a sure thing. If that is the actual case, then her evaluation as it stands is correct. But if Lisa's evaluation is based on not questioning the bid, it should be revisited. "Sure things" just don't happen when you are estimating future values. So, what happens if she adds uncertainty to her evaluation? Upon further reflection, she concludes that the bid might go down a little, or up as much as 10%. As a result: her high = $24,800, most likely = $22,000, and low = $21,800.

With Lisa's reevaluation, the team belief is now 40% (not shown here, but calculated in *Accord*). For this quantitative evaluation, Anne's pessimism has reduced the fused team satisfaction level. For a qualitative evaluation, Anne's opinion would have had little effect, due to her uncertainty. But for this quantitative evaluation, her influence on the result is significant. Which brings us to a key point: *Where qualitative evaluation fuses uncertainty that is due to lack of knowledge, quantitative evaluation includes uncertainty in the estimated values.* (The way this is determined is explained in appendix A.)

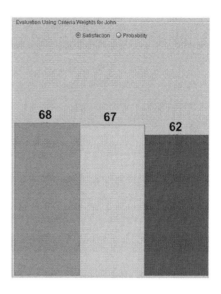

Figure 9.13: The entire team's evaluation from John's viewpoint.

After all the team members' evaluations have been considered and the team beliefs have been computed, you can calculate overall satisfaction from each viewpoint and answer the key questions.

Let's look at John's importance weighting first. His overall satisfaction with each of the alternatives appears in figure 9.13. Compare this to figure 9.7 and you will see that satisfaction with the middle alternative, Able Industries, has changed significantly with the addition of the other evaluations. The other two are only slightly changed. Thus, using John's importance weightings, Grex and Able are almost the same and Swale is only slightly behind. Clearly, we can't answer any of the key questions using only John's viewpoint. So don't read too much into these results yet—the other viewpoints will change them.

Multiple Team Viewpoints

To get John's viewpoint as shown in 9.13, the team beliefs were multiplied by his importance weightings and then added together. This allows us to see how the whole team would evaluate the criterion if they all agreed with John's ideas about importance. The same process yields results from the other evaluators' viewpoints. Team satisfaction analyses use all the evaluation information from the Belief Maps and number lines, only with different weightings. Figure 9.14 shows the results from Anne's viewpoint. Comparing this with John's results, seen in figure 9.13, we find some disagreement on the results. While John favors Grex and Able about equally, Anne favors Swale. Bob's and Lisa's viewpoints yield results in between those of John and Anne.

There are three important points to take away from these results:

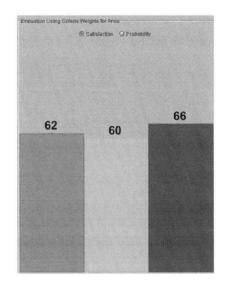

Figure 9.14: The entire team's evaluation from Anne's viewpoint.

- There is no right answer at this point; these results only show the team's disagreement. Clearly there is not yet buy-in for any one choice.
- It should not be surprising that the three alternatives are very close. All the weak proposals were filtered out, and if there were a clear winner this evaluation would not have been necessary.
- The disagreement is not a bad thing. It will help determine what-to-do-next, the topic of the next chapter.

It is important to reiterate that overall team satisfaction utilizes all the evaluation data from the Belief Maps and number lines, and the viewpoint (i.e. importance weightings) of only one decision maker at a time. This allows the team to study the evaluation results from the viewpoint of stake-

	John	Anne	Bob	Lisa	Ramon
Training time	0.25	0.12	0.27	0.37	0.42
Ease of use	0.31	0.21	0.35	0.20	0.11
Team experience	0.25	0.30	0.23	0.17	0.14
Cost	0.19	0.37	0.15	0.26	0.33
Total	1.00	1.00	1.00	1.00	1.00

Table 9.4: Criteria weightings.

holders not represented on the team. For example, let's say the team wants to look at the evaluation through the eyes of the "big boss," Ramon, shown in table 9.4. The only information the team collects from Ramon (or inputs for him by proxy) is the criteria weightings that he thinks are important. This is a very powerful method that allows the information that has been entered on the Belief Maps to be viewed from many different perspectives.

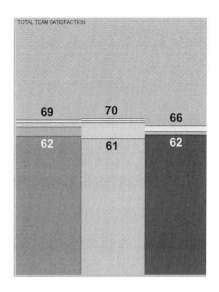

Figure 9.15: The composite team satisfaction.

The satisfaction results for the team are shown superimposed on each other in figure 9.15. You can't tell from the figure which results come from which team member, but for our purposes here, it makes no difference. It is very tempting to average these together to find the "mean" team satisfaction. But as I mentioned earlier, doing so loses valuable detail, and all the options would come out with about the same satisfaction scores (remember, this is one of the drawbacks of the Decision Matrix). Also, it violates a basic theorem of decision making that says averaging can give you "garbage."[2] To get around these limitations, I highly recommended that you resist averaging evaluation results, regardless of the method you use to make a decision. Rather, look at a composite, as shown in figure 9.15, and use other information to give you guidance about what-to-do-next. In this figure, the results based on each of the weightings are superimposed on each other to show the range and distribution of results. In contrast, it is easy to see how averaging would show all the alternatives with about the same level of satisfaction.

It now appears that we can't answer any of the key questions for the team. There is no clear "best" and we are not sure about buy-in or what-to-do-next. But ambiguity at this point should not come as a surprise. As I mentioned earlier, these alternatives all passed the filter criteria, and if there had been a standout, this exercise would not have been necessary. But don't lose heart! There is very good information here, and the team will tease it out.

Are There Buy-in, Consensus, and Accountability for the Decision?

The ideal situation is to have the entire team buy into and be accountable for any decision that it makes. When I introduced buy-in in the first chapter, I said that you know you have buy-in when:

- Everyone can paraphrase the issue to show that he or she understands it.
- Everyone has had a chance to contribute to the solution of the problem.
- Everyone has had a chance to describe what is important to him or her.

All the material I've presented up to this point has supported the development of these buy-in goals. We won't get to a decision on our example problem until the next chapter, but some great work has been accomplished:

- Through the effort to develop criteria and evaluate data relative to them, everyone involved now understands the issue well.
- Everyone has had an *equal* chance to contribute to the resolution of the issue. The methodology and Belief Maps has evened the playing field, regardless of individual decision-making styles.
- By seeing the results from different viewpoints, everyone has been able to visualize how what is important to them affects the overall results. Further, once they see that, even though they disagree about what is important, they agree with others about the result, which avoids needless discussion.

You find the term "consensus" in the title of this section. To some people consensus is a goal; to some, a pariah. In the "goal" sense, it is the same as buy-in. In the "pariah" sense it means to compromise and agree on a single "team story." But used here, the word has a different context; in robust decision making, teams actually use an analytical method to find consensus. Here's how it works.

Figure 9.10 shows the team's evaluation of Grex's ease of use. It is clear that John and Bob's evaluations of this criterion are similar. Bob knows less than John, but he agrees on the Level of Criterion Satisfaction (the vertical axis). But Lisa does not agree, and claims a similar knowledge level to that of John and Bob.

Consensus is a combination of how well the team agrees about the level of criterion satisfaction, tempered by the amount of knowledge on the team. Thus, consensus is not great on this evaluation (*Accord* calculates it to be 56%), as everyone claims medium to high knowledge and there is wide disagreement on the level of criterion satisfaction. Full agreement by the team yields consensus = 100%, and full disagreement yields consensus = 0%. If Lisa changed her evaluation to say that her knowledge was very low and moved her point to the far left, the consensus would rise to 83%. This is because Anne is only in slight disagreement with John and Bob. If Anne now moves her point between Bob's and John's, the consensus would jump to 96%, because Bob, Anne, and John agree on Level of Criterion Satisfaction regardless of their Level of Certainty. Generally, consensus values over 60% are considered satisfactory. Is the lack of consensus on this specific evaluation important? The team really doesn't know yet, but it will find out in the next chapter.

A third term that is often used and mixed with "buy-in" and "consensus" is "accountability." Accountability implies 1) responsibility for the team's actions and 2) the ability to explain them to others. Without buy-in, no one wants to be accountable in this way. But Belief Maps and satisfaction analysis clearly support buy-in, and from that accountability ensues.

In some cases, teams have used the methodology in this book, reached a recommendation, and carried it forward to management, only to have it overturned. Sometimes this occurred because the team didn't have all the information the manager had; sometimes the criteria had changed; sometimes the importance had changed. This kind of result implies that the process itself is broken, that the team's work is, to a certain extent, wasted. But when teams use a well-documented process like the one in this book, there is a clear history of how the decision was made and where the accountability for it lies.

The Risk That the Alternative Will Not Turn Out As You Expect

The second of the five key questions—"What is the risk that our decision will not turn out as we expect?"—really requires that you answer three questions, which you first encountered in chapter 3:

- What can go wrong if I choose option X?
- How likely is it to happen?
- If it does go wrong, what are the consequences?

In decision making, the only way you can truly know you are "wrong" is after the fact—if your choice doesn't meet one or more of your criteria to a sufficient degree after you've put the choice into action. Since when you make decisions you are looking forward in time, **decision risk is defined as the expectation that an alternative will not meet the criteria.** By using expectation (in the statistical sense), the first risk questions are answered with a numerical value (expected value) about each criterion.

In the design of physical or economic systems there is often a "risk analysis" step, in which the risk of failure is determined by using mathematical models. The goal is to identify features of the system that may be in peril as a result of both foreseen or unforeseen factors. This analysis is usually performed after a specific alternative has been chosen and detailed.

In decision management, however, you need to take a slightly different tack and assume that:

- You must address risk during decision making, *not* as a task to complete after you have selected an alternative. This is because decision risk is a measure of your lack of knowledge, as well as other uncertainties you need to consider when you make a decision.
- There is risk associated with every feature of every alternative. Traditional risk assessment separately addresses financial risk, performance risk, and schedule risk. But when including risk as a part of the decision-making process, you must integrate the uncertainty inherent in all the features at once, because it is the combination of them that drives your decision.
- You can get a good assessment of uncertainty, and thus risk, by fusing the evaluations of all the members of your team.
- You can collect sufficient information using the Levels of Criterion Satisfaction and Certainty on the Belief Map to calculate risk as part of the decision-management process.

To better understand the differences between "system risk," or traditional risk analysis, and decision risk, consider table 9.5. The table describes our

		System Risk	Decision Risk
The three risk questions	What can go wrong?	A component or system fails	A poor choice is made
	How likely is it?	Probability of occurrence dependent on system history, simulation, and sensitivity analysis	Probability dependent on team's uncertain knowledge and their belief in information and models
	What is the impact?	Money, time, and possibly lives are lost as the system fails	Money, time, and possibly lives are lost as the poor decision is put into action
Analysis methods applied		Traditional probabilities (Frequentist methods)	Bayesian probability methods specifically designed to fuse uncertain incomplete, inconsistent and evolving evidence

Table 9.5: System risk vs. decision risk.

three questions about risk along with the analysis methods we might apply for both types of risk. When you look at the differences, you will see that decision risk calls for analytical methods that are different from those traditionally used; it calls for Bayesian methods.

The best way to see these differences in action is to rejoin the system selection team's effort to choose a proposal. We will explore with them the methods to use to find risk associated with a single alternative relative to a single criterion. Please note that in *Accord,* for each alternative this risk is fused across all the criteria and all team members.

First, let's consider a qualitative example: John's evaluation of Grex's ease of use. In figures 9.9 and 9.10 he assessed his criterion satisfaction as high (he thinks the probability is high that Grex's product will be easy to use) based on his high level of knowledge. This translated to a belief of 0.68, which, for our purposes here, we will round off to .70. So now the question becomes: What is the risk, based solely on John's evaluation, that this 70% belief in Grex's ease of use may be wrong?

There are two levels of risk for us to consider. First, John's 70% satisfaction indicates quite directly that there is a 30% (100% - 70%) chance that Grex's product will not be easy to use. This is the first-level risk associated with choosing Grex. We can consider this value to be an assessment of risk because it combines the consequences (not meeting the criterion is 1 - the Level of Criterion Satisfaction) with the probability of this occurring (Level of Certainty), and it is an expected value. However, due to uncertainty, this

30% number may be too low. We can estimate the second level of risk, the amount of *potential increase* in risk, in three steps:

1   First, we compute the chance that the alternative does not meet the target (that Grex is easy to use). Belief is the probability that it does meet the target, so 1 minus belief is the chance that it does not. In John's case this is 1 - 0.7 = 0.3.

2   We know that the consequence of not meeting the target is that the belief drops from 0.7 to 0.0.

Now we can compute the risk as (the chance that the alternative does not meet the target) x (the consequence of not meeting the target). The result is that risk = 0.3 x 0.7 = 0.21, or 21%. What this means is that if everything goes as badly as it can, John's satisfaction evaluation could be as low as 70% – 21% = 49% (or the inverse; the risk is 30% + 21% = 51%).

John initially said that he thought that Grex's product would rate high in ease of use (75%), but due to his lack of knowledge, his belief is 70%. But when we factor in uncertainty, the risk that it won't be easy to use is actually 51%. This value describes what can go wrong (that Grex's product won't be easy to use) and how likely that outcome is (there is a 51% chance), and we know that the consequence is that time and money will be lost. A 51% risk is a huge number; further on I'll show how including his teammates' evaluations will reduce it.

Belief	Risk	Worst possible
1.0	0.0	1.0
0.9	0.09	0.81
0.8	0.16	0.64
0.7	0.21	0.49
0.6	0.24	0.36
0.5	0.25	0.25
0.4	0.24	0.16
0.3	0.21	0.09
0.2	0.16	0.04
0.1	0.09	0.01

Table 9.6: Qualitative risk values.

Table 9.6 summarizes the general relationship between belief, risk, and worst possible performance in qualitative evaluations. This method of computing risk is automated in *Accord*.

If John's evaluation had been a quantitative assessment, the logic would be a little different. When we estimate numerical values, the risk is less than when we estimate purely qualitative evaluations. Unfortunately, qualitative risk is also more difficult to estimate, because it is based on all the number line judgments that team members make. I'll present a simple risk evaluation estimate. But we can only obtain accurate estimates through more

Belief	Risk	Worst possible
1.0	0.00	1.00
0.9	0.02	0.88
0.8	0.04	0.76
0.7	0.06	0.64
0.6	0.08	0.52
0.5	0.10	0.40
0.4	0.12	0.28
0.3	0.14	0.16
0.2	0.16	0.04
0.1	0.18	0.00 (bounded)

Table 9.7: Quantitative risk values.

complex methods, such as those built into *Accord*.

Qualitative risk is approximately 20% of the difference between satisfaction and unity (1, or 100%). The exact value depends on the distribution on the number line of the high and low estimates around the most likely value. For example, if the satisfaction for an alternative is 60%, the risk is about 20% of (100 - 60 =) 8%. So if everything goes as badly as it can, then the satisfaction could go as low as (60 - 8 =) 52%. Table 9.7 shows the average 20% degradation for risk and the worst possible performance for quantitative criteria.

Both the qualitative and quantitative risk estimations address single alternative/criterion evaluations. For anything more complex than that, you need a computer.

For our current example, figure 9.16 shows the effect of risk as a gray area at the bottom of the team's satisfaction curves. The team is 60 - 68% satisfied with Grex. But because of the risk factor these scores may be 8% too high. Thus the total risk is 40 - 48%, ((100 - (68 - 8)) = 40 and 100 - (60 - 8) = 48), depending on the individual team members' viewpoints.

The main points I'd like you to take away from this discussion are:

- Decision risk is the expectation that an alternative will not meet the criteria you have established. It answers:
  - What can go wrong if I choose option X?
  - How likely is it to happen?
  - If it does go wrong, what are the consequences?

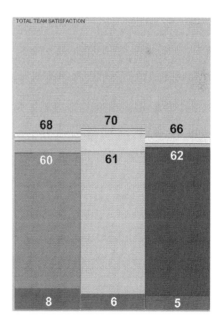

Figure 9.16: Team satisfaction showing risk.

- Decision risk is not the same as system risk and must be analyzed differently.
- Risk can be found easily by using *Accord.*

Now let me recap what we've covered in this chapter and where the team is in making its decision.

Summary

We have accomplished a lot in this chapter, but the team we've been following still can't answer any of the five key questions. If you look at figure 9.16, you'll find that the team can readily see that there is little to differentiate the three alternatives. The risk is slightly higher with the first alternative, Grex, but there is better agreement about the third alternative, Swale. All but one member of the team likes the middle one, Able, the best. At the same time, it's clear that the team still has some work ahead of it.

On the bright side, though, they now have tools to help them with important steps in robust decision making. They can:

- Find satisfaction for the alternatives
- Fuse the team's evaluations
- See the results from multiple viewpoints concerning importance
- Understand the probability of an alternative being the best one
- Calculate consensus
- Analyze decision risk

Not bad! In the next chapter we will tackle calculating what-to-do-next. When we add that piece to the capabilities we gained in this chapter, we will be fully able to answer the five key questions.

If you are not interested in using *Accord,* there is still much to take away from this chapter:

1 You can estimate a single evaluator's satisfaction to help answer the first key question.
2 You can appreciate the complexities of fusing multiple estimations. To determine the level of satisfaction, you can use a team estimate for each point on a Belief Map and treat these points as if a single evaluator had developed them.

3   You can appreciate the effects of differences in viewpoint and apply them to either of the items above.

4   You can estimate levels of consensus by looking at the distribution of points on Belief Maps.

5   You can estimate levels of risk to support answering the second key question.

Decide What-to-Do-Next
—Analyzing the benefit of further effort

10

Introduction

The team we've been following has gone through the initial evaluation, but so far no best proposal has emerged. All three have strengths and weaknesses, but it's not yet clear which to choose. And at this point, answering the five key questions is impossible:

1. Which is the best alternative?
2. What is the risk that our decision will not turn out as we expect?
3. Do we know enough to make a good decision yet?
4. Is there buy-in for the decision?
5. What do we need to do next to feel confident about our decision, within the scope of our limited resources?

So now the team is faced with deciding what-to-do-next to reach a conclusion. In this chapter we will join Anne as she focuses the team's efforts on the fifth question. In answering it, they will also work to arrive at satisfactory answers to the first four.

Remember the Arthur C. Clarke quote from chapter 1? "The only real problem in life is what to do next" sums it up well. Think about it: Once you've made a difficult decision, it's like a weight has been lifted from your shoulders. You can *act* on the decision. But trying to figure out what-to-do-next to reach a decision can be debilitating. Many decision makers get stuck, do useless analysis, and fail to make a decision simply because it is not clear what-to-do-next. This is the hard part—we're in the belly of the beast now. It's also the part that has been virtually ignored by other books and methods.

Personally, it was an intellectual leap for me to get from decision making = choosing an option, to decision making = choosing what-to-do-next, with choosing an option as the ultimate goal but with many paths to follow to achieve it.

Previous chapters encouraged you to change your thinking and consider all information to be uncertain. This chapter advocates a second change: namely, to adopt the mind-set that the goal of decision making is not selecting an alternative, it's deciding what-to-do-next. Of course, in the end you need to select an alternative, but the path you take to get there is critical and is, in fact, a series of what-to-do-next sub-decisions.

An important distinction to make is that deciding what-to-do-next is part of the decision-making process; it is not the action that follows—implementing the decision. Also important to note is that decision making is not a single pass effort; it is iterative, as it must be if you are to arrive at a robust decision.

The strategy to determine what-to-do-next, summarized in figure 10.1, is the core of robust decision methodology. The clockwise arrows show the progression through the strategy. Each step in the process takes more time and effort to resolve. Each radial arrow, stated as an "if, then" rule, points to the activity you should take to help make the decision and resolve the issue. We will work through the rules, numbered one through six in the figure, alongside Anne's team as we move through the chapter.

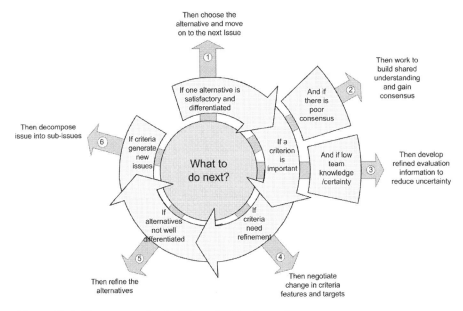

Figure 10.1: The strategy for deciding what-to-do-next.

What-to-Do-Next Rule 1: If You're There, Then You're Done

Is the team at a point where it can choose a proposal and move on to another issue? If it has found that, regardless of individual members' viewpoints, a satisfactory, low-risk alternative has been identified, then it has reached agreement. Then all that is left to do is document the selected alternative and put the decision into action. But looking at their results from the previous chapter, in figure 10.2, you can see that Anne favors the third option, Swale, Inc., while the others favor the second one, Able Industries—and just barely.

There is no clearly satisfactory and differentiated alternative, regardless of whose viewpoint is considered. It is clear, then, that the first rule in figure 10.1 does not apply; the team is not ready to choose an alternative, and has more work to do.

What the team would like to see, and what you would like to see in a real-life situation, is one alternative that stands out from the others, one for which satisfaction is significantly higher from every viewpoint. To be differentiated, it is sufficient for an alternative to be 5% more satisfactory than the others. However, even if it is differentiated, you should also examine its level of satisfaction. Let's say, for example, that Grex had a satisfaction of 40% and all the others were at 30%—should you choose Grex? 40% is a pretty low level of satisfaction, but this level is dependent on the targets that have been set for both the quantitative and 5-point criteria. If a "delighted" value of one important criterion is set at an unrealistic level, then none of the alternatives can score very high.

In addition, when you invoke this rule, remember that your satisfaction calculations may be flawed because they may have been calculated from

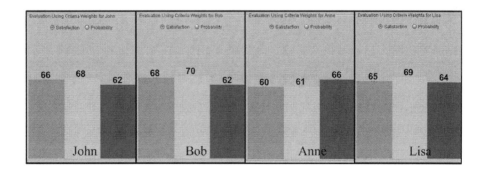

Figure 10.2: The results of the first pass by the team.

sparse information, or they may be based on limited knowledge or low levels of certainty. These limitations are easy to see on the Belief Maps in terms of Levels of Certainty and Criterion Satisfaction. However, even with low knowledge on all alternatives, one alternative may have higher satisfaction than the others. You can see the complexity involved here.

Clearly though, the team has not finished its work. But since it's using *Accord*, it has an advantage, because the program produces a What-To-Do-Next Report, shown in figure 10.3. This report automates the logic in figure 10.1, and the team can use it to help manage its decision as it progresses through its deliberations.

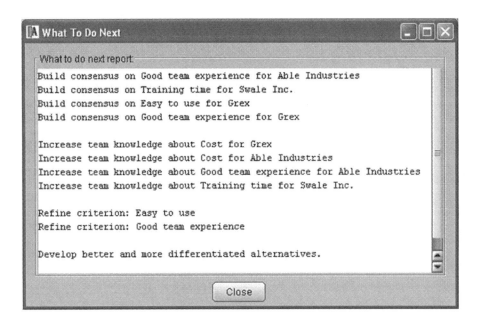

Figure 10.3: Initial What-to-Do-Next Report.

What-to-Do-Next Rule 2: If You're at Odds, Then You'd Better Find Out Why

To tease apart the virtual tie among the three proposals, the team must look for the easiest things to do first, in order to use the least amount of resources. Looking at the logic in figure 10.1, it's clear that it's necessary to work on critical evaluations where the team members' evaluations don't agree. The evaluations to work on are specifically identified in the first section of the What-To-Do-Next Report.

The team knows that, in general, the least expensive activity to undertake is to discuss, clarify, and refine the evaluation information. As a catch-all term, this can be referred to as "developing consensus." Essentially, if consensus about an alternative's ability to meet a criterion is low and this criterion can change the satisfaction results significantly, then the team knows that it should further interpret and discuss the evaluation information: Clarify alternatives and criteria, and refine Belief Maps.

The evaluations that merit this effort can also be found by looking at the Belief Maps and importance weightings. If a Belief Map shows a poor Level of Criterion Satisfaction agreement for an evaluation that is important to many of the stakeholders, then it is a candidate for this activity. The What-To-Do-Next Report in figure 10.3 identifies four evaluations worthy of discussion. The report orders the evaluations based on an analysis of which has the potential to make the greatest impact. And since discussion to build consensus is less expensive than doing additional work to reduce uncertainty, this is the place to start.

The way to begin to develop consensus is to ensure that all the decision makers are evaluating the same information. We know that no two people will have exactly the same mental model of the alternatives or criterion. They can't, since each person's understanding is based on prior experience and knowledge. Thus, a good place to check for consistency in understanding of the alternatives and criteria is on the team's Belief Map.

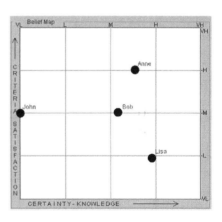

Figure 10.4: Team Belief Map revisiting team evaluation of Able Industries' team experience.

The first evaluation to revisit is Able Industries' team experience, modeled on the Belief Map in figure 10.4. There is only 55% consensus on this criterion. (This value was calculated in *Accord.*) This is a low level of consensus, but both John and Anne think this feature is important.

The lack of consensus on this evaluation is caused by one of the following:

- **The evaluators may have a different understanding of the alternative.** In other words, Lisa brings different knowledge and experience to the evaluation than her colleagues do. This type of disunity of understanding is especially common if the knowledge level about the alternative is not very high. If the alternative is not well refined, then there is a chance that the evaluators may not be evaluating exactly the same thing.

- **The evaluators may be using different interpretations of the criterion in their evaluations.** Although they are supposed to be using the same criterion, they may have different interpretations of what is included in features measured. This type of interpretation problem is especially common if the criterion is qualitative; then the evaluation may be inconsistent among team members. But this can also happen with something as refined as, say, "unit cost." The definition of a "unit" may not be consistent.

- **The evaluators' experience leads them to different conclusions.** In other words, they just plain disagree on how well the alternative meets the criterion. This is fine, as long as it is not confounded by the inconsistent definitions in the previous two reasons for poor consensus.

The first cause of lack of consensus encourages both discussion about and refinement of the alternatives. Often, team discussion will help produce a uniform understanding of the proposal and even help refine it. The second cause requires refining the criterion. The third cause implies that the evaluators who disagree may not know as much as they thought. If they were measuring exactly the same alternative against exactly the same target, their conclusions should not differ greatly. Thus, if the team members seem to have the same understanding, they should reconsider their knowledge assessment or consider generating more evaluation information.

After some discussion, Anne now realizes that her evaluation of Able's experience level was out of step with

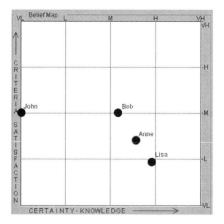

Figure 10.5: Anne's reevaluation of the Able team's experience.

the others on the team, as she defined "highly experienced" differently than they did. She also learned from her team that a key person had left Able. As a result, she moved her point to reflect her new evaluation, as shown in figure 10.5. This change lowers the fused team satisfaction with Able by about 5%. With this one evaluation change, Able is no longer the favorite in any evaluator's eyes. The methodology has identified the most sensitive and inconsistent evaluation to focus on, and its re-evaluation has changed the results.

The next items on the What-to-Do-Next report also have relatively low consensus and high importance. Anne could have found these by reviewing the belief maps, but the report makes it easier. After similar discussions about Swale's training time, and Grex's ease of use and team experience, the satisfactions have changed, as reflected in figure 10.6, with the satisfactions shown superimposed on each other. And the What-to-Do-Next report has been updated as shown in figure 10.7. The What-to-Do-Next Report still

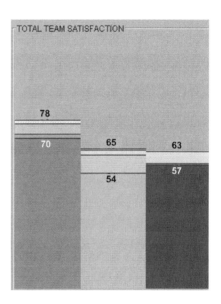

Figure 10.6: Updated total team satisfaction.

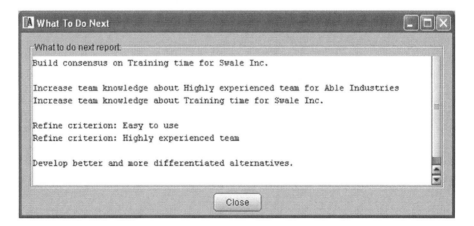

Figure 10.7: The updated What-to-Do-Next Report.

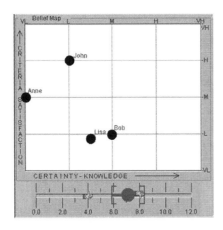

Figure 10.8: The Belief Map for Swale's training time.

shows that the team has not reached consensus on Swale's training time. They just don't agree about how to evaluate the evidence they have, and that's okay. Note that this evaluation appears in the report as needing more team knowledge, i.e., more certainty. Anne could also have seen both of these points (low certainty and lack of consensus) by looking at the Belief Map shown in figure 10.8. What is evident here is that uncertainty is high (certainty is low to medium) in every team member's evaluation, that John does not agree with Lisa or Bob on satisfaction, and that Anne has abstained. It's no wonder this has been identified as an evaluation of interest.

So where does the team stand at this point with respect to the five key questions? Its answers are:

1 Which is the best alternative?
   As figure 10.6 indicates, it's Grex, the first one.
2 What is the risk that our decision will not turn out as we expect?
   The risk ranges from 22 to 30%, with an additional 5% found by analyzing the worst that can happen, for a total risk of 27 to 35%. Anne thinks this is acceptable.
3 Do we know enough to make a good decision yet?
   Not yet. According to the What-To-Do-Next Report, the team still needs to look at Able's team experience and Swale's training time.
4 Is there buy-in for the decision?
   Nearly everyone favors Grex—at the moment.
5 What do we need to do next to feel confident about our decision, within the scope of our limited resources?
   Gain knowledge in the two weak evaluations.

Anne can decide to stop right here and go with Grex, but because of her team's answers to the five questions, she chooses to see the process through one more step.

What-to-Do-Next Rule 3: If You Don't Know Much, Then You'd Better Learn

This rule suggests that the team identify alternative evaluations that are highly important but have low team knowledge or high uncertainty, as indicated on the Belief Map and suggested in the What-to-Do-Next Report.

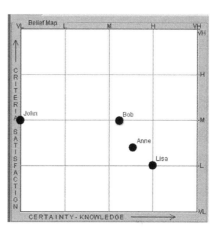

Figure 10.9: The Belief Map for Able's team experience.

As the Belief Map in figure 10.9 shows, the team considers Able's team experience to be not so poor, but it's poor enough and important enough to be identified in the report. More obvious is the uncertainty about Swale's training time (figure 10.10). A simple example will show why these areas have been identified, and demonstrate how easy it can be to jump to the wrong conclusion.

Anne convenes the team to reevaluate Able's team experience. During the ensuing discussion the team questions why they are talking about this evaluation, since their level of consensus is reasonable and they are much more satisfied with Grex than Able. So Anne shows the team the result of a simple experiment. She moves John's evaluation from the default position on the left side of the Belief Map (figure 10.9) to

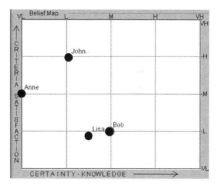

Figure 10.10: Swale's training time.

the location shown in figure 10.11, which also shows the resulting change in team satisfaction.

This evaluation is so sensitive that one person evaluating an alternative in the upper right corner has made Able appear to be as appealing as Grex. A similar result can be shown with Swales' ease of use.

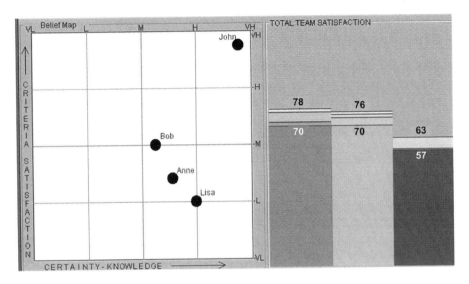

Figure 10.11: Anne's experiment with John's evaluation of Able's team experience.

To increase its knowledge, or certainty, about either of these evaluations, the team can do one or more of the following:

- Develop some form of analysis, either formal or informal
- Perform some experiments
- Hire consultants who have knowledge they do not have
- Speak to the vendor representatives
- Reference prior documented work
- Leverage team knowledge using the knowledge of individual team members (i.e., build a better shared understanding, or have the knowledgeable individuals tutor the others)
- Restrict variation through contractual agreements

Note that these activities may cost more than would having a discussion to reach consensus. That's why this rule is placed later in the logic, after working to reach consensus.

Before beginning experiments, analyses, or initiating other methods to gather information, consider the fact that increasing knowledge or certainty requires the commitment of resources. It takes time and money to do experiments, perform analysis, hire consultants, or chase down knowledge in any other way. And these costs cannot be recovered. Before you do more work, consider the potential effect or benefit relative to the cost of increasing your knowledge. Engineers and other analysts can be sorely tempted to refine analytical models, simply because that is what they know how to do well. But this can quickly lead to analysis paralysis, and consequently, no progress at all. If there isn't a clear indication that refinement will help the team to differentiate alternatives, resist temptation. Don't do it.

After looking at the information they have, Anne and the team can choose to either select Grex or follow the recommendations in the report. They decide to nail down Swale's training time, and it's a good thing they do. After they take this step and reexamine the answers to the five key questions, they discover that Grex is in fact a better option than Swale, achieving even less risk. Now they can choose Grex, feeling confident in their choice and in the methods with which they reached that conclusion (see figure 10.12). Even though the entire team doesn't agree on Grex being the best option, there is strong buy-in for the decision and accountability for it. Happy ending!

But what if all of the team's deliberations still hadn't led them to positive answers to the key questions? Fortunately, there are other what-to-do-next options to consider.

What-to-Do-Next Rule 4: Negotiate New Criterion Features and Targets

Often, the decision-making process leads you to refine your criteria. In robust decision making we have worked hard to isolate differences about

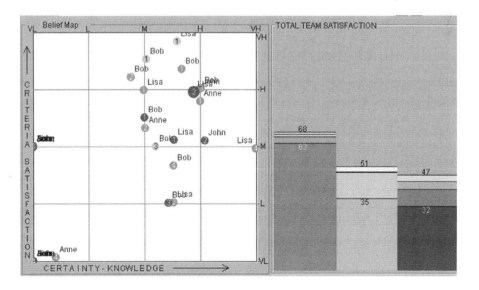

Figure 10.12: The team decides on Grex.

criteria in the importance weightings. We work to agree on the criteria and their targets and agree to disagree on their importance. But sometimes there's a benefit to negotiating new features and targets for your criteria. You can tell it is time to do this when:

1 The criteria are not helping you differentiate the alternatives
2 A criterion needs to be refined because:
   a It isn't measuring what it is supposed to
   b It can be refined from qualitative to 5-point or quantitative measures to show better differentiation
   c It is measuring a similar feature as some other criterion (i.e., it is not independent)
   d It is not measuring all the alternatives in the same way (i.e., it is not universal)
   e It is measuring more than one feature
   f It is too detailed—it is measuring a feature that can't be controlled by this issue (i.e., it is not external)
3 New criteria are being discussed, covering features that are not currently being measured.

I haven't used the term "negotiate" in the book up to this point. I introduce it here because negotiation often revolves around the criteria, their targets, and their importance. Negotiation has implications that are not conducive to robust decision making, itemized in table 10.1[1]

If your criteria are not helping you to differentiate among the alternatives, then it is time to refine them; the baggage that comes with negotiation is the price you pay. For example, the team may agree that their "easy to use" criterion needs refining. To do this, they may discuss breaking it down into the number of steps it takes to do "x," or the perceived ease in accomplish-

Robust decision making	Negotiation
Common interests dominate	Conflicting interests dominate
Depends on a shared perception of information	Information is used judiciously since premature disclosure may weaken position
Is a search for solutions	Predetermined solutions by each party
Emphasis on managing the logical process and determining the course of action	Emphasis on structuring exchange that will achieve an acceptable settlement
Results in implementable solution	Results in agreement

Table 10.1: Robust decision making compared to negotiation.

ing "y." Generally speaking, adding new criteria takes effort and you should not undertake it unless the earlier rules do not yield results.

Turning back to Anne's team, we see that the What-to-Do-Next Report has identified two qualitative criteria as possibly needing to be refined. The team had also begun to talk about compatibility with other systems they are already using—a new criterion—but has decided that it isn't worth adding to the list.

If refining criteria doesn't help, then the focus needs to turn to generating new alternatives.

What-to-Do-Next Rule 5: Generate New Alternative Solutions

At the end of the first round of evaluations, the three proposals that the system selection team were considering were virtually tied. This could imply that the team needs to go out for more bids. But luckily, by applying the preceding rules, the team was able to break the deadlock and avoid the pain of reopening the proposal process.

Generating new alternatives is something that often happens as a by-product of performing the kind of detailed decision evaluation I suggest in this book. This is especially true when the issue requiring a decision involves the design of new products or processes. The new ideas that evolve through discussion and developing a shared vision can be a beneficial outcome, but new ideas can also be one of the negative outcomes. It depends on the timing. Early in the decision-making process, new ideas are gifts that come from the knowledge gained by working on the problem. But later in the process, as people start to make commitments, new ideas can delay closure.

There are two signals that indicate you may need new alternatives:

1   The alternatives you have are not differentiated.
2   Your level of satisfaction with the best alternative is
    too low.

How low is "low"? It depends on many factors, as well as on how risk-averse you are. If all your criteria are qualitative, then 70% is a conservative boundary. If an acceptable alternative shows greater than 70% satisfaction from all viewpoints, then the team should be comfortable accepting it. For quantitative criteria, it all depends on how realistically you've set your "delighted" targets. If all your targets are outside the range of all of your alternatives, then your satisfaction level with any of them won't be very high.

Even though the What-to-Do-Next Report for Anne's team suggested that they develop new alternatives, they didn't have to take that step because less-resource-demanding activities could be brought to bear to break the deadlock.

What-to-Do-Next Rule 6: Decompose the Issue into Sub-issues

The final rule, which Anne's team didn't need to put into practice, is decomposing, or breaking down, the problem issue into sub-issues. This happens when you develop measures for a given criterion—yes, there are criteria for a criterion. Let's see what happens if the team starts to discuss the "easy to use" criterion and realizes that they have a set of measures for it, such as: the number of steps to do activity A; the number of steps to do activity B; the time it takes to print a report; the percentage of people who understand charts at first sight.

Then "select a system that is easy to use" can be treated as a sub-issue and the result of that sub-issue evaluation can be used as part of the proposal selection process. Some problems naturally decompose into sub-issues. You need to forcibly decompose other problems in order to help the decision makers look at smaller problems. This decomposition can often be accomplished quite easily, but at other times the sub-issues are so interdependent that any consideration of them is problematic at best.

Summary

Counterintuitive as it may seem, in robust decision making deciding what-to-do-next is of primary importance; it is even more critical than selecting an alternative. That's because it will lead you to the best possible choice. If you take nothing else from this book, take away two concepts, one from early in the book and one from this chapter: the importance of uncertainty and the need to carefully analyze what-to-do-next.

You can accomplish what-to-do-next analysis solely with Belief Maps and knowledge about criteria importance from your stakeholders. But it is much easier with *Accord*, because it has an internal rule base that uses the results of your analysis to suggest courses of action.

The what-to-do-next step does more to put on a level playing field the mix of individual problem-solving styles we encountered in chapter 4 than any other activity in the book. It controls the pace of the deliberation and forces the entire team to examine what is important.

As you take your knowledge from this chapter with you into your deliberations in the workplace, at a minimum keep figure 10.1 in mind, and be aware that the further around the figure your discussion goes, the more it will generally cost, both in time and in other resources. Focus first on consensus, and then on knowledge/certainty using Belief Maps as your guide. Only if these fail to bring about positive answers to the five key questions should you focus your team's efforts on refining alternatives and criteria. Apply this logic, and you will receive the highest benefit for the least cost.

Decision Documentation and Rationale

11

Making Robust Decisions

I began this book with a definition of a robust decision: the best possible choice, one found by eliminating all the uncertainty possible within the scope of available resources and then choosing, with known and acceptable satisfaction. The bulk of the book details methods that focus on this goal. By now you should have a good appreciation of the importance of considering and managing the uncertainty.

Obviously, you don't need to use every method in this book in order to be able to make better decisions. In fact, your first decision is choosing which methods to use in a given situation. A good approach is to use the checklist on the following page to help guide you. It corresponds to figure 1.2 (page 32).

First, you can use it to take an inventory of your current decision-making process. Second, you can use it as a basis for developing a plan, and commit to phasing in all the unchecked items. The steps in the checklist are in a logical order, with the latter items generally being dependent on those above them.

A third use of this list is to support you when making everyday decisions. If you are in a situation where you need to make a choice, start at the top of the list and work your way down until it is no longer useful to do so. The more important the decision and the larger the team, the farther down the list you may need to work. For critical decisions, you should use the entire list.

Note that the strength of robust decision making is not found solely in *Accord* software, which only directly supports the last three items. In fact, the software's usefulness is dependent on all the preceding items. So, if diving in all the way is not possible in your organization, start pushing on the early items in your meetings.

The decision checklist

- ☐ Recognize that there is a decision to be made.
- ☐ Write or state the issue as a single sentence.
- ☐ Develop multiple alternatives for resolving the issue.
- ☐ List the stakeholders.
- ☐ Work to generate a set of discriminating criteria and their targets.
- ☐ Understand who thinks which criteria are important.
- ☐ Evaluate the alternatives relative to the criteria and note the reasons for the evaluations.
- ☐ Manage and visualize the evaluation uncertainties (using Belief Maps, for example).
- ☐ Fuse the evaluations using a structured method to find:
    Alternative satisfaction
    Alternative risk
- ☐ Base future activity on a what-to-do-next evaluation.
- ☐ Document the decision and the reasoning behind it.

In the next section I will introduce the concept of decision rationale—the effort to capture the reasons behind a decision for purposes of reuse and review. This is the last item on the list, and leads to the topic of decision documentation: recording the items on the checklist along with the rationales for them.

Decision Documentation

It has long been a common practice in engineering to carefully document the final results of the design process as a set of drawings and other specifications. These drawings are used as directions for manufacturing the product. They are also the results of literally thousands of decisions. The same is true about business documents. They are only a snapshot of the final results, conveying little detail about the decisions that led to them.

In engineering, if you want to know what decisions were made, you reverse engineer the product, working back from the drawings, to understand why each feature is the way it is. The story you develop is a best guess at least, but the details are lost, and you may repeat previous mistakes.

One way to ensure that the actual decisions will be known is to document them as they occur. This sounds like something that would be done as a matter of course, but it usually isn't. Here are suggestions about what should be documented:

At a minimum:
A sentence describing the issue
A description of the alternatives considered
A list of the people involved and their role
A description of the criteria including measures, units, and targets
The final decision—the alternative selected or what was done next

At a maximum:
The importance of each criterion by viewpoint
Evaluations made by each evaluator, complete with the uncertainty
Results such as:
Satisfaction
Risk
Accord's what-to-next-report
A description of the rationale behind the decision
Iteration history

You can use a simple form to record decisions. You can fill it in for each major decision and file it either in hard copy or electronic form. Below is a sample template. It was produced automatically by *Accord*. (More types of information may be included in this report than are listed.)

Title: Choose client/server communication protocol

Date: August 3, 2006

Rationale:
Evidence points to Callable code with VBA. Dan pushed hard for this and he is managing this project. Dave suggested a proof of concept prototype, which is being built to confirm that information is easily sent back and forth between the server and client.

Team members evaluating the issue:
Daniel Bridenbecker
Dave Ullman
Keith Price
Robert Williams

Alternatives considered:
- Transform using XML map & XSL
- Callable code with VBA
- Callable code with .NET
- Transform in server

Criteria for evaluating alternatives:

Measured

Feature	Type	Units	Delighted	Disgusted
Elapsed time	less-is-better	weeks	7	8
Dan time	less-is-better	hours	50	100
Keith hours	less-is-better	hours	100	150
Robert hours	less-is-better	hours	200	300
Clean client/ server interface	qualitative	—	—	—
Office application compatible	qualitative	—	—	—
Simple client delivery	qualitative	—	—	—
Easily upgradeable for developer	qualitative	—	—	—

Results
Range of satisfaction for each alternative and the risk (amount the satisfaction may be reduced):

Alternative Satisfaction Range (0.0–1.0)

	Low	High	Risk
Transform using XML map & XSL	.67	.71	0.04
Callable code with VBA	.76	.88	0.03
Callable code with NET	.41	.59	0.03

What-to-Do-Next
Callable code with VBA has high satisfaction and probability of being the first choice is high from all viewpoints

Produced by *Accord* from Robust Decisions, Inc.:
www.robustdecisions.com

The last two items in the "maximum" list are worthy of exploration—the rationale and iteration history.

Decision Rationale

A rationale is the reasoning behind a decision, describing why and how the conclusion was reached. At a minimum, it is a written statement that describes the issue, the alternatives considered, and the conclusion, but it can be much more. Let's extend the definition of a rationale to include the reasons for bothering to record it. Namely:

> A decision rationale is the **capture of the deliberation** that leads to a decision in a manner that can be **easily queried** to **answer questions about how the decision was made** for **future review and reuse.**

So, not only should the rationale tell what the decision was, but how it was reached. It should also be structured for review and reuse. The previous report does part of this, but certainly can only answer superficial questions about how the decision was made. Any other information will need to be inferred or re-engineered. Ideally, the rationale should include a record or history of argumentation, documentation, and communication. This sounds good, but it is exceedingly difficult to do.

In fact, I spent from 1990 to the present devising methods to capture and manage rationale. My work focused on mechanical designs, so it began with trying to capture and manage the evolution of drawings, but much important information was still missing. About 1995 it became evident that, as I stated in chapter 1:

> Business and technical progress is the generation and refinement of information, punctuated by decision making.

Thus, the obvious place to capture the information was at the decision points. Here the drawings, the analysis, and other information are all supporting evidence for the deliberation. The preceding report is a first cut at documenting the rationale, but it can be much more than that. The following material makes use of *Accord* software, as automation is needed to fulfill all the needs of a rationale support system.

Accord records each change to the framing of the problem or each major

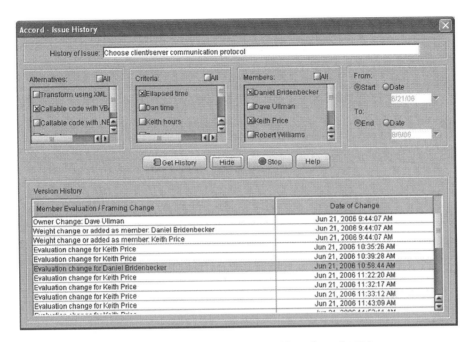

Figure 11.1: Query for elapsed time to develop callable code with VBA.

change in evaluation in a database in an effort to provide a rationale and re-use capability. (Note that this feature is not included in the free version you can download with this book.) If changes in framing are documented and each evaluation is annotated with the reason behind it (why a point is where it is on the Belief Map), then the records in the database form a detailed history. Further, if you can search or query to see the effect of a criterion on an alternative or the impact of one of the evaluators on the decision, then you have achieved a rationale system. This is what can be done with *Accord*.

The ability to view the history of a decision and make queries about it is a unique feature of *Accord*. It allows you to easily search, review, and reuse past work and study the rationale behind a decision. In *Accord*, you can view the history of the current issue or find an issue with certain characteristics.

In *Accord*, you can select the profile of what you are looking for by choosing the members, alternatives, and criteria of interest. Selecting "all" (default) will produce the same result as checking all the boxes in an area. You can also specify the date/time parameters for a search. For example, in figure 11.1 a query is built to see Dan and Keith's evaluations for the "elapsed time" needed to develop "Callable code with VBA." The list at the bottom of the window is each record where this evaluation was made. The text tells whether the new record was in response to a change in framing, weighting,

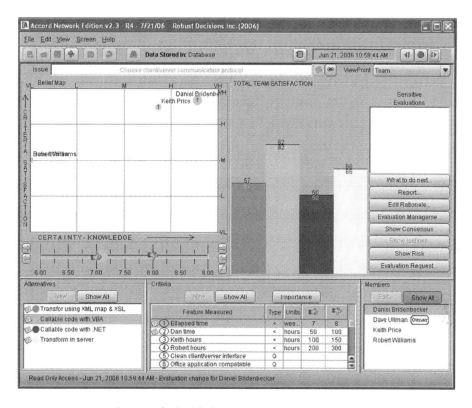

Figure 11.2: Accord *screen for highlighted item in Figure 11.1.*

or an evaluation. Selecting "Get History" for the highlighted item in figure 11.1 results in the *Accord* screen in figure 11.2. Note that *Accord* looks as it usually does, but with a bar along the bottom announcing that the information is read-only and showing the date and action of the historical image. You can then easily step through all the changes to see how the decision changed with the addition of information about topic(s) in your query.

Reuse and Decision Templates

Tracking the history of deliberation gives you many opportunities to reuse deliberation. You can revisit issues partway through and use the state of the deliberation as a starting point for another issue. Another way to reuse previously worked problems is to use decision templates. This concept arose from the observation that you can reuse sets of criteria for similar problems. For example, say you have to decide whether to buy a product or manufacture it in-house, or you have to choose a new employee. In either case, when you have done this once, you have a template for doing it the next time. Essentially, the template consists of an issue statement and a set of measures for evaluating alternatives that may resolve the issue. While it's true that not every problem is the same and some of the measures may be different, templates offer a strong starting point for many types of common decisions. The next chapter contains many common decision templates.

Criteria Templates

12

Not All Decisions Are Unique

Many decision problems occur repeatedly, with evaluation measures remaining fairly constant from issue to issue. You can develop templates to address such recurring problems, thereby reducing the time and effort involved in reaching robust decisions and adding consistency to the decision-making process.

At a minimum, a template consists of a specific issue and the measures used to evaluate alternatives for it (remember that criteria are measures with units and targets). Beyond this bare minimum, templates can also include specific targets for the measures, as well as the relative importance of the criteria.

Below is a list of some areas that lend themselves to templates. The remainder of this chapter will present templates for some of these; you can use them as a starting place to solve similar issues. The issues covered in the chapter are in bold.

1 Business issues
   a **Vendor selection**
   b **Portfolio assessment**
   c **Proposal evaluation**
   d **Product differentiation**
   e Choose a new plant location
   f Decide on which investment to make
   g Choose a new employee
2 Technology issues
   a **Make/buy decisions**
   b **Technology readiness**
   c Architecture selection
   d Concept selection

    e Design decisions

    f Trade study management

3 Military issues

    a Choose the best course of action

    b Acquire new systems

    c Perform Analysis of Alternatives (AoA)

4 Homeland security issues

    a Determine if a group is a threat to homeland security

    b Determine which location is the most likely target for a bomb

    c Choose the best security method for protecting a building from terrorists

Basic Template Steps

Templates for these and other areas can be developed by following these steps:

1 Define an issue that will be addressed repeatedly. Reduce it down to a specific statement, e.g., "Choose an employee from a pool of candidates."

2 Develop a representative list of issue applications that may be considered with the template. For example, you might use a template to assist you in hiring a CEO, an engineer, and a human resources officer.

3 Consult experts to determine a set of measures that are common to the alternatives. Continuing with the hiring example, such measures might be:

    a Years of experience

    b Salary requirements

    c Fit to job description

    d Hiring cost (moving costs, bonuses, start-up costs)

Note that these are measures only; targets and importance are not listed. Specific targets will depend on the particular position you are looking to fill, as will the importance of each of the measures.

For each of the issue applications, add targets and importance weights, and test a set of alternatives. For each of the criterion measures listed in item 3, ask, "Does this measure help discriminate among the alternatives?" Additionally, ask, "Are there other measures that help discriminate among the alternatives?" Use these two questions to refine the list you developed in step 3. Remember that you may list a measure that has no importance for some specific issue. In that situation, it can be weighted at zero to eliminate it from the problem; in other situations, its weight may be nonzero.

Take care with the lists below and the ones that you develop to be clear about the type of criteria you are forming. If they measure the probability that something occurs, or yes-ness, they are qualitative. If they measure the degree to which something occurs, they are quantitative. Identifying this is especially critical when using 5-point scales (see chapter 6 for details).

Following are templates for some common issues. For each, consider the list of measures as a starting point and use your expertise and specific knowledge of your organization to refine it.

Selecting a Vendor or Make/Buy Decisions

A common issue in technology, business, and service industries is which vendor to select to make a part or supply a service. This decision is the same if one of the alternatives is to do it in-house; in that case it is called the make/buy decision.[1] The days of accepting the lowest bid are gone, and the complexity of making this kind of decision is evident in the list of important measures that need to be considered.

Measure: High product quality
Details: Evaluate the anticipated relative quality of the product. Product quality includes finish and function.

Measure: Low development costs
Details: Evaluate the anticipated relative capital cost of preparing for production. This includes equipment, facilities, personnel, and other expenditures. Be sure that the costs compared are based on the same starting and ending conditions.

Measure: Low product costs
Details: Evaluate the anticipated relative cost of producing the product. This needs to include all costs required to get the product ready for insertion into an assembly or delivery to the customer. Be sure that the costs compared are based on the same starting and end conditions.

Measure: High product life cost stability

Details: Evaluate the anticipated relative stability of the cost estimates. How might the costs change over a two- or five-year period? What controls are in place to manage the cost?

Measure: Low development lead time

Details: Evaluate the anticipated relative lead time to get the product ready for production.

Measure: Low order lead time

Details: Evaluate the anticipated lead time needed between placing an order and receiving the product.

Measure: Strong intellectual property control

Details: Evaluate the anticipated relative control you will have over intellectual property. If intellectual property is not an issue, do not evaluate this criterion.

Measure: Good control of order volumes

Details: Evaluate the anticipated relative control you will have over the size of the orders and how well the volume matches your needs.

Measure: Easy to change product

Details: Evaluate the anticipated relative ability you will have to change the product.

Measure: Good product support

Details: Evaluate the anticipated relative ease with which you will be able to support the product.

Measure: Good control of supply chain

Details: Evaluate the level of control you have over suppliers.

Portfolio Assessment

Portfolio assessment or portfolio management is the effort to rank order a list of projects or products to determine which should be undertaken first. The template below is very extensive, presented as a hierarchy in two levels.[2]

Either use this list while considering only the five top-level measures, or expand to each of the second-level items and use all eighteen measures.

Measure: Technical success
Second-Level Measures:
1 Technical "gap"
2 Program complexity
3 Technical skill base
4 People availability
5 Facilities availability

Measure: Commercial success
Second-Level Measures:
1 Market need
2 Market maturity
3 Competitive intensity
4 Newness to company

Measure: Reward
Second-Level Measures:
1 Five-year cash flow
2 Technical payback
3 Time to start up

Measure: Business strategy fit
Second-Level Measures:
1 Company fit
2 Impact on company

Measure: Strategic leverage
Second-Level Measures:
1 Proprietary position
2 Platform for growth
3 Durability
4 Fit in company

The strengths of this list are:

Does not place undue emphasis on financial measures
Captures multiple goals
Each project is measured by a complete set of criteria (insures
    consistency and nothing is overlooked)
Forces review in greater depth and a forum for discussion
Recognizes that some measures are more important than others
Yields a single score

Proposal Evaluation

Many companies, government agencies, and other organizations request proposals from vendors and need to evaluate them to determine which to fund. Usually, the call for proposals is made through an RFP and the proposals are reviewed by a team of experts responding to a set of criteria. A typical set is given below as a template for proposal review.

Measure: Ability to meet objectives
Details: Degree to which the proposal describes a thorough
    and credible approach to meeting the business and technical
    objectives of the RFP.

Measure: Cost and schedule realism
Details: Degree to which the proposal's cost and schedule reflect a
    clear understanding of the technical/management complexity of
    the effort, and the associated schedule and budget risks.

Measure: Maturation status
Details: Degree to which the proposal provides substantiation that
    the proposed methods are sufficiently mature to achieve the
    outcome. This could be labeled "feasibility," as it is the degree
    to which the proposal is convincing that it is possible to carry out
    the project and finish it with the planned results and outcomes.

Measure: Management plan
Details: Degree to which the management plan describes
    a thorough and credible approach for communicating and

controlling project and task management functions and resources.

Measure: Capability and experience of the proposed management staff
Details: Degree to which the proposed management team and participating organizations have demonstrated the requisite experience and organizational capability to plan and deliver the proposed goods or services.

Measure: Cost
Details: The proposed cost, its volatility, and methods to control it.

Measure: Creativity
Details: Degree of innovation or originality.

Product Differentiation

Using these measures, you can assess how well your product is differentiated from its competition. These are based on the $APPEALS method for assessing product differentiation developed by Peter Marks, Managing Director of Design Insight.[3]

Measure: Price differentiation
Details: Evaluate the customer's potential for finding a bargain relative to the competition—high performance and ease of use at a good value. A very high rating means:
　1 Value is good relative to the competition
　2 Price or payment terms are matched to the customer

Measure: Availability to the customer
Details: Evaluate how well the channel matches the customers' buying behavior. This means meeting deadlines competitors can't touch. A very high rating means:
　1 Product is available when the customer wants it
　2 There are few middlemen who don't add value
　3 Buying, installing, and using are intrinsically enjoyable
　4 Expert advice is available to simplify the buying process

5 Solution is tailored to the customer

6 Product is sold in the way the customer wants to buy

Measure: Packaging differentiation

Details: Evaluate how well the customer can see the value of the product and its differentiation from the competition. A very high rating means:

1 The invisible is visible so customers can see the differentiation

2 The product sells itself in the communication medium used

3 A range of sizes, colors, and visual aspects match the range of customer tastes and intellectual styles

4 Look and style are consistent with cultural norms

Measure: Performance

Details: Evaluate how well the product does what it is designed to do. How does your customer measure performance and how does the product measure up? A very high rating means:

1 Very good performance in terms of the customer's cognitive perception and measurable features

2 Tools are available to help the customer track its performance

Measure: Ease of use

Details: Evaluate the delight the customer will take in learning about the product and its ease of use. This requires matching the "impedance" of the product to our human senses and capabilities; customer tries to assess sensory and learning matches while buying. A very high rating means:

1 Learning and use are obvious and intuitive

2 User interface is intrinsically rewarding

3 Accommodates different cognitive styles

Measure: Assurances

Details: Assurances inspire confidence in the product and company. The goal is to relieve the customer's fears. Typically, these include looking foolish to peers, paying too much, and rapid obsolescence. The more exclusive the assurances, the higher the market share. A very high rating means:

1 There are ways to address customer's voiced and unvoiced fears
2 Good promises are followed by good execution

Measure: Life-cycle costs
Details: Lower cost of ownership serves as a differentiator, especially if it is identified for the customer. A very high rating means:

1 The cost of ownership is made evident to the customer
2 There is a clear measure of the life-cycle cost relative to the competition

Measure: Social sanctions
Details: Social sanctions are measures of who influences your customer's buying decisions. For new products it is important to win the support of respected early adopters and to develop a community for them. It is also important to be sensitive to the cultural norms of customer groups. A very high rating means:

1 It appeals to early adopters
2 It leverages off the social sanctions of the customer

Technology Readiness

As we saw in chapter 8, technology readiness is used by the military and NASA to measure the degree to which a technology is ready for off-the-shelf use. Unfortunately, many technology readiness assessments are made very ad hoc and with little guidance. The following measures can help add rigor to the development of a technology readiness score. Although they are designed for hardware assessment, they can easily be converted for software or business readiness assessment.

Measure: Critical parameters that control the function are known
Details: Every design concept has certain parameters that are critical to its proper operation. It has been estimated that only about 10 to 15% of the dimensions on a finished component is critical to the operation of the product. It is important to know which parameters (e.g., dimensions, material properties, or

other features) are critical to the function of the device.

1 Critical parameters are unknown

2 Some critical parameters are itemized based on gut feel

3 Critical parameters are itemized based on
functional model

Measure: Safe operating latitude and sensitivity to variation of
the parameters are known

Details: In refining a concept into a product, the actual values
of the parameters may have to be varied to achieve the desired
performance or to improve manufacturability. It is essential to
know these operating limits and the sensitivity of the product's
operation to them. This information is only known in a rough way
during the early design phases; during the product evaluation it
will become extremely important. This is an essential measure of
the technology's robustness.

1 There is no modeling of latitude or sensitivity to
variation

2 Estimates are made on some critical parameters

3 Analysis is done on paper to model some operating
latitudes and sensitivity to variation

4 Design of Experiments or Taguchi Robust Design
experiments are completed on some critical parameters

3 Analysis is done on paper to model some operating
latitudes and sensitivity to variation

5 Design of Experiments or Taguchi Robust Design
experiments are completed on all critical parameters

Measure: Failure modes and risks are known

Details: Every type of system has characteristic failure modes
and faces risks. It is a useful design technique to continuously
evaluate the different ways in which a product might fail.

1 No formal failure or risk analysis has been undertaken.

2 Failure modes and risks are estimated

3 Failure modes and risks are based on minimal
functional model

4 Failure modes and risks are fully modeled and/or based
on historical data

5 Failure modes and risks are fully modeled and/or based on experimental data

Measure: Manufacturing Fidelity

Details: Part of the new technology's maturity is the evolution of the manufacturing process for it and/or the procurement of new capabilities or vendors to produce it.

1 Not defined

2 Lab demo is assembled

3 Proof-of-concept prototype is constructed

4 Proof-of-product prototype is manufactured

5 Processes and equipment, or vendors, are in place to produce the technology

Measure: Test Fidelity

Details: Testing is a big part of any new technology.

1 No testing has been done

2 Lab tests of component parts has been done

3 Lab tests on complete technology has been done

4 Testing has been done in simulated environment

5 Testing has been done in actual environment

Applications of Robust Decision Making 13

Introduction

In this chapter, you will see how the robust decision-making methods I have introduced in this book have been put to practical use. To begin, we'll examine three case studies. The first comes from Hewlett-Packard (HP); there, a non-technical team selected a technology platform. The case study itself was written by the manager of the issue to demonstrate his team's success to others in his organization, and offers few details.

The second case study has affected you directly. It was the decision about how to publish this book. It affected your becoming aware of it, as well as the price you paid for it. While this decision was strictly my own, I actually evaluated it from three different viewpoints to help me arrive at the decision.

The third case study comes from Pratt & Whitney. They were working to select a conceptual design for a rocket engine, for which they sought government funding. Throughout this process, and with other projects in which they have used the decision-making methods described in this book, they have referred to their efforts as "trade studies." This term refers to trade-off criteria; it reflects an effort to find an alternative that maximizes satisfaction with the criteria by trading off success among them.

Trade studies are often used in the aerospace and automotive industries. To refine this concept, you will find a section in this chapter containing details about trade-off methods. This is a reprint of a published paper.

Finally, I've included a section on unsticking the OODA Loop, a model of the decision-making process that I introduced in chapter 2. There, I suggested that people often get stuck in the early parts of the loop and end up making an "OO-OO-OO" sound. It is worth revisiting the OODA Loop with what we have learned since, in an effort get past this problem.

Case Study: HP Decision Management[1]

Often, the most difficult part of problem solving is knowing where to start. In the following case study, members of a Hewlett-Packard knowledge sharing team had been struggling with a technology decision for two years. Then they discovered a facilitated decision-making process called Bayesian Team Support and *Accord* software. This case study is a good example of how any technical or non-technical team can approach a difficult decision when the facts and trends are uncertain.

Background

In its global business model, HP uses video sharing to get information from technical and business presentations to the desktops of individuals far from where the knowledge originates. The existing system, VidNet, originally started in 1998 as an effort to preserve the content of technical presentations captured on videotapes whose content was decaying. Events captured as early as 1982 are still being used to educate new engineers and for legal defense of intellectual property. Not only did VidNet digitally encode this valuable reference library, it eliminated an extensive inventory of video tapes stored in locked cabinets at a dozen "learning center" locations in North America, Europe, and Asia.

By 2002, VidNet supported HP's Imaging and Printing Group's (IPG) 24,000 employees, including nearly 9,000 engineers and scientists, with nearly 1,000 online assets. Upgrading the VidNet inventory was officially sanctioned as a Workforce Development (WD) group project in 2003. By 2004, the team had added 235 new assets, and it expected to add another 400 in 2005. The program started tracking visitors in November 2004, and in the first nine months of tracking, had more than 250,000 visits from more than 9,300 unique users in 43 countries.

Problem: Selecting a Technology Platform

In its early days the IPG team (not yet officially organized as VidNet) decided to offer streaming video using Real Media Player. The decision to use RealPlayer 8 was easy in the late 1990s; there were only two widely available players, RealPlayer 8 and Microsoft's Windows Media Player. Because the target audience of the initial video content included engineers developing products for use in Windows, UNIX, Linux, and Apple Macintosh environments, the player needed to operate in all of them. Since Microsoft's product exclusively supported Microsoft operating systems, the VidNet team chose to use the more flexible Real Media Player.

By 2004, that decision needed to be reexamined: VidNet's reliance on Real Media Player was now appearing to limit functionality in getting streaming assets to its intended audience. This limitation was due to two factors: First, although the focus of development at HP had shifted significantly toward Microsoft products, non-developers (most employees) operating in the Microsoft environment were finding the Real Media Player installation process overly cumbersome. Second, those on alternate operating systems were simply not accessing VidNet resources. Still, the issues surrounding the decision to switch streaming technology were daunting. Although the VidNet team frequently discussed the issues and their ramifications, no clear path forward could be seen. There were simply too many variables to consider and there was too much uncertainty in the technologies.

Getting the Decision on Track

After many months of discussion, the issue of whether to change from the Real Media Player, and if so, to which other technology platform, was no closer to resolution. At the same time, the number of VidNet users was increasing, and the disconnect between Real Media Player and these users was not going away.

Some members of the VidNet team had learned of success in resolving similar issues using a methodology called Bayesian Team Support™ (BTS) from Robust Decisions, Inc. HP had already used decision-support software based on this methodology for about two years to help the company choose inkjet architecture and select ink chemistries, and people involved were enthusiastic. In the words of one of the product managers, "We've used other decision-making software and methods, and none have provided the same level of understanding of the issues, and confidence in the outcomes... [The approach] enabled us to be more rigorous, quickly brought our team members to a common plane, and better quantified the inputs and results." The VidNet team decided to apply the methods and software to their issue of choosing which technology platform to use going forward.

The VidNet team started by inviting a group of fifteen people into the decision-making process: the six core members of the VidNet Program, several technology partners (those who operated the physical IT infrastructure), and some managers representing key viewer populations of the streaming products. Since team members were physically located in different geographies, a series of teleconferences was used to itemize alternative platforms and the criteria that would be used to evaluate them.

Once the team felt there was enough raw data to move forward, it was gathered together physically for training on BTS and the decision support software.

The teleconferences and a face-to-face session were facilitated to help learn the structured decision-management BTS process and how to use *Accord* software. Under the guidance of the trainer/facilitator during a full-day session, the team developed two initial conclusions:

1 Before this effort the team hadn't even fully understood the issues.
2 The criteria to be used for making a choice were not well articulated or agreed upon.

Although it seemed evident in retrospect, under the guidance of the facilitator the team quickly realized that VidNet viewers didn't want to load any media players onto their PCs and they certainly didn't want to configure any settings in order to make the online viewing experience possible. In short, they wanted the media player to be transparent.

Following this session, the core team of six set out to better understand the issues involved. First, they divided the problem into two new issues—the technology required to capture and stream content, and the format used to archive it. Next, a new set of six criteria was created to replace the fifteen criteria in the previous exercise. These criteria were much better focused on the most important issues and provided a greater level of discrimination for examining the various alternatives:

- *Cost of storage* (disk space, floor space, wages for staff, licensing, servers)
- *Cost of transition* (current and future transcoding, wages, licenses, equipment)
- *Longevity of storage* (does the asset deteriorate over time?)
- *Obsolescence of format* (Is the format—such as a codec—subject to obsolescence?)
- *Time to view* (from end-of-capture to availability of hot on-demand link)
- *Creation Cost* (cost to create a single hour of asset)

Team members worked individually, gathering data on the six criteria, and then came together to review the findings. Over the course of three short meetings the team steadily narrowed its options. Starting with twenty unique alternatives and supported by *Accord* software, the group gradually eliminated candidates based upon their ability to meet concretely defined criteria. Eventually, the group was left with a single alternative: using Microsoft Media Player for capture and streaming and storing archive copies on a server using MPEG format.

The BTS process provided the VidNet team with important benefits beyond the technology decision for streaming and storing its knowledge transfer assets. It also answered a host of long-standing questions, created the program's first set of operating philosophies, and developed a framework for revisiting the operating system decision annually.

What the Team Learned

The uncertainty inherent in the technologies evaluated and the original difficulty in defining decision criteria made robust decision-making methods an essential part of the team's success. Uncertainty about the technologies being evaluated and difficulty in defining decision criteria are both characteristic of many technical and non-technical decision processes.

The following six steps summarize the decision-making process and describe additional lessons learned quickly through the BTS process and with the support of *Accord* software:

1 **Define the issue**—While the issue was determined up front, it changed as the team learned more about the decision. The decision-support software provided a free-text window in the application to capture the issue. As simple as that seems, getting the group to agree on the issues and how to word them in writing proved to be a valuable exercise in the process.

2 **Identify the decision makers**—In preparing for the first round, the team felt strongly about including a broad range of decision makers and influencers. However, while the end users are important, they don't have the interest or patience to do more than offer an opinion. The BTS process focused on including the appropriate people and only those who have a stake. Initially the team erred early on the side of too much inclusion; progress came more quickly as the right people were identified and participated.

By listening to its customers, the team gained focus on the issues, but it could have obtained the same information in less time by simply talking with them as part of the data-gathering exercises.

3   **Define and characterize the decision criteria**—The BTS process dictates that decision criteria be determined *before* discussing alternatives. In so doing, the team managed to keep preconceptions and prejudices to a minimum. There were fifteen decision criteria in the first round. By the second round the team had identified the six most critical of these, and ultimately, only two of these six provided any differentiation between the alternatives. The BTS methodology emphasized and supported identifying the discriminating criteria.

4   **Identify the alternatives**—At one point in the process the team was feeling overwhelmed by the number of options available. The software was useful in keeping track of each alternative and helping the decision group remain focused upon the ultimate objective. It also weeded out inferior choices.

5   **Evaluate, discuss, and decide**—The final decision was not the alternative that had the highest satisfaction as analyzed by the software. However, the discussion around why one alternative came out on top helped the team to understand the problems inherent in that option. The software allowed each person to work separately and then to easily integrate their work back into a common work space, allowing the team to develop a shared vision of the issues.

6   **Rinse and repeat as necessary**—The VidNet team entered the first phase fully expecting to arrive at a decision by the end of the initial workshop, but more work was needed. BTS showed how to keep performing successive iterations until the whole group was comfortable that the outcome reflected the available data within the levels of certainty currently available.

Summary

The VidNet team had struggled for two years, unable to make a decision, before using the BTS process. The training, facilitation, software, and meetings all took time, but in the end we gained a solid decision with good buy-in from all stakeholders. Further, we are much better prepared for the next situation that requires a difficult decision in an environment where the facts and trends are uncertain.

Consider the number of nagging, persistent issues you deal with on a regular basis and imagine what a guided decision-making process such as that described in this case study might do to lighten your load. If the process is progressive, includes the appropriate people, and concludes with a robust decision, the time invested in following the process saves time later—slow is fast. In our case, once the decision was made, all participants already knew what needed to be done when they left the room, and implementation was swift. In your business, taking time up front to make effective decisions will create a similar impact on the effectiveness and speed of your implementations.

Case Study: How to Publish This Book

It is always best to practice what you preach, so I applied robust decision-making methods to choosing how to publish this book. I had published books before using traditional publishers, and I had used a Publish on Demand (PoD) house that printed books as they were ordered. In fact, I had a contract offer from a very good traditional publisher in my hand, but I was not sure whether to accept it or not.

Figure 13.1 shows a screen shot of *Accord* that models this problem. In it, the different alternatives I considered are listed. They are (with some clarification):

- Go with a traditional publisher (this was the offer I had in hand).
- Go through an agent to a traditional publisher.
- Self-publish on the web. (Publishing on the web was a new area that had shown some success, but I didn't know much about how to do it.)
- Self-publish on the web with professional help (to minimize time, I could hire professional help with web publishing).
- Self-publish, using a standard book printer (I was familiar with a number of people who had self-published books).
- Publish on demand (PoD) and hire an editor.

The criteria for differentiating among these are shown in table 13.1:

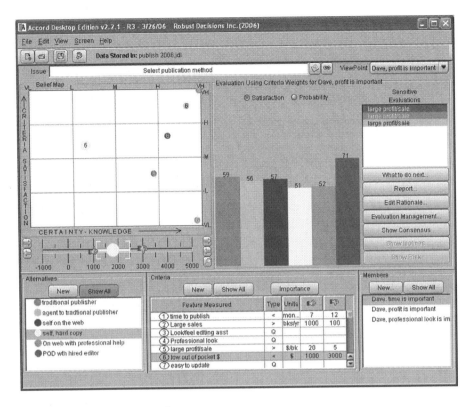

Figure 13.1: Accord Screen shot.

I then used three different "team members":

- •Dave: time is important
- •Dave: profit is important
- •Dave: professional look is important

In reality, I entered all the evaluation information using just one of these (I was the only evaluator). However, I set the importance weightings differ-

Measured Feature	Type	Units	Delighted	Disgusted
Time to publish	less-is-better	months	7	12
Large sales	more-is-better	bks/yr	1000	100
Look/feel editing asst	qualitative	--	--	--
Professional look	qualitative	--	--	--
Large profit/sale	more-is-better	$/bk	20	5
Low out of pocket $	less-is-better	$	1000	3000
Easy to update	qualitative	--	--	--
Maturity of method	qualitative	--	--	--

Table 13.1: Book criteria.

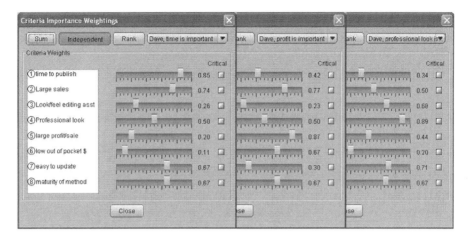

Figure 13.2: Importance weightings from different viewpoints..

ently on each of them to reflect differences in viewpoint. You can readily see this in figure 13.2.

Before I was through, I had entered fifty-six evaluation points. In some cases I knew very little, and in others I had first-hand experience. The results, regardless of viewpoint, showed that PoD was the right way to go. One example output is shown in figure 13.1. This result was somewhat surprising, as it costs more up front and I have to worry about marketing. Still, no matter how I weighted the data and reviewed my evaluations, the results were pretty much the same. And that is how you came to purchase or borrow a book that was published on demand.

Case Study: Pratt & Whitney[2]

Pratt & Whitney (P&W, formerly known as Rocketdyne, then as Boeing Space and Defense Group) in Canoga Park, California, designs and manufactures the liquid fuel rocket engines that power the NASA Space Shuttle and propel other systems into space. With a system as complex as a rocket engine and with large financial resources at stake, robust decisions are essential; poor decisions can result in significant and expensive reworking

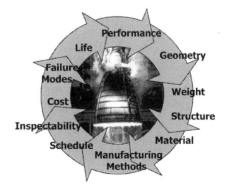

Figure 13.3: Trade-offs in rocket engine design.

289

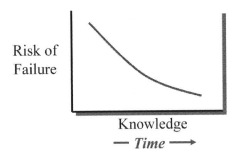

Figure 13.4.

later. When making rocket engine decisions, there are many trade-offs that have to be considered, as shown in figure 13.3. Usually, not all the targets for all these different parameters can be met, and performance in one must be traded off for performance in another. Managing these trade-offs is the subject of this case study.

A central challenge for P&W is managing these trade-offs as early as possible in the process and then refining them as more work is completed—as information becomes more certain. Essential to good design is having the required knowledge at the time design decisions need to be made. Graphically, figure 13.4 shows how the risk of failure decreases as time progresses and knowledge increases. Nonetheless, there is no way around making decisions when uncertainty, and thus the risk of failure, is high.

This case study concerns the selection of a rocket nozzle modification for the Delta rocket engine. The Delta engine was first used in the 1960s and has undergone many changes and much evolution. In response to a request for proposals, we needed to develop a concept that was appealing to our customer and, at the same time, was one we were sure we could deliver if we won the contract. Thus, the issue we faced was to select a Delta Rocket nozzle modification to propose in an uncertain environment characterized by:

- Unrefined information—some even qualitative
- Conflicting information—evaluation and importance varied across team members
- Evolving information—the problem changed with time
- Incomplete information—evaluation wouldn't be completed until we got the contract

We had faced this kind of issue many times before and had developed a "traditional" approach to the problem. This was based on a modified Pugh's method, figure 13.5. The steps in this process were:

1   Identify trade parameters
2   Assign weight to individual criteria, using a Pair-wise comparison
3   Total weight equal to 100 percent
4   Rate criteria against design concept
5   Use a scale of time 1 to 10 in matrix form
6   Multiply weight and rating
7   Add total scores and compare

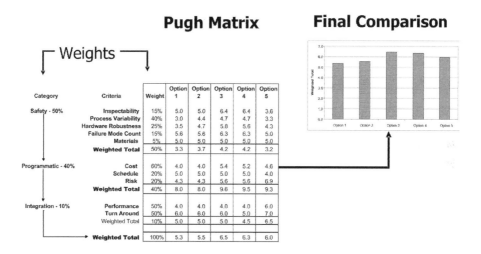

Figure 13.5: Modified Pugh tool.

Although this approach worked well in helping get our thoughts organized, there were clearly some problems with it:

- It assumed that all alternatives had the same level of knowledge for each criteria
- Strong voices could dominate
- "Ignorance is bliss"—we often didn't deal with uncertainty
- It assumed that all experts had the same experience base for the options
- It was hard to achieve consensus
- It was difficult to determine the best option when final comparison was close

In developing a bid for the Delta nozzle project, we decided to try Bayesian Team Support (BTS) and the *Accord* software tool. This project took on two goals, 1) choose the best nozzle to propose and 2) evaluate *Accord*

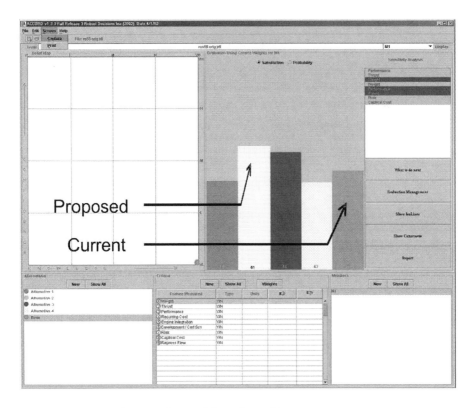

Figure 13.6: Accord *screen shot modeling the problem*

and its underlying methodology. Although the results are anecdotal, they gave us clear evidence for how to improve our process. Figure 13.6 shows a "sanitized" screen shot of *Accord* that models our problem. Here, the trade parameters used in our deliberation are:

- •Weight
- •Thrust
- •Performance
- •Recurring cost
- •Engine integration
- •Development schedule certainty
- •Risk
- •Capital cost
- •Repress flow

There were twelve team members representing different parts of the organization. We evaluated four new concepts versus the current nozzle.

Based on this evaluation, we chose one for the proposal.

Our findings about the use of *Accord* in our environment were:

1   *Accord* **was faster than the method we had traditionally used.** Using the traditional method, decisions usually took months. With Accord, this one had only taken a few hours. This seemed to be because of its graphical nature and its ability to even the decision-making playing field (see next item).

2   *Accord* **helped manage strong personalities.** Typically, the process had been hijacked by the strongest personalities on the team (they are all rocket scientists, after all). Accord dulled their ability to do so; consequently, everyone got to have his say.

3   *Accord* **handled the mix of information.** The traditional method couldn't handle the mixture of quantitative and qualitative data. For example, one time-consuming feature of our traditional approach was working all the trade parameters to be measured on a 1 to 10 scale. But this wasn't necessary in *Accord*, as it can handle qualitative, quantitative, and 5-point scale parameters.

4   **It was easy to develop importance weightings.** Traditionally, we had used a Pair-wise comparison approach for criteria weight development. This was time consuming and we had no evidence that using it was any better than the methods in *Accord*. Additionally, *Accord* allowed the exploration of the trades with different weightings, giving us the impression that we had a better handle on the problem.

5   *Accord* **supported information evolution.** During the evaluation, the data were e-mailed to experts; options were rated and recombined. This supported the evolution of the proposed nozzle and gave a basis for continued use during the development of the actual product.

6   *Accord* **managed uncertainty.** Uncertainty characterized much of our information and was a discriminator for close options. Our traditional approach had no mechanism to manage this, whereas it is the foundation of *Accord*.

7   *Accord* **suggested next steps.** *Accord* results provided a clear indication of what to work on next to generate the best proposal in the time we had available.

The team came away from the exercise with high confidence in the nozzle being proposed. In fact, the proposal was accepted and the project was funded. Based on this experience we are continuing to ramp up our use of *Accord* and BTS methods.

Trade Studies Theory[3]

The following paper was originally published in the Proceedings of the 2006 INCOSE conference. The paper is reprinted as it appeared, so there is some redundancy. It is an extension of the trade studies done at Pratt & Whitney. It is somewhat technical, but if you are interested in trade studies, it will give you much to think about.[4]

Introduction

With the increasing demand for complex and interrelated systems comes the challenge of managing the decisions being made by a team of collaborating experts, each working on a piece of the puzzle and all vying for their share of scarce resources. In early-stage design, this process is especially challenging, as there is limited knowledge, uncertainties are high, and the decisions made have far-reaching effects on the directions pursued thereafter, and hence the affordability, reliability/safety, and effectiveness of the final product. It is clearly more viable and less expensive to refine a design at the time that it is being conceived. Therefore, efforts toward making good decisions at this stage have high payoffs.

During every stage of the design process, designers trade off performance, cost, and risk in an evolutionary process whose goal is to find a satisfactory solution. This paper explores a recent method to manage the trade study process, especially when uncertainty is pervasive and decisions are a mix of quantitative and qualitative information. We believe that it is possible to support a trade study process that is sensitive to the uncertainties in evolving system information, a key ingredient in managing risk, robustness, changes, and spiral development.

In this paper we explore what is needed to support such activities. To do so, we follow an example as it gets increasingly complex and realistic. As the issues addressed increase in computational need, we make use of *Accord*, a decision-support system based on Bayesian Team Support methods.

What Are Trade Studies?

A trade study is the activity of a multidisciplinary team to identify the most balanced technical solutions among a set of proposed viable solutions.[4] These viable solutions are judged by their satisfaction of a series of measures or cost functions. These measures describe the desirable characteristics of a solution. They may be conflicting or even mutually exclusive. Trade studies, often called trade-off studies, are commonly used in the design of aerospace and automotive vehicles and the software selection process to find the configuration that best meets conflicting performance requirements.[5]

The measures are dependent on variables that characterize the different potential solutions. If the system can be characterized by a set of equations, we can write the definition of the trade study problem as: Find the set of variables, xi that give the best overall satisfaction to the measures:

$$T_1 = f(x_1, x_2, x_3.....)$$
$$T_2 = f(x_1, x_2, x_3.....)$$
$$T_3 = f(x_1, x_2, x_3.....)$$
$$...$$
$$T_N = f(x_1, x_2, x_3.....)$$

Where T_j is a target value and $f(...)$ denotes some functional relationship among the variables. Further, the equality between the target and the function may be a richer relationship, as will be developed below. If the equations are linear, as in the production volume example used as a starting point below, then this problem is solvable using linear programming techniques. Generally, one or more of the targets is not fixed at a specific value and it is desired to make these T values as large or small as possible. These are generally referred to as cost functions, and the other measures are treated as constraints.

If the situation was as described above, formal optimization or linear programming methods would work and there would be no need for this paper. However, in practice needed information is:

- Uncertain—to be detailed below
- Evolving—new information is being developed that affects the trades
- Both qualitative and quantitative—at Honeywell the most important trade studies have predominantly qualitative information
- Coming from conflicting sources—in systems engineering, many

> people have some of the information needed; no one person has it all
> - The best choice comes from a team, building a shared mental model of the situation

Trade studies are essentially decision-making exercises—choose an optional concept or course of action from a discrete or continuous set of viable alternatives. In the *FAA Systems Handbook* the decision analysis matrix (aka Pugh's method) is suggested to support the activities, but this method cannot support uncertainty, a mix of quantitative and qualitative information, or teams.[6] To manage uncertainty, the authors suggest supplementing point estimates of the outcome variables for each alternative with computed or estimated uncertainty ranges. "The Standard Approach to Trade Studies," an INCOSE paper from 2004, suggests a similar approach.[7]

The *NASA Systems Engineering Handbook* suggests using multi-attribute utility theoretic (MAUT) or the Analytic Hierarchy Process (AHP).[8] But these too are not good with uncertainty, mixed information, and teams. The authors suggest using probability-based methods to maximize utility when uncertainty predominates, but give little detail on how to approach this.

Another approach to supporting trade study information is to use Bayesian Team Support (BTS) methods. These methods were designed to manage the types of information itemized in the list above. In this paper we will introduce BTS and apply it to a trade study example to explore its applicability.

The Effect of Uncertainty on Trade Studies

What makes early system design and trade studies most challenging is that much of the critical information is uncertain, evolving, and may be lacking in fidelity. Further, with team members from many disciplines and with different values about what is important, information may be conflicting. These terms—"uncertain," "evolving," "fidelity," and "conflicting"—permeate this paper and thus need clarification.

There are two types of uncertainty. The first, variability (i.e., stochastic uncertainty, irreducible uncertainty, or common cause variability) is the result of the fact that a system can behave in random ways. The weather will change, material properties are variable, and there will always be chip junctions failures. In general, even though some portion of variation can be controlled (e.g., insulation from weather changes) there is always variation that is either uncontrollable or too expensive or difficult to warrant controlling.

The second type of uncertainty results from the lack of knowledge about a system (i.e., subjective uncertainty or state of knowledge uncertainty). It is a property of the team members' cumulative experience and the amount of time they have spent on the current or similar concepts. Both types of uncertainty are direct causes of risk—as, in a world with no variability and perfect knowledge, there would be no risk.

Typically, probability theory has been used to characterize both types of uncertainty. Variability is usually analyzed using the frequentist approach associated with traditional probability theory. However, traditional probability theory is not capable of capturing lack of knowledge uncertainty, which in early design is a large cause of risk. One method for managing lack of knowledge uncertainty is Bayesian methods, as will be discussed later.

During the design process information is **evolving.** It begins with customers' criteria and matures to the final drawings, specifications, and code. Through this development, the trade-offs and risks are changing as the systems evolve. Managing this evolution is crucial in systems, as changes in one system will affect others. Sometimes these interactions are missed—leading to rework, compromised performance, or system failure.

As part of design activities, experts run simulations to predict performance and cost. Early in the design process these simulations are at low levels of fidelity, some possibly qualitative. **Fidelity** is the degree to which a model or simulation reproduces the state and behavior of a real-world object. Increased fidelity requires increased refinement and increased costs to the project. Generally, with increased fidelity comes increased knowledge, but this is not necessarily so, as it is possible to use a high-fidelity simulation to model garbage and thus do nothing to reduce uncertainty. Often, especially in early trade studies, there are no formal simulations, and all or most of the evaluations are qualitative. These evaluations are no less valid than detailed simulations. In fact, it has been argued that gut feel is the key to good decisions.[9, 10]

Finally, the team members' interpretation of the available information may be **conflicting**. Conflicting interpretations occur naturally due to differences in background, role in the project, interpretation of the information, expertise, and problem-solving style. Conflicts are not good or bad, just different interpretations of the available information.

Traditional solution methods cannot take these uncertainties into account. If they are small compared to the actual values, then these methods can be used, assuming the uncertainties exist, to find a solution and then take into account the uncertainties using sensitivity analysis. However, if the uncertainties are significant, another philosophy needs to be followed.

A Production Volume Example

Consider a simple example of a trade study taken from a textbook on optimization.[11] A company manufactures 2 machines, x_1 and x_2. It wants to find the number of x_1 machines and x_2 machines to manufacture so that profit will be maximized. It is known that:

- Profit on machine x_1 is \$400 and profit on machine on x_2 is \$600.
- Using available resources, it takes twice as much time to make machine x_2 as it does machine x_1.
- The company can make a maximum of 14 x_2 machines a day.
- Using available resources, sales can sell up to 14 x_1 or 24 x_2 machines per day.

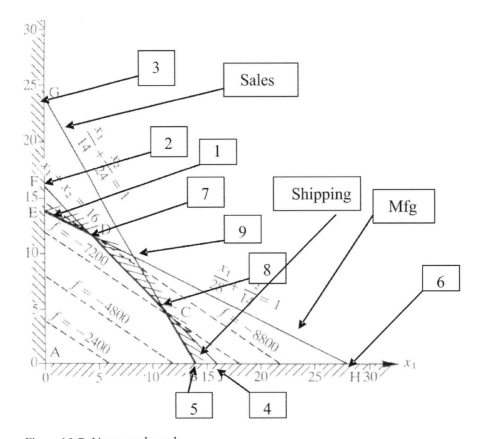

Figure 13.7: Linear trade study.

•Shipping can only handle 16 x_1 or x_2 machines a day.

This is a simple trade study problem with only one measure (profit) and two variables (# of x_1 machines and # of x_2 machines). Further, the way the problem is set up, there are linear relationships for the cost, manufacturing, sales, and shipping. Namely:

•Profit/day = 400 x_1 + 600 x_2
•x_1/28 + x_2/14 <=1, for manufacturing
•x_1/14 + x_2/24 <=1, for sales
•x_1 + x_2 <=16, for shipping

Since all these equations are linear, this problem can be solved by linear programming methods. The equations can be plotted as shown below with x_1 horizontal and x_2 vertical and using a method like Simplex, or in this simple case by inspection; point #7 is seen to give the best profit and meet all the other goals. Thus, the company should make 4 Type x_1 machines and 12 Type x_2 machines. Doing this, its profit will be $8,800/day.

This is a good textbook problem. It will be used as a basis while we explore:

•Target uncertainty
•Evaluation uncertainty
•Importance uncertainty
•Mix of qualitative and quantitative criteria
•Fusion of multiple team members' evaluations
•Determining what-to-do-next to ensure that the best possible decision is being made

To make this problem more interesting, assume that we explore points 7, 8, and 9 in our effort to choose the best option. In many actual trade studies, the options are discrete, as the functions relating variables are unknown or at best uncertain.

Target uncertainty

Target uncertainty reflects flexibility in what is desired of each measure in the problem. In order to discuss targets, first rewrite the equations that represent this problem as:

- Profit/day = 400 x_1 + 600 x_2
- x_1 x .5+ x_2 $\leq$14, for manufacturing
- x_1 x 1.71+ x_2 $\leq$24, for sales
- x_1 + x_2 $\leq$16, for shipping

Considering the manufacturing, sales, and shipping equations first: Each has been normalized to show a number of x_2 units that reflects capacity. It makes no difference if these equations are normalized on x_1 or x_2. The main point is that manufacturing thinks it can produce 14 normalized machines, sales can sell 24, and shipping can ship 16. But how accurate are these targets? For this example, let us assume that these normalized target values are our best guess. Further, if manufacturing, for example, is asked to produce 15 normalized machines, this can probably be worked in. Maybe even 16 can be accommodated based on what is known about manufacturing. However, at some volume, there will be a need for overtime, additional equipment, or some other painful change. Likewise in the negative direction, at some volume less than 14, there will be idle people or equipment. Thus, **target uncertainty** reflects the flexibility that exists in most targets to accommodate satisfying other criteria or maximizing satisfaction with the choice made. Consider buying a car, camera, or house. You set a target for the cost, but then, if other features are really great, you adjust the target. The better the system is understood and the less flexibility possible, the lower the target uncertainty.

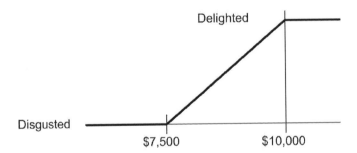

Figure 13.8: Sample utility curve.

We will model each of the targets as a simple linear utility function. Target uncertainty can be characterized by two values: a delighted value and a disgusted value. For example, a profit of $10,000 will delight the company and one of $7,500 will disgust it. This is a more-is-better target as shown in figure 13.8.

Similarly:

- Manufacturing Target Uncertainty: As described above, delighted at 14 x_2 units, disgusted at 11 and 17. This is referred to as a specific target best and the utility curve is a two-sided distribution.
- Sales Target Uncertainty: Sales works on commission, so the more sales the better. They will be delighted at 26 x_2 units, disgusted at 20.
- Shipping Target Uncertainty: Shipping is lazy, so the less they have to do, the better. They will be delighted at 16 x_2 units, disgusted at 19.

Figure 13.9, a screen shot from *Accord*, shows this information entered as Criteria. Note the "Type" symbols indicating the shape of the utility function.

Evaluation and Viewpoint Uncertainty

Next, consider the equations that are used to represent the measures. For example, the equation for manufacturing is $.5 \times x_1 + x_2 \leq 14$. We have already discussed the uncertainty in the target—14 units—and now focus on the

Criteria				
New Show All	Importance			
Feature Measured	Type	Units	🖐	🖐
① Profit	>	K$	10	7.5
② Manufacturing	=	units	14	17
③ Sales	>	Units	26	20
④ Shippng	<	Units	16	19

Figure 13.9: Screen shot of the criteria and members area

terms on the left side of the equation. **Evaluation uncertainty** is the fidelity with which the equation represents reality. This equation has been written as a linear equation, but it is difficult to believe that the relationship is that simple, and that the coefficient is .5. In fact, the actual relationship may be more complicated and the coefficient some other value. Even more challenging is that the relationship may be different for different functions within the organization, or that the relationship is completely unknown.

For the example, assume that the uncertainty in the equations may be as much as 10% of the nominal value calculated. If, for example, x_1 = 8 units and x_2 = 10 units (point 9) then, using the equation above, manufacturing can produce 8 x .5 + 10 = 14 units. If the equation is 10% high, then it will estimate 17 units (rounded to the nearest whole unit), and if low it will estimate 11 units. This may seem like a high uncertainty. However, for production lines that are just being designed or not yet mature, this is a conservative number. The same holds for sales and shipping.

Table 13.2 shows a spreadsheet that was used to calculate the nominal values and the +10% and −10% deviations from them.

pt #	x_1 units	x_2 units	profit K$	profit +	profit-	mfg	mfg +	mfg -	sales	sales +	sales -	ship	ship +	ship -
						# of x_2 units			# of x_2 units			# of x_2 units		
7	4	12	8.8	9.7	7.9	14.0	15.4	12.6	18.8	20.7	17.0	16.0	17.6	14.4
8	11	5	7.4	8.1	6.7	10.5	11.6	9.5	23.8	26.2	21.4	16.0	17.6	14.4
9	8	10	9.2	10.1	8.3	14.0	15.4	12.6	23.7	26.0	21.3	18.0	19.8	16.2

Table 13.2: The spreadsheet calculations.

Accord merges this information with the utility information to calculate overall satisfaction (amongst other analyses) for each alternative considered (here points 7, 8, and 9). The results can be weighted for different viewpoints.

The importance of each of the measures may vary with function in the company. Some may believe that profit is really the only important measure, whereas other may want to equally weight manufacturing and sales capacity. Importance uncertainty reflects differences in what targets are most important to meet in finding a solution to the problem.

The satisfaction calculated by *Accord* when only profit is important (all the other measures are weighted at zero) is shown in the left section of figure 13.10. Here the bars represent the percent of satisfaction with each of the alternatives. The results show:

- Point 9 is best, with point 7 second and point 8 last. This order is obvious from table 13.2 or from the linear trade study diagram (figure 13.7).
- Point 9 is only 57% satisfactory as the company said it would be delighted at $10K, which is only met with the most optimistic estimate ($10.1K). The pessimistic estimate is not far above the disgusted level.

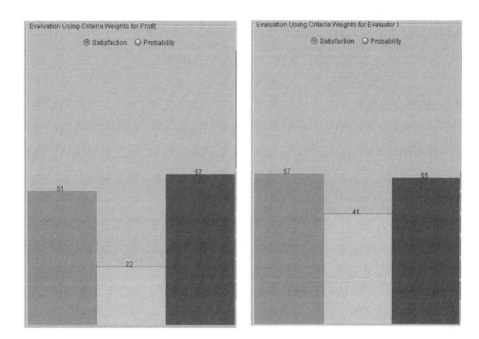

Figure 13.10: Two different results for points 7, 8, and 9, in order.

- There is a 43% risk that the company will not be satisfied with profit. This risk is actually an expected value of not being satisfied.

In the right half of Figure 13.10 the satisfactions are shown when Shipping and Manufacturing are both considered important. Here Point 7 is best, just barely. This shows that satisfaction can change with the eye of the beholder.

Qualitative criteria

Usually, not all the important features of alternatives are measurable, even though good practice encourages us to measure everything. The reality is summed up well by a quote attributed to the Noble Laureate Frank Knight. After reflecting on Lord Kelvin's statement, "When you cannot measure it… your knowledge is of meager and unsatisfactory kind," Dr. Knight said, "Oh, well, if you cannot measure, measure anyhow." The reality is that to refine something that is not readily measurable requires time and effort that may not be available.

In this case, some difficult-to-measure features are market perception (i.e., if you make too few of one product you might be perceived as abandoning that product), and affects on suppliers (i.e., if you don't order parts

Criteria					
New	Show All		Importance		
Feature Measured	Type	Units	🗨	🗨	
① Profit	>	K$	10	7.5	
② Manufacturing	=	units	14	17	
③ Sales	>	Units	26	20	
④ Shippng	<	Units	16	19	
⑤ Positive Effect on Customers	Q				
⑥ Positive affect on suppliers	Q				

Figure 13.11: Added qualitative criteria

needed for x₁ the vendor may discontinue making them). These qualitative measures can be added to the list of criteria in *Accord* and are denoted with a "Q" as shown in Figure 13.11. We will show the effect of the addition of these qualitative criteria in a moment. Qualitative criteria are evaluated using a Belief Map.

The Belief Map provides a novel, yet intuitive, means for entering/displaying qualitative evaluation results in terms of knowledge, certainty, satisfaction, and belief. Belief Maps offer a quick and easy-to-use tool for an individual or a team to: ascertain the status of an alternative's ability to meet a criterion; visualize the change resulting from analysis, experimentation, or other knowledge increase or uncertainty decrease; and compare the evaluations made by the team members. Each point on the Belief Map is color coded to match the alternatives and numbered to match the criteria.

For qualitative evaluations the vertical axis represents the "criterion satisfaction": how well the alternative being evaluated satisfies the criterion. This is analogous to the numerical rating given in a Decision Matrix (aka Pugh's Matrix). The horizontal axis is referred to as "certainty-knowledge," as the evaluator's certainty or knowledge is the basis of the assessment.

The logic behind the belief values is easily explained. If an evaluator puts her point in the upper right corner, then she is claiming she is an expert and is confident that the alternative fully meets the criterion. If she puts her point in the lower right corner, she is expert and confident that the alternative has a zero probability of meeting this criterion. If she puts her evaluation point in the upper left corner she is hopelessly optimistic: "I don't know anything about this, but I am sure it will work"—she believes that the alternative meets the criterion, even though she has no knowledge on which to base this belief. This is referred to as "the salesman's corner." If she puts her evaluation point in the lower left corner she is pessimistic: "I know nothing, but it will be bad." This is called the "engineer's corner," for obvious reasons.

Accord changes all points on the belief map into probabilities for fusion with other evaluation information. The Belief Map for all the evaluation in the example is shown in Figure 13.12.

Fusion of multiple team members' evaluations

Usually, decisions are made based on the fusion of many people's knowledge and opinions. Where only one estimate may be made for profit or other important measures in most organizations, there are other models with other results that are often ignored. It is not that the one used is right and the others are wrong; it is that multiple estimates of the situation are difficult to manage. This is exacerbated when the measures are qualitative because there are no numbers to fall back on.

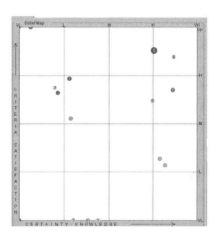

Figure 13.12: Sample Belief Map.

A strength of the BTS methodology is its ability to fuse the evaluations from multiple evaluators or team members. There is not room to describe the methodology here, but the reduction of all information to probabilities and expected values allows this fusion. To demonstrate this, two additional evaluators are added to the example problem. Fusing their estimates of profit and the other measures based on other models and knowledge with what is already in *Accord*, Point 9, satisfaction grows even stronger relative to the other options.

What-to-do-next

In *Accord* there is a "What-to-Do-Next" analysis (see figure 13.13). This generates a report based on all the input and calculated data. Using an internal rule base, the What-to-Do-Next analysis takes the information developed and generates an ordered list of what the decision maker(s) should do next to improve the differentiation in satisfaction between the highest ranked alternative or the probability that the highest ranked alternative is best. The top items on the list are generally the most effective for the effort required to address them.

In the text, the "what-to-do-next" suggestions are typically one of three types:

- Evaluation can be improved by gaining consensus on specific items. This means that the information from the various sources does not agree and a formalized process to resolve the inconsistency can result in increased shared knowledge and confidence in the evaluation.
- Evaluation can be improved by gathering more information or doing more analysis on specific evaluations. Again, only those areas that can significantly affect the satisfaction level are identified.
- Refine qualitative criteria.

The goal of this display is to reduce the cognitive load on the decision makers while providing them with the best possible information for making a decision. Based on this report, the team worked on the items identified.

Conclusions

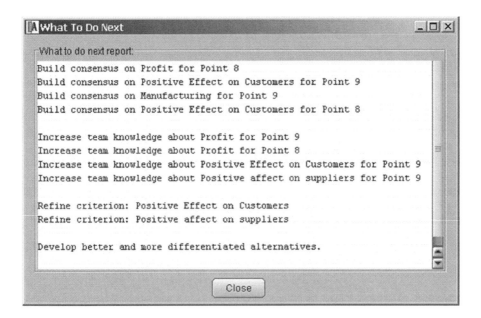

Figure 13.13. What-to-Do-Next-report.

For the example problem and based on the current evaluation, Point 9 is the best choice and potentially gives more profit than Point 7. Where the deterministic approach finds Point 9 out of the region of acceptable solutions, adding uncertainty and multiple evaluators has resulted in its being best. There may be even a better point that has not been evaluated, as suggested in the What-to-Do-Next report. Considering that Points 7 and 9 require 4 to 8 x_1 machines and 10 to 12 x_2 machines, it seems logical to consider other options in this range.

In general, trade studies are difficult to support, especially when information is uncertain, incomplete, inconsistent, and evolving. Analytical methods only apply when the system is well known and they can't support multiple opinions and uncertainty. This paper has demonstrated the application of Bayesian Team Support as instantiated in *Accord* to manage a trade study. It has helped address:

- Target uncertainty
- Evaluation uncertainty
- Importance uncertainty
- Mix of qualitative and quantitative criteria
- Fusion of multiple team members' evaluations
- Determining what-to-do-next to ensure the best possible decision is being made.

Applying Robust Decision-Making Methods to Unstick the OODA Loop

I introduced the OODA Loop in chapter 2 as a model of decision making that isn't, on the surface, totally consistent with the model developed here. However, it relies on the same building blocks. In chapter 2 we talked about getting stuck in the OODA Loop and making an "OO-OO-OO" sound. Now that we have explored all the details of making decisions, it's time to itemize some OODA Loop guidelines to help you stay unstuck and make robust decisions.

Overall guideline

1 Identify the OODA Loops in your organization and their interactions. Each OODA Loop provides the environment for other, interacting OODA

Loops. Each OODA Loop represents a decision or series of decisions to be made.

2 Each OODA Loop addresses an issue. Make sure the issue is known by all.

Observation Guidelines

1 Observations are used to collect evaluation information. In order to know what to evaluate, you must know what to observe—which alternative measures to gather data about. This means that the alternatives and criteria must be known and organized.

2 Make sure that you know the properties of Observations. Each piece of information comes with details about its stability, consistency, certainty, completeness, and dependence on the observer. Note these and formalize them, if possible.

3 All Observations are uncertain. Anytime anyone supplies you with an estimate, the results of a simulation or experiment, or an opinion, you should tag it with a level of certainty. You need to make this explicit. Engineers and financial analysts in particular are prone to giving single values for information that is really a distribution. Push back on them to find the distribution, even if it is put in terms like "very sure," "about," or "sort of."

Orientation Guidelines

1 Since Orientation is so important, it is amazing that more emphasis isn't put on its component parts. The major function of Orientation is making sense of observations. Since all observations are understood only in relation to what the Orienteer knows, "sense" is different for each person presented with the Observations. Thus, one sticking point happens when the person responsible for the OODA Loop doesn't have sufficient knowledge to Orient—and knows it. It may take a while for this realization to sink in. So if you are responsible for a decision and it isn't happening, ask yourself whether that's because you lack sufficient knowledge to make sense of the situation. If that's the reason, find people who do have the knowledge.

2 If a problem is sufficiently complex that a team is involved, then each person on the team has a different context for Orienting. Here, sense-making is communal and challenging, as no one person has either a complete picture or the capability of developing one. It is possible to have meetings to discuss the Observations without significant sense-making. The key here is to set up environments that support sense-making by sharing key information needed for the Decision. Implicit knowledge needs to be made explicit in a form that can be understood by others who have a different context for understanding the Observations.

3   If you are in a team situation, during Orientation there will be multiple viewpoints about what is important. It is essential to separate opinions about what is important from the sense-making itself. For example, the cost of a course of action may be very important to some and not so important to others. This fact needs to be kept separate from the estimated cost of each course of action being considered. The uncertainty in the estimate may swamp the differences in importance, but only if these separate parts are made explicit. Further, disagreements about what is important can be an asset, as management of them can support collaboration, leading to Action and buy-in.

4   Since Observations are uncertain, Orientation methods need to be able to manage uncertain information, whether quantitative or qualitative. The only way to know about and manage the risk is by managing this uncertainty.

5   During Orientation, make sure you consider multiple courses of action and can itemize them. Develop methods within your organization that encourage multiple alternative courses of action to be considered. Find ways to help the champions of each idea compare and contrast his or her alternative with those of others.

Decision Guidelines

1   Making a Decision is essentially deciding what-to-do-next. The default is to do nothing—getting stuck at "OO-OO-OO." Being stuck is a clear call for you to either:

- Build consensus with the information you have. This pushes back on Orientation: managing viewpoints, sharing implicit knowledge, and developing new courses of action. This is the first choice about what to do, as it is the most cost effective.
- Perform more analysis to refine the Orientation information. This is generally more expensive than working with the information

you have, and can lead to "paralysis by analysis," the risk-averse activity of trying to drive out all uncertainty by undertaking increasingly higher-fidelity simulations of the situation. When the fidelity of the simulations outstrips the certainty of the Observations, time and money are wasted.

- Return to Observation and collect more information. This is usually more expensive and time consuming than the previous two options. But, if the information that will reduce the risk and unstick the decision is available to collect, this step may be worthwhile.

2   Work toward robust decisions. To know how well you are doing, keep track of the decisions you make and the Actions that follow. This is seldom done in a fashion that makes it possible to learn from OODA loop successes and failures.

The Technical Basis for Bayesian Team Support

Introduction

A master once told his student, "decisions are only hard when the there is little difference between the choices." The master was Professor Lofti Zadeh, the father of fuzzy logic. The student was Bruce D'Ambrosio, later a Professor of Artificial Intelligence at Oregon State University and co-developer, with the author, of Bayesian Team Support (BTS). Like fuzzy logic, Bayes methods require a change in the way uncertain problems are approached. Bayes methods fit team decision making in ways that fuzzy logic cannot. Much of the detail on Bayes methods presented here is Professor D'Ambrosio's.

Bayesian decision theory has its roots in the work of an obscure eighteenth century cleric, Reverend Thomas Bayes, who worried about how to combine evidence in legal matters. But its modern form traces to the work of John von Neumann, mathematician and computer pioneer, in the 1940s, and L.J. Savage in the 1950s.[1] Bayesian methods rely on measuring and managing the degree to which a person believes a proposition. The basic equations Bayes developed are used as the basis for updating beliefs in the light of new information; such updating is known as Bayesian inference.

Bayes' methods rely on probabilities. However, they are used quite differently from traditional probabilistic methods. Traditionally, what is deemed probable is not propositions believers entertain (as is the case with Bayesian methods), but events considered as members of populations to which the tools of classical statistical analysis can be applied. For example, you can measure the heights of a population of people and use these results with traditional event-based statistics to predict the height of your new child. However, if you want to decide whether to have a picnic tomorrow, event-based statistics may not give the best help, as we shall see.

Bayesian decision theory is a well-founded computational theory for applying general knowledge to individual situations characterized by uncertainty and risk.[2] It excels in situations where the available information is imprecise, incomplete, and even inconsistent, and in which outcomes can be uncertain and the decision makers' attitudes toward them vary widely. Bayesian decision analysis can indicate not only the best alternative to pursue given the current problem description, but also whether a problem is ripe for deciding, and if not, how to proceed to reach a decision.

In Savage's formulation, a decision problem has three elements: (1) preferences over the possible outcomes of alternate actions; (2) a set of action alternatives; and (3) beliefs about the world. Given a problem description, the theory prescribes that the optimal action to choose is the alternative that maximizes the subjective expected utility.

A well-known problem in applying Bayesian decision theory to decisions involved teams: There was no known sound way to integrate the preferences of multiple decision makers. This has been solved (and patented[3]) with Bayesian Team Support (BTS). BTS assumes that the information collected is uncertain, incomplete, inconsistent, and evolving. As evidence accumulates, the greatest degree of belief in one of the alternatives will emerge as the best choice. The BTS methodology is the basis for *Accord* software. *Accord* is the first commercialized team decision-support method based on Bayesian Team Support. Other methods cannot fuse team knowledge nor support uncertain and incomplete information.

Before we continue, it is important to compare and contrast Bayes probabilities to what we learned in school. Bayesian probabilities look at the world differently from traditional probabilities (called frequentist probabilities to differentiate them from Bayesian). Frequentists see probability as the long-run expected frequency of occurrence. $P(A) = n/N$, where n is the number of times event A occurs in N opportunities. Thus, frequentists worry about measuring what has already happened to estimate the probabilities of future events. However, the Bayesian view of probability is related to degree of belief. It begins with a hypothesis about reality (often called a "prior") and updates this as more is learned. It is a measure of the probability of an event given incomplete knowledge. The difference between frequentist and Bayesian approaches can be summarized in table A1.

Here's a simple example. I want to have a picnic at noon tomorrow. I need to make a decision by 9 tomorrow morning whether or not to cancel it, which I will if it is going to rain. From my frequentist perspective, I have data about the probability of rain tomorrow, and even some data that tell

	Frequentist	Bayesian
View	Based on measurements of past events	Based on estimates of future events
Evidence	Measures past results	Uncertain estimates of the world
Statistical results	Based on data description	Based on the chance of parameters meeting targets
Rigidity	Must follow a set design	Updated as new information becomes available
Use in making decisions	Can only give evidence for decisions	Tailored for decisions

Table A1: Frequentist and Bayesian approaches.

the probability of it raining tomorrow based on the barometer and other data about today. All of this is based on past measurements that result in statistics such as "it rains 70% of the time on September 5." The only results I can get from this data are what have been designed into the reduction of the past data (i.e., I can't say anything about the probability of mice falling from the sky if that type of precipitation was not measured and modeled). This frequentist view helps me make a decision only by providing me with evidence for a future event, but this is not enough.

The morning of the picnic I look outside. I am armed with the frequentist prediction of 70% chance of rain. I look at the sky, the barometer, and my Ouija Board, and update the 70% (i.e., the prior) with new information: a Bayesian view. I would like a clear day (my target), but there are some clouds that make this possibility uncertain. Based on my best estimates I believe that the chance of rain is 60% and this is almost low enough for me not to cancel the picnic. The phone rings and it is my friend who lives thirty miles west of me. It is clearing over his house and the weather always comes from his direction. Based on this new information, I update my 60% prior to a 40% chance of rain and decide to have the picnic. I am truly a Bayesian.

From this basis, we can now develop how we use Bayesian logic to support making complex decisions.

Elements of a Bayesian Decision Model

As I stated earlier, a Bayesian decision model, as specified by Savage, has three elements: (1) a preference over the possible outcomes of action; (2) a set of decision alternatives; (3) a set of beliefs about the world. We will assume that for any decision problem, we have a set of alternatives to choose among—the second element—and so we will focus on the first element, the preference model (i.e., the criteria) and the third element, beliefs about how well the alternatives meet the preferred outcomes.

A preference model is a set of objectives or criteria that are used to judge the alternative solutions. This is simple when there is only one criterion, but when there are multiple criteria, exactly how to combine the evaluations to model the preference is problematic. A typical simplification is to use a simple *additive* model, in which one first decomposes overall preference into a set of *objectives* (i.e., features), here embodied in criteria, and then assigns importance weights to each criterion. This assumes that the team member is willing to trade off losses in one objective for gains in another. While this is sometimes the case, it does not always hold. We will explore how to model these "critical criteria" in a later section.

Beyond how to combine criteria, there is a second problem with preference models: There are strong theoretical reasons why it is impossible to combine preferences from multiple decision makers. BTS uses two methods to manage team evaluations. I will develop these here. But before I do this, I must address the third element of Savage's Bayesian decision model.

The third element, modeling beliefs about the world, must, first of all, be simple and intuitive. Complex models that require vast amounts of precisely specified information may be theoretically attractive, but are useless to the busy practitioner. Much of the following explanation is about how we model beliefs about the world and how we fuse multiple beliefs. We do this in two steps. First, we may have multiple people evaluating the same thing and we need to fuse their beliefs. Then we must fuse the evaluations across the preference model to gain a measure of each alternative's satisfaction. The following material first refines information fusion, then explains how we do this, with qualitative evaluations followed by quantitative evaluations.

Information Fusion

The challenges with information fusion are easily seen in figure A1. Here there are three team members (DM1, DM2, and DM3) using three criteria to evaluate a single alternative. The first criterion is qualitative and the team's evaluations are shown on the three Belief Maps in the upper left corner of the diagram. The second and third criteria are quantitative and evaluated on the number lines shown in the top middle and right. For each of the criteria, the evaluations are fused to find a team belief. This is each team member's individual evaluation combined, using Bayesian methods,

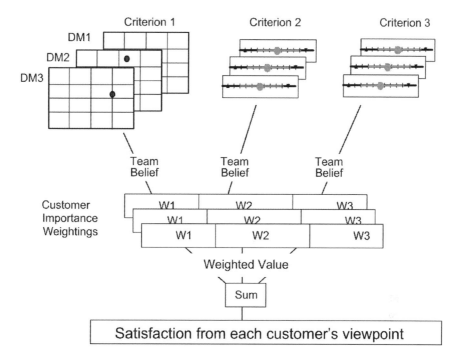

Figure A1: Bayesian information fusion.

to the evidence. Member 2 adds to the evaluation of Member 1, just as my friend's information about clouds added to my prior estimate about the probability of rain.

Then the team beliefs are fused using the importance weighting (i.e., the preference model) of one of the team members. There are three sets of importance weightings shown; there could be more or less, but each weighs the team beliefs to generate an overall satisfaction. What is shown in this diagram is the core of the BTS methodology and is programmed in *Accord*. Beyond what is shown, there are many other statistics calculated in *Accord*. These are discussed further on.

One important point in the diagram is that the underlying mathematics for both qualitative and quantitative measures generates team beliefs that can be combined consistently to generate the satisfaction, as well as other statistics. First, we will develop the math of qualitative criteria evaluations.

Qualitative Evaluations

It may seem that the *alternative/criterion* representation for a decision problem is rather simplistic and ad hoc. However, support for this representation comes from extensive research into modeling decision-making processes. In addition, there is a straightforward mapping to an influence diagram, as shown in Figure A2. Our model of qualitative argumentation is derived from this graphical representation.

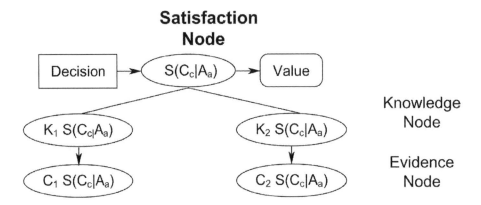

Figure A2: Influence diagram.

Figure A2 represents a single alternative/criterion evaluated by two people. The box labeled "Decision" takes as values the alternatives for resolving the issue represented by the diagram. The circle labeled $S(C_c|A_a)$ represents the satisfaction of criterion C_c given alternative A_a and will be called a *satisfaction* node. Here the subscript a is the specific alternative being addressed; c is the criterion. While we show only one, there will be one satisfaction node for each alternative/criterion combination. For qualitative evaluations we allow only Boolean *(satisfied/unsatisfied,* or *yes/no,* or *agree/disagree)* satisfaction levels. Therefore, we are measuring the probability that the alternative will satisfy the criterion, not the degree to which satisfaction is achieved. In other words, we measure the degree of belief that the criterion will be met. After the fact, once we can look at the result, the answer will be "Yes, it met the criterion" or "No, it did *not* meet the criterion."

The pair of two node chains hanging from $S(C_c|A_a)$ represents opinions posted by two evaluators. There can be any number of such chains hanging from each of the $S(C_c|A_a)$ satisfaction nodes: one for each opinion. The higher of the two ovals represents the state of participant knowledge about the ability of the alternative to meet the criterion (i.e., Level of Knowledge).

It represents the probability that what is believed is actually correct. The lower oval is used to encode probabilistic evidence for criterion C_c satisfaction (i.e., the Level of Criteria Satisfaction or Evidence). It represents what is believed.

The conditional probability distribution for the *knowledge node* given the actual satisfaction has two degrees of freedom. We reduce this to a single degree by assuming symmetry to simplify knowledge acquisition. That is, we assume:

$$P(K_p) = yes | S(C_c | A_a) = yes) = P(K_p) = no | S(C_c | A_a) = no).$$

What this says is that for each participant's (subscript p) evaluation the probability (P) that what is believed is correct ($P(K_p)$ = yes) when criteria c is satisfied by alternative a, $S(C_c | A_a)$ is the same as the probability that what is believed is incorrect ($P(K_p)$ = no) when the criteria is unsatisfied. This single degree of freedom is the *knowledge* the participant has about the alternative/criterion pair, because this single parameter encodes how accurately the participant's belief reflects the actual world state. The complete distribution for a knowledge node, then, is shown in table A2.

$S(C_c|A_a)$	$P(K_p S(C_c|A_a)=yes)$	$P(K_p S(C_c|A_a)=no)$
Yes	$K_{c,a,p}$	$1 - K_{c,a,p}$
No	$1 - K_{c,a,p}$	$K_{c,a,p}$

Table A2.

We allow $K_{c, a, p}$ to range between 0.5 and 1.0, where 1.0 represents perfect knowledge (i.e., high certainty) and 0.5 represents complete ignorance (i.e., flipping of a coin or high uncertainty).

We will refer to the lower node as the *Evidence* node, E_p. The evidence node has only one value and all that matters is the ratio of the probabilities for that value given K_p (i.e., this node holds the user-stated probability that the alternative meets the criterion given the state of knowledge, normalized to a 0 to 1 range). That is, we treat the participant as making a noisy or soft observation (report) on his or her belief. We encode this as a pair of numbers constrained to sum to one, as shown in table A3.

$S(C_c|A_a)$	$E_p(S(C_c|A_a))$
Yes	$E_{c,a,p}$
No	$1 - E_{c,a,p}$

Table A3.

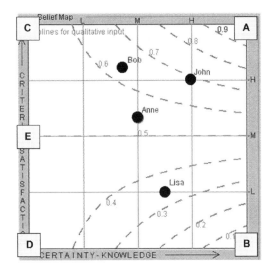

Figure A3: Belief Map.

This says that evidence for yes results in criterion satisfaction, and that the evidence for not satisfying the criterion is 1 - the evidence. Note that this model assumes uncorrelated evidence from team members—this is for a single team member evaluating a single alternative/criterion pair. While modeling correlation among opinions is straightforward, it is an extra burden on the team that outweighs the advantages in most situations; thus, we do not do it.

We can find the probability of satisfaction by combining the knowledge and evidence. Namely, the probability of satisfaction for an alternative/criterion pair is $P(S_p(C_c|A_a)$ = yes) and is the sum of knowledge that the evidence is correct times the probability that it is correct and the knowledge that the evidence is incorrect times the probability that it is incorrect. In equation form this is:

$$P(S_p(C_c|A_a) = yes) = (E_{c,a,p} K_{c,a,p} + (1.0 - E_{c,a,p})(1.0 - K_{c,a,p}))$$

This equation is fundamental to and original to Bayesian Team Support. Let's explore this equation using a Belief Map. In figure A3, letters A through E have been added to figure 8.7. The figure shows the evaluation of a single alternative relative to a single criterion by a team of people and includes isolines that result from the equation above.

Consider:

Point A: K = 1.0 (very high knowledge), E = 1.0 (very high evidence for criteria satisfaction), P = 1.0 = 1.0 × 1.0 + (1.0 - 1.0) × (1.0 - 1.0)

Point B: K = 1.0 (very high knowledge), E = 0.0 (very low evidence for criteria satisfaction), P = 0.0 = 1.0 × 0.0 + (1.0 - 1.0) × (1.0 - 0.0)

Point C: K = 0.5 (very low knowledge), E = 1.0 (very high evidence for criteria satisfaction), P = 0.5 = 0.5 × 1.0 + (1.0 - 0.5) × (1.0 - 1.0)

Point D: K = 0.5 (very low knowledge), E = 0.0 (very low evidence for criteria satisfaction), P = 0.5 = 0.5 × 0.0 + (1.0 - 0.5) × (1.0 - 0.0)

Point E: K = 0.5 (very low knowledge), E = 0.5 (no evidence, Medium criteria satisfaction), P = 0.5 = 0.5 × 0.5 + (1.0 - 0.5) × (1.0 - 0.5), default position

John: K = 0.875 (high knowledge), E = 0.75 (high evidence for criteria satisfaction), P = 0.69 = 0.875 × 0.75 + (1.0 - 0.875) × (1.0 - 0.75)

Bob: K = 0.72 (medium knowledge), E = 0.8 (high+ evidence for criteria satisfaction), P = 0.63 = 0.72 × 0.80 + (1.0 - 0.72) × (1.0 - 0.80)

Anne: K = 0.75 (medium knowledge), E = 0.60 (medium+ evidence for criteria satisfaction), P = 0.55 = 0.75 × 0.60 + (1.0 - 0.75) × (1.0 - 0.60)

Lisa: K = 0.81 (medium-high knowledge), E = 0.25 (low evidence for criteria satisfaction), P = 0.34 = 0.81 × 0.25 + (1.0 - 0.81) × (1.0 - 0.25)

To combine the individual assessments, the following formula effectively computes their normalized product. Normalization combines $P(S_p(C_c|A_a) =$ yes) (the equation that results in the isolines) with $P(S_p(C_c|A_a) =$ no).

$$P(S(C_c|A_a) = \text{yes}) = \alpha \, \Pi_p \, (E_{c,a,p} \, K_{c,a,p} + (1 - E_{c,a,p})(1 - K_{c,a,p}))$$

with α as a normalization factor:

$$\alpha = 1/(\Pi_p \, (E_{c,a,p} \, K_{c,a,p} + (1 - E_{c,a,p})(1 - K_{c,a,p}))$$
$$+ \Pi_p \, (E_{c,a,p} \, (1 - K_{c,a,p}) + (1 - E_{c,a,p})K_{c,a,p}))$$

And Π_p being the product over all participants.

This results in the "team satisfaction" noted in figure A1. It is the probability that the team believes that the alternative meets the criterion. For our team, as shown in figure A3, the equations give:

Team Satisfaction =

$$\frac{(0.69 \times 0.63 \times 0.55 \times 0.34)}{(0.69 \times 0.63 \times 0.55 \times 0.34) + (0.31 \times 0.37 \times 0.45 \times 0.66)} = .70$$

Where Anne and Bob support John, Lisa's evaluation counters that support. Without Lisa, this value would be 0.82.

Now this value can be combined with those for evaluations relative to other criteria to find the overall satisfaction for the alternative using the preference model. Where many methods average over preference models, in BTS we only use one preference at a time, as discussed earlier. Thus, the overall satisfaction for an alternative according to a specific preference viewpoint is:

$$S(A_a) = \Sigma_c W(C_c) \times P(S(C_c|A_a) = yes)$$

Where $W(C_c)$ is the importance weight assigned to criterion C by a single participant.

These are the details of how we find the alternative satisfaction for a specific alternative as determined relative to a qualitative criteria. In the next section we develop a method that is consistent with this for quantitative criteria.

Quantitative Evaluations

Quantitative evaluations are different from qualitative. Where qualitative focuses on agreement, satisfaction, or yes-ness, quantitative is a measure of degree. There is still the need to represent the three decision elements, but here the first (a preference over the possible outcomes of action) and third (a set of beliefs about the world) are different. This can be seen on a number line; figure A4 shows an example. Here the delighted target for cost is $20,000 with a disgusted value of $25,000. These values describe the preference for the outcome. In her evaluation, Anne judges the most likely cost at $25,000 with a low estimate of $22,500 and a high estimate of $27,000. These constitute her belief about the cost of Grex. Thus, the number line gives all the information needed to model Anne's evaluation.

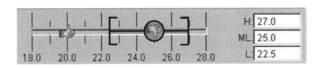

Figure A4: Anne's evaluation of the cost of Grex's proposed cost.

Utility curves based on the delighted and disgusted values give a simple representation of the preference model, figure A5. More sophisticated utility curves could be used than the simple two-point type used here. But it is hard enough getting people to think about two target values without worrying about more sophisticated models. Additionally, there is so much uncertainty in all the estimates that a more sophisticated model is frankly not warranted.

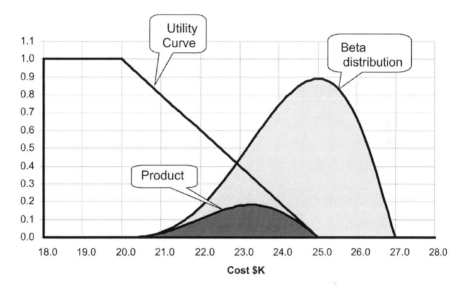

Figure A5: Utility curve.

The belief about the world is based on the high, low, and most likely estimates. These are used to define a Beta distribution. This is similar to the common Normal distribution or Bell curve, but it allows asymmetrical distributions to be easily modeled.

I will explain what is done with a simple example. We will use Anne's data but lower her "low" estimate to $20,000 to make the example graphically more interesting. In figure A.5 the utility curve is plotted along with the Beta distribution based on Anne's estimated values and the resulting product of the two. The utility curve shows complete utility (1.0) for any cost less than $20,000 and no utility if greater than $25,000.

The Beta curve is based on the three evaluation points input by Anne. Beta curves look like normal distributions when symmetrical, but can represent skewed distributions as shown. The area under the distribution curve

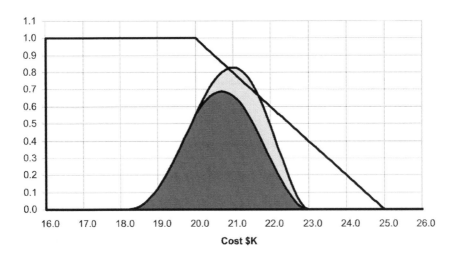

Figure A6: Utility curve.

=1.0; however, the vertical scale in the figure has been increased for ease of visualization.

If you multiply the distribution by the utility, the area under the resulting curve gives the satisfaction with the evaluation. Note that Anne's evaluation greater than $25,000 has counted for nothing. In this case the area under the product curve equals 0.19, showing Anne's generally low judgment of the cost.

If she had evaluated it at low = $19,000, most likely = $21,000, high = $23,000, then the curves would look as in figure A.6. Here the distribution based on the data is partially in the delighted region and is thus fully counted. That part greater than $20,000 is discounted by the utility curve. The resulting area under the probability of satisfaction for this alternative/criterion pair is 0.81 or 81%.

The satisfaction calculated here is combined with the others found for either qualitative or quantitative evaluations using the preference formula from page 320, extended for inclusion of quantitative evaluations.

$S(A_a) = \Sigma_c W(C_c) \times$ (if qualitative $(P(S(C_c|A_a) = yes))$, or if quantitative (Satisfaction))

or

$S(A_a) = \Sigma_c W(C_c) \times (TS(C_c|A_a))$ where TS = team satisfaction.

Beyond finding the overall satisfaction for an alternative, many other measures can be developed from the basic mathematics.

Value of Information (VOI)

A major component of BTS is Value of Information (VOI) analysis. VOI analysis is a decision analytic technique that explicitly evaluates the benefit of collecting additional information to reduce or eliminate uncertainty. VOI analysis is at the heart of the what-to-do-next analysis. VOI analyses are becoming increasingly used in health care and other fields.[4]

VOI analysis is based on the extent to which a change in information will reduce the decision uncertainty. VOI provides a principled methodology that enables acquiring information in a way that optimally trades off the cost of information gathering with the expected benefit. Several analytical challenges that inhibit greater use of VOI techniques include issues related to modeling decisions, valuing outcomes, and characterizing uncertain and variable model inputs appropriately.[5]

A good quote that sums up the benefits of VOI analysis is: "Value of information (VOI) analysis is useful because it makes the losses associated with decision errors explicit, balances competing probabilities and costs, helps identify the decision alternative that minimizes the expected loss, prioritizes spending on research, quantifies the value of the research to the decision maker, and provides an upper bound on what should be spent on getting information."[6]

Value of Information analysis is a type of sensitivity analysis unique to Bayesian methods. Where a traditional sensitivity analysis explores the sensitivity about a deterministically calculated result to changes in the independent variables, a VOI analysis is based on the uncertainty input as part of the evaluation information. I will explain this.

In the ideal world, for each qualitative criterion the team would have an expert with authoritative knowledge who could evaluate how well each alternative met the criterion. For each quantitative variable they would know the exact value with no variation. However, these ideals are seldom the case. Decisions are usually made with knowledge and certainty that are evolving and for which there may be no experts. Value of Information analysis adds a virtual expert to the team to find out what might happen if resources are committed to increase team knowledge and control the uncertainty. The effect of this "expert" on the satisfaction gives a clear picture about the value of actually committing resources to improve the evaluations.

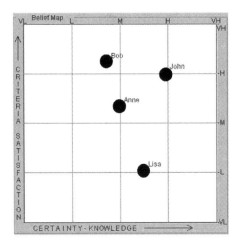

Figure A7: The actual team evaluation of Grex's ease of use.

The methodology is best explained through an example. In evaluating Grex's "easy to use" criterion, the team placed their points on the Belief Map as shown in a figure A7.

Here, the team has moderate consensus and knowledge about Grex's proposed ease of use. Before expending effort to improve the consensus or to gain better "ease of use" knowledge, it is worth noting whether additional information will have any effect on the satisfaction results. This we will find out.

A "virtual expert" is assumed to have perfect knowledge and very highly agrees that Grex's proposed product will be easy to use. The expert's point has been added to the Belief Map in figure A8.

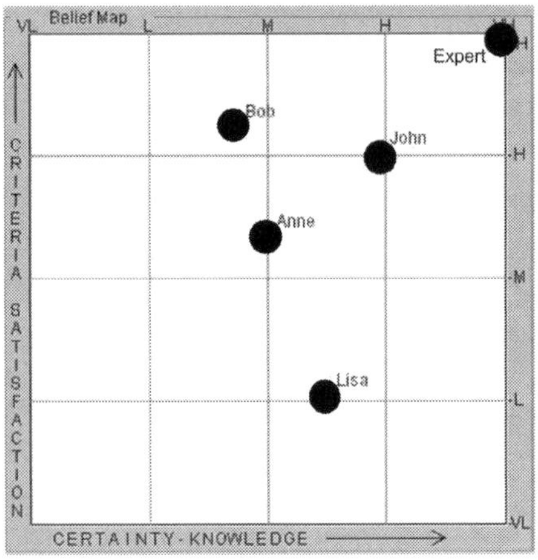

Figure A8: The virtual expert's evaluation.

The effect of the addition of a virtual expert to the team can be seen in figure A9. This is a reprint of the satisfaction results from figure 9.14, with the additional effect of the expert's evaluation of "ease of use" shown superimposed, raising the satisfaction from 62 to 68%. Also, the downward bar shows the evaluation in the event that the expert is sure that Grex cannot meet the "ease of use" criterion. To find this, the expert's point is placed in the lower right-hand corner of the Belief Map, signifying that he or she has perfect knowledge and is completely confident that Grex *cannot* meet the "ease of use" target.

Before interpreting the results, note that the expert's evaluation overwhelms the evaluations made by the rest of the team. An expert evaluator who is fully confident that an alternative meets (or cannot possibly meet)

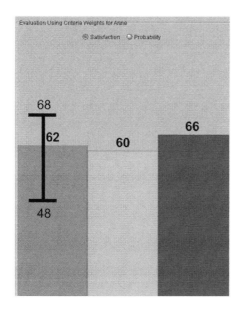

Figure A9: The entire team's evaluation from Anne's viewpoint.

the target set by the criteria will dominate all other assessments. This makes sense, as it often occurs in real-life scenarios. This calculation of value of information clearly illustrates the highest and lowest satisfaction levels that are achievable if the knowledge about each of the alternative/criterion pairs is complete and criteria satisfaction is as high or low as it can be. This calculation also shows how any additional knowledge can change the evaluation.

Examination of the results of the expert analysis from Anne's viewpoint is shown in figure A9. The best the value satisfaction can achieve due to changes in evaluation of "ease of use" is 68% as shown; the worst is 48%. The 6% increase (14% decrease) in "ease of use" evaluation may be important or not. It needs to be put in perspective. The highest potential increase, using Anne's importance weightings, is for the team experience of Swale—25% increase—and the greatest decrease is for the team experience of Grex—23%. These should not be surprising, as Anne ranked team experience as her second most important criteria.

The value of information analysis is the limit to the possible change. If further research proves that John and Bob's initial evaluation is correct, and Lisa and Anne agree with them, then satisfaction with Grex will move toward 68%, at least from Anne's viewpoint. In general:

> The results of the value of information analysis are a function of:
> the current importance weighting
> the current knowledge or certainty indicated by the team
> the current criterion satisfaction indicated by the team

The value of information analysis can be done without *Accord* by exploring the extremes of each evaluation in whichever method is used. However,

Accord does it automatically and uses the result as one of the major inputs for the what-to-do-next analysis.

What-to-Do-Next

The what-to-do-next analysis is an expert system that uses the VOI results, combined with the level of consensus, knowledge, and type of criteria to generate statements that guide the team to the most cost-effective actions that will resolve the issue. This is a virtual cost/benefit analysis, in that through the VOI we know the benefit and we can infer the cost. The VOI gives a rank ordering of which alternative/criterion pairs can have the greatest effect on the results. We then use the other data and the assumption that it is less expensive to work on reaching consensus than it is to increase knowledge or reduce uncertainty. Further, it is less expensive to do either of these than it is to refine criteria, as refinement usually requires collecting new information. Finally, all of these are less expensive from a decision viewpoint than is developing new criteria. Thus, the rule base recommends one or more of the following:

- •<Alternative x> has high satisfaction and probability of being the first choice is high from all viewpoints. You may want to choose it.
- •<Alternative x / Feature y> is sensitive and consensus is low. Discussion about this is advised.
- •Knowledge of <Alternative x/ Feature y> is sensitive and consensus is low. Develop more information using experiments, analysis, or experts.
- •<Criteria x and y> are weak, yet important. Refine these criteria features and targets.
- •The team is having difficulty differentiating between alternatives. Either generate new criteria that better measure features that vary from alternative to alternative, or generate new alternatives.
- •None of the alternatives has very high satisfaction. Generate new alternative solutions.
- •The importance weightings vary too much among team members to reach consensus. Discuss importance weightings.

This is automated in *Accord*.

Probability of Being Best

Probability of being best is a unique BTS solution to the problem of combining preferences from multiple team members' evaluations. As discussed before, combining evaluations across team members must be done with care, as methods like averaging wash out the true information and can lead to ambiguous or wrong conclusions. Earlier, we addressed this by keeping the weightings separated and not combining them at all. A second method is to generate a measure that samples across the entire space of preference functions bounded by the individual member preferences. In other words, consider the example shown in figure A3. Here, the four team members found that their satisfactions when evaluating Grex's "easy to use" were 0.69, 0.63, 0.55, and 0.34. These four values define a distribution for the satisfaction of this criterion by this alternative, thus sampling across the importance weightings. Similar distributions can be found for all the alternative/criterion pairs. If an alternative/criterion has only a single evaluation, then the distribution is defined by that single value.

Using these distributions, BTS then runs a Monte Carlo simulation. The way this works is:

1 Using the distributions, pick a value for the satisfaction of each alternative/criterion pair. This value is random, but determined by the distribution. In our example, you can see by inspection that the simulation is much more likely to pick a value of 0.60 than it is 0.40.

2 Using the individual criterion satisfactions, calculate the overall satisfaction for each alternative. This is done using only one of the team's importance weightings.

3 Record which of the alternative is best: has the highest satisfaction for this single simulation.

4 Go back to Step 1 and do the process again. Repeat this thousands of times.

5 Using the total number of times each alternative was best as accumulated in step 3, normalize these to total 100% and you have the probability that each is best.

This additional statistic gives the relative preference for each of the alternatives as probabilities that sum to 100%. Coupled with the satisfaction, the probability of being best gives a good indication of how well the alternatives meet the criteria.

Risk

As I discussed in chapter 9, risk is both the lack of satisfaction and the amount that satisfaction might decrease due to uncertainty. This "downside risk" of an alternative is the risk that, if you choose the alternative, it won't turn out as expected. That is, it is the expectation over outcomes less than the overall expected value, for that alternative. This is one-sided first moment about the overall expected value (the mean). To find this risk we sample across the evaluation distributions. For each sample expected value (SEV) less than the overall expected value (OEV), the consequence is the amount the SEV is less than the OEV. The risk is simply the sum of the consequences where the sum embodies the probability of occurrence: Risk = Σ (OEV-SEV).

Critical Criteria

Not all criteria can be traded off against each other, as implied in the simple summation formula:

$$S(A_a) = \Sigma_c W(C_c) \times (TS(C_c|A_a))$$

Some criteria must be made. Most of these are filter criteria, but some few discriminate and must be part of the overall satisfaction calculation above. However, if an alternative fails to meet one of the critical criteria, the satisfaction will be very low. One traditional way of managing critical criteria is to multiply the team satisfactions together so that the equation becomes:

$$S(A_a) = \Pi_p (TS(C_c|A_a))$$

There are two problems with this equation. First, if critical criteria do not have 100% satisfaction, the overall satisfaction calculated by this formula becomes quite small (e.g., four critical criteria at 90% team satisfaction yields 27% overall satisfaction). This does not square with intuition. Even more limiting is that, in general, most criteria can be traded off and only one or two are critical. There is no way to combine these two types of criteria using the equations above.

Our solution to this is embodied in the following equation. Here there are a total of i criteria. Of these, j criteria are critical and the remaining i-j can be traded off (this could be zero). The overall satisfaction[7] is:

$$S(A_a) = \Pi_j \, TS_j \times \Sigma_{i\text{-}j} \, (W_i \times TS_i)$$

where:

W$_i$ is the weighting renormalized across i-j
TS$_i$ is the team's fused belief on criterion i

The best way to show how this works is through example. Say there are four criteria (i = 4) and one of these is critical (j = 1). Further, say that the team satisfactions are as shown in the following table.

	Team satisfaction (TS$_i$)	Importance weight(W$_i$)	Criterion type
1	67%	24%	Trade off
2	83%	32%	Trade off
3	37%	44%	Trade off
4	85%		Critical

Table A4: Team satisfaction, importance weight, criterion type.

If only the trade-off criteria are used the satisfaction is::

$$S(A_a) = (0.24 \times 0.67 + 0.32 \times 0.83 + 0.44 \times 0.37) = 0.59$$

With the addition of the critical criterion:

$$S(A_a) = 0.85 \times (0.24 \times 0.67 + 0.32 \times 0.83 + 0.44 \times 0.37) = 0.50$$

If criterion 3 becomes critical and criterion 4 is a trade-off, then:

$$S(A_a) = 0.37 \times (0.24 \times 0.67 + 0.32 \times 0.83 + 0.44 \times 0.85) = 0.30$$

Here you can see the strong effect of a critical criterion.

Summary

The Bayesian Team Support (BTS) model used here provides the first complete, integrated answer to needs in technical and business team decision-making. It allows a consistent method for collecting and analyzing evaluation information to generate a number of useful measures that can be used by teams to make robust decisions.

Robust Decisions & *Accord* Details

Robust Decisions, Inc.

The methods in this book were developed by Robust Decisions, Inc. (RDI). RDI was founded by the author, Dr. David Ullman, and his colleague Dr. Bruce D'Ambrosio. The two began developing these methods in 1995 when they realized that Ullman's interest in supporting the decision making process, his expertise in the mechanical design process, and his knowledge of robust design complemented D'Ambrosio's expertise in Bayesian decision theory. In 2003, RDI began to market the methods contained in this book, as well as its decision-making software, *Accord*.

Robust Decisions, Inc.'s web address is www.robustdecisions.com.

Accord Products

At the time of publication of this book, the current version of *Accord* is 2.3. This version, released in 2006, is available in three configurations:

Accord Desktop

Desktop was the first and is the most basic form of *Accord*. It runs on any Windows 2000 or Windows XP PC. It has all the functionality of *Accord* shown in this book. Its ability to support teams is limited as follows: The issue is framed and saved on one PC by the issue manager. The saved file (*.jdl) is e-mailed as an attachment to others who also have *Accord* loaded on their machines. They each enter their importance weightings and evaluations, and then e-mail the file back to the issue manager. The manager can then merge the data files into his in order to manage the issue.

You can download a free thirty-day trial version of this program by following the instructions below. It comes complete with a user's manual and example problems.

Accord Network

The commercial version of *Accord* is a client-server application that allows team members to more easily share data. The problem is framed by the issue manager and saved to a database. Team members are assigned levels of authority. Team members enter their importance weightings and evaluations on their own computers and their information is automatically merged and saved to the database. The database can be replayed and queried to review a history of the deliberation or to reuse information.

Requirements for *Accord* Network
- •Server
  - Intel® Pentium® III or AMD AthlonTM PC with 500 MHz, 256 MB RAM
  - Microsoft Windows 2000 Professional (SP2 or later), Windows NT 4.0 (SP6a or later), Windows XP; call for others
  - Disk space: 60 MB
- •Client
  - Java Runtime Environment 1.5+
  - 1024x768 16-bit high-color display or greater

Accord Browser add-in

In 2006, *Accord* Network was extended to include a browser add-in. This add-in provides a simplified user interface for users who have had no training on inputting evaluations. It allows the issue manager to send evaluators an e-mail that contains a link. This link opens an *Accord* window in a browser to allow easy collection of importance and evaluation information. Collected information is input directly to the server database.

How to Download *Accord*

You can download Accord Desktop free for thirty days at: www.robustdecisions.com/accorddownload.html.

With this download you will get the following files:
- •*Accord* Desktop, full version, thirty-day license
- •*Accord* User's manual
- •Example problem used in chapter 9
- •Example problem as updated in chapter 10
- •Other example problems

Newsletter

Robust Decisions, Inc. produces *The Decision Expert Newsletter*. This monthly one-page newsletter contains information to help you make the best possible decisions, as well as case studies. To sign up for *The Decision Expert Newsletter*, visit www.robustdecisions.com/newsletter.html.

Notes

1 Robust Decisions

1. Paul C. Nutt, *Why Decisions Fail*. San Francisco: Berrett-Koehler Publishers, 2002.

2. Research by Stauffer and Ullman showed that during the mechanical design process, designers broke problems into smaller and smaller chunks. In fact, this partitioning results in cognitive episodes that are about one minute long. In other words, designers who were solving problems followed the methodology shown on a minute-by-minute basis. Similar results have been found from other types of problem solving. (L.A. Stauffer and D.G. Ullman, "Fundamental Processes of Mechanical Designers Based on Empirical Data," *Journal of Engineering Design*, Vol. 2, No. 2, 1991, 113–126; D.G. Ullman, T.G. Dietterich, L. A. Stauffer, "A Model of the Mechanical Design Process Based on Empirical Data," *Artificial Intelligence in Engineering Design and Manufacturing*, 2(1), Academic Press, 1988, 33–52.)

3. Based on a list by Richard Schmuck. See Richard A. Schmuck, Patricia A. Schmuck, *Group Processes in the Classroom*, paperback 7th edition. New York: WCB/McGraw-Hill, 1996.

4. An introduction to Taguchi's philosophy can be found in David Ullman, *The Mechanical Design Process*, 3rd edition (New York: McGraw-Hill, 2003). Further detail is available in many books, the best of which are Clyde M. Creveling, *Tolerance Design: A Handbook for Developing Optimal Specifications* (Reading, MA: Addison Wesley, 1997) and Genichi Taguchi et al., *Taguchi's Quality Engineering Handbook* (New York: Wiley InterScience, 2004).

2 A Focus on Decisions

1. David Ullman, *The Mechanical Design Process*, 3rd edition. New York: McGraw-Hill, 2003.

2. *A Guide to the Project Management Body of Knowledge (PMBOK Guides)*. Project Management Institute, 2001.

3. "Letter to Joseph Priestley," *Benjamin Franklin Sampler*. New York: Fawcett, 1956.

4. David Ullman, "'OO-OO-OO!' The Sound of a Broken OODA Loop," *CrossTalk*, September 2006.

5. Available on the web: www.d-n-i.net/boyd/pdf/c&c.pdf.

6. The sound "OO-OO-OO" was described in a presentation by Harvey S. Gold, Lead Design for Six Sigma Black Belt, DuPont CR&D, June 2005.

7. Ullman, *The Mechanical Design Process*, 74.

8. M. George, *Lean Six Sigma for Service.* New York: McGraw-Hill, 2003.

9. D. Ginn and E. Varner, *The Design for Six Sigma Memory Jogger.* Goal/QPC, 2004.

10. Stuart Pugh, *Total Design: Integrated Methods for Successful Product Engineering.* Reading, MA: Addison Wesley, 1990.

11. Actually, it is much worse than this, as by averaging you can easily violate Arrow's Impossibility Theorem. Say that there are three team members, one who orders the options A > B > C, another who evaluates B > C > A, and a third who says C > A >B. All three voters have rationally ordered preferences, but on the average (in two out of three cases), they prefer A to B, and prefer B to C, and also C to A. The resulting social order is not rational, and provides no basis on which to make a decision. See M.J. Scott and E. Antonsson, "Arrow's Theorem and Engineering Design Decision Making," *Research in Engineering Design*, Vol. 2, No. 4, 2000, 218-228.

3   Often Wrong But Never in Doubt

1. This curve itself is an estimate based on a modest sample size. Although not statistically correct, it makes the point needed. Only basic knowledge of normal distributions is assumed here.

2. A primary source is M.G. Morgan and M. Henrion, *Uncertainty: A Guide to Dealing With Uncertainty in Quantitative Risk and Policy Analysis* (New York: Cambridge University Press, 1990).

3. Ladislow Reti, *The Unknown Leonardo.* New York: McGraw-Hill, 1974, 181.

4. James Surowiecki, *The Wisdom of Crowds.* New York: Doubleday, 2004.

5. Sherry Sontag, *Blind Man's Bluff.* New York: HarperCollins, 1999.

6. Bent Flyvbjerg, Mette Skamris Holm, and Søren Buhl, "Underestimating Costs in Public Works Projects: Error or Lie?" *Journal of the American Planning Association*, Vol. 68, No. 3, Summer 2002, 279–95.

7. Standish Group, *Chaos Reports* 2000 and 2004. https://secure.standishgroup.com/.

8. Ullman et al., unpublished research for unnamed sponsor 2005.

9. If you are interested in trying this simple experiment with your organization, you can download the questionnaire from www.robustdecisions.com/dishexperiment.html. We only ask that you share the results with us.

10. Ilan Yaniv, "Precision and Accuracy of Judgmental Estimation," *Journal of Behavioral Decision Making*, Vol. 10, 1997, 21-32.

11. With the mean of the distribution of mean estimates at 18 min and the standard deviation at 6 min, then using normal distribution tables, the 90% mean estimate is 26 min (close to the mean 90% result of 29 min in the experiment). If the standard deviation is 8 min (the 90% value) the 90% mean estimate is 28 min, even closer.

12. D. Peters and G. Dewey, "Beware of the Bid, Bad Bias: Overcoming Poor Project Estimating," *Crosstalk*, April 2000.

13. E.F. Loftus and J.C. Palmer, "Reconstruction of automobile destruction: An example of the interaction between language and behavior," *Journal of Verbal and Learning Behavior* 13 (1974), 585-589.

14. M. Jorgensen, "Uncertainty Intervals versus Interval Uncertainty: An alternative method for eliciting effort prediction intervals in software development projects," 2002.

15. Peter L. Bernstein, *Against the Gods: The Remarkable Story of Risk.* New York: Wiley, 1996.

16. Flyvbjerg, Holm, and Buhl, "Underestimating Costs in Public Works Projects: Error or Lie?", 279.

17. Jack B. Soll, J. Klayman, "Overconfidence in interval estimates." Center for Decision Research, Graduate School of Business, University of Chicago, January 2003.

18. S. Plous, *The Psychology of Judgment and Decision Making.* New York: McGraw-Hill, 1993.

19. This model was developed in conversation with Jaris Hihn and Art Chmielewski of the Jet Propulsion Laboratory, Pasadena California.

20. Washington State Department of Transportation, "Major project program cost estimating guidance." www.fhwa.dot.gov/programadmin/mega/cefinal.pdf, June 2004.

21. L. Leach, *Critical Chain Project Management,* 2nd edition. Artech House, 2005.

22. D. Ullman and L. Leach, "The Promise of Simulation Training to Deliver the Benefits of Lean Project Management," for AFRL/MLMP December 2004.

23. D. Ford and J. Sterman, "Overcoming the 90% Syndrome: Iteration Management in Concurrent Development," *Concurrent Engineering* 11 (2003), 177–86.

24. Washington State Department of Transportation, "Major project program cost estimating guidance."

25. E. Russo and P. Schoemaker, "Managing Overconfidence," *Sloan Management Review,* Vol. 33, No. 2, Winter 1992, 7–17.

26. K. Tupman, "Get accurate project estimates," *Tec Republic,* February 6, 2003, www.zdnet.com.au/insight/0,39023731,20271841,00.htm

27. M. Jorgensen, "An Attempt to Model Software Development Effort Estimation Accuracy and Bias." Simula Research Laboratory, 2003. www.simula.no/photo/easejorgensenfinal.pdf.

28. In NASA's *Probabilistic Risk Assessment Guide,* undesirable consequences are tied to accident (i.e., event) scenarios. "Probabilistic Risk Assessment: Procedures Guide for NASA Managers and Practitioners," Office of Safety and Mission Assurance, NASA Headquarters, August 2002.

29. Thanks to Brian Seitz (formerly of IBM and now with Microsoft) for clearly articulating these.

4 Teams Don't Make Decisions, But...

1. P.R. Scholtes et al., *The Team Handbook*, 3rd edition. Madison, WI: Oriel Inc, 2003.

2. D.D. Wheeleer and I.L. Janis, *Practical Guide for Decision Making*. New York: Free Press, 1980.

3. J. Payne, J. Bettman and E. Johnson, *The Adaptive Decision Maker*. New York: Cambridge University Press, 1993.
   This book is about how people choose the strategy they use when making a decision. The authors build a model of the strategy showing people's behavior is contingent on the problem (task variables, context variables), the person (cognitive ability, prior knowledge), and the social context (accountability, group membership). Their basic thesis is that the use of various decision strategies is an adaptive response of a limited-capacity information processor to the demands of complex task environments.
   Their research shows that people often try to minimize their cost by using a lexicographic heuristic. This strategy is to determine the most important criteria and compare the alternative to it. The alternative with the best value on the most important criteria is selected. If there is a tie, then the next most important attribute is considered.
   There is a very short discussion about teams, but the book is really focused on individual decision makers.

4. Studies on descriptive problem solving can be found in:
   Stauffer and Ullman, "Fundamental Processes of Mechanical Designers Based on Empirical Data."
   C.J. Altman et al., "A Comparison of Freshman and Senior Engineering Design Process," *Design Studies*, Vol. 20, No. 2, March 1999, 131-152.
   S.L. Ahmeed, S. L. Blessing and K. Wallace, "The Relationship Between Data, Information and Knowledge Based on a Preliminary Study of Engineering Designers," DETC99/DTM-8754, ASME Design Theory and Methodology Conference, Sept 1999, Las Vegas.

5. Prescriptive methods are discussed in:
   R.I. Keeney and H. Raiffa, *Decisions with Multiple Objectives*. New York: Cambridge University Press, 1993.
   T.L. Saaty, *Decision Making for Leaders: The Analytic Hierarchy Process for Decisions in a Complex World*, 1999/2000 Edition. Pittsburgh: RWS Publications, 2000.
   Saaty, *The Analytic Network Process*. Pitttsburgh: RWS Publications, 1996.

6. The measures used here are roughly equivalent to the Five-Factor (aka Big Five) model measures as follows:
   • Energy Source (Internal–External) = Extroversion
   • Information Management Style (Facts–Possibilities) = Originality or Openness
   • Information Language (verbal–visual) = none
   • Deliberation Style (Objective–Subjective) = Accommodation or Agreeableness
   • Decision Closure Style (Flexible–Decisive) = Conscientiousness or Consolidation
   Note that I have not included the measure for Emotional Stability.

Reference material for the Big Five can be found at:. The Big Five Quickstart: An Introduction to the Five-Factor Model of Personality, http://www.centacs.com/quickstart.htm.

7. The measures used here are roughly equivalent to the Myers-Briggs measures as follows:
• Energy Source (Internal–External) = Introverted (I)–Extraverted (E)
• Information Management Style (Facts–Possibilities) = Sensing (S)–Intuitive (I)
• Information Language (verbal–visual) = none
• Deliberation Style (Objective–Subjective) = Thinking (T)–Feeling (F)
• Decision Closure Style (Flexible–Decisive) = Perceiving (P)–Judging (J)
Books that describe the Myers-Briggs method:
D. Keirsey and M. Bates, *Please Understand Me,* 5th ed. Del Mar, CA: Prometheus Nemesis, 1978. O. Kroeger and J. M. Thuesen, *Type Talk at Work.* New York: Delta, 1992.
Kroeger, *Type Talk.* New York: Delta, 1989.
Web sites are: www.myersbriggs.org and www.keirsey.com

8. Tom Judd, Cognition Corp, "Taking DFSS to the Next Level." WCBF, Design for Six Sigma Conference, Las Vegas, June 2005.

5 Everybody Hears Only What He Only Understands

1. George Lakoff, *Don't Think of an Elephant.* White River Junction, VT: Chelsea Green, 2004.

2. Nancy Lee Jones, "The Americans with Disabilities Act (ADA): Statutory Language and Recent Issues," Updated June 13, 2005, Congressional Research Service, The Library of Congress.

3. From Ullman, *The Mechanical Design Process.*

4. A study of five design engineers included video taping them as they solved a design problem. The resulting video was then decomposed to track their activities. It was found that they broke their problem solving into small micro-issues (called episodes in the cognitive psychology literature). These micro-issues averaged 56 seconds in duration. In other words, their entire problem solving activity was broken into small problems. This result may seem at odds with experience, but it is consistent with models of how humans cognitively process information. Similar results have been found in other studies. D.G. Ullman, T.G. Dietterich, L. Stauffer, "A Model of the Mechanical Design Process Based on Empirical Data," Academic Press, *Artificial Intelligence in Engineering Design and Manufacturing,* 2(1), 1988, 33–52.

5. Norbert Dylla, "Thinking Methods and Procedures in Mechanical Design." Dissertation, Technical University of Munich, 1991, in German.

6. Ullman, *The Mechanical Design Process,* 162.

7. Based on an example in "Tools for the Imagination Phase of the Direct Creativity Cycle." www.riectedcreativity.com/pages/ToolsImagine.html.

8. For information on TRIZ, see www.trizjournal.com.

9. E. Domb and H.W. Dettmer, "Breakthrough Innovation In Conflict Resolution: Marrying TRIZ and the Thinking Process," *Proceedings of the APICS Constraint*

Management Special Interest Group, March 1999, www.triz-journal.com/archives/ 1999/05/b/

10. Here, the method has been greatly shortened. In traditional TRIZ practice the contradictions are used with a large table to find which Inventive Principles might best be used. The table is too big for inclusion here and exploring the 40 Principles is not much more time consuming than using the table.

11. The entire list of inventive principles is at www.triz-journal.com/matrix/ index.htm or in the appendices of Ullman, *The Mechanical Design Process.* This list converted to business alternatives can be found in D. Mann and E. Domb, "40 Inventive (Business) Principles With Examples," *The TRIZ Journal,* www.triz-journal.com/archives/1999/09/a/index.htm.

12. Two good sources for details on the EC are H. William Dettmer, *Breaking the Constraints to World-Class Performance* (Milwaukee: ASQ Quality Press, 1998) and Detmer, *Strategic Navigation* (Milwaukee: ASQ Quality Press, 2003). Also see Larry Leach, *Critical Chain Project Management,* 2nd edition. Norwood, MA: Artech House, 2005.

13. Adapted from a more detailed similar problem in Detmer, *Breaking the Constraints to World-Class Performance.*

14. Larry Leach emphasized this point in personal communication.

6   Measuring the Ideal

1. From the Hoechst AG–U.S Scoring model in Robert Cooper et al., *Portfolio Management for New Products.* Reading, MA: Addison Wesley, 1998

2. Based on a method described in M. Mollaghasemi and J. Pet-Edwards, "Making Multiple-Objective Decisions," IEEE Computer Society Technical Briefing, 1997, 7–9.

3. MindManager is a product of Mind Jet, http://www.mindjet.com/us/

4. Criteria hierarchies are the foundation of the Analytical Hierarchy Process (AHP), discussed in chapter 7.

5. Ralph L. Keeney, *Value-Focused Thinking: A Path to Creative Decisionmaking* (Cambridge, MA: Harvard University Press, 1992). A good application of this methodology is in a USAF Thesis by David M. Jurk, "Decision Analysis with Value Focused Thinking as a Methodology to Select Force Protection Initiatives for Evaluation." AFIT/GEE/ENV/02M-05, March 2002, http://www.stormingmedia.us/ 80/8070/A807004.html.

6. Items in the table were taken from www.utmen.edu/~rarreola/quest.php and appear in other sources. This site also gives good guidance on developing Likert questionnaires.

7   Importance Is in the Eye of the Beholder

1. This is often called the lexicographic method. Dictionaries are lexicographic, as they are set up so you first look for the first letter, then the second, and so forth. The first is most important; the second is next, and so on. Details on this and other patterns can be found in John W. Payne, James R. Bettman, and Eric

J. Johnson, *The Adaptive Decision Maker* (New York: Cambridge University Press, 1993).

2. Ward Edwards for one: Ward Edwards and F. Hutton Barron, "SMARTS and SMARTER: Improved Simple Methods for Multi-attribute Utility Measurement" and F. Hutton Barron and Bruce Barrett, "Decision Quality Using Ranked and Partially Ranked Attribute Weights."

3. $w_k = (1/K) \sum (1/ i)$ as i goes from k (the number of the criterion with 1 being the highest weighted and K being the lowest) to K (the number of criteria)

4. Saaty, *Decision Making for Leaders.*

5. Ibid.

8 Decisions Are Based on Your Belief About an Uncertain Future

1. Bernstein, *Against the Gods: The Remarkable Story of Risk.*

2. John Fox, *Quality Through Design.* London: McGraw-Hill, 1993.

3. The Level of Certainty is a measure of standard deviation. When the high estimate is on delighted and the low is on disgusted this is a little less than + 3 sigma distribution as detailed in appendix A.

4. Only the very basics of the Wright Brothers are discussed here. For more complete information see: T. Crouch, *The Bishop's Boys* (New York: W.W. Norton, 1989) and M. McFarland, ed., *The Papers of Wilbur and Orville Wright* (New York: McGraw-Hill, 1953, reprinted by Ayer Company, 1998).

5. Otto Lilienthal, *Birdflight as the Basis of Aviation,* 1889. Reprinted in 2001 by American Aeronautical Archives.

9 Robust Decision Making

1. The actual math is: Team belief $\approx \Pi$ Bi / $(\Pi B_i + \Pi (1- B_i))$ where Π is the product symbol and B_i is the individual belief of each team member. This product can be calculated or is an output from *Accord.*

5. This violates Arrow's Impossibility Theorem (see chapter 2, note 11).

10 Decide What-to-Do-Next

1. Based on *Negotiation Strategy and Tactics,* 2nd edition. Nashua, NH: Situation Management Systems Inc., 1989.

12 Criteria Templates

1. Although the list is not from this paper, a good source of make-or-buy information: Charles H. Fine and Daniel E. Whitney, "Is the Make-Buy Decision Process a Core Competence?" MIT Center for Technology, Policy, and Industrial Development, Working paper, February 1996.

2. From the Hoechst AG—U.S Scoring model in Cooper et al., *Portfolio Management for New Products.*

3. Peter Marks, *The Origins of Winning Products.* Self-published 1998.

13 Applications of Robust Decision Making

1. John L. Morris, Hewlett Packard, September 27, 2005.

2. Jeffry Fint, and Joseph Onstott, Pratt & Whitney. This case study was presented as a PowerPoint presentation at the Jet Propulsion Laboratory New Design Paradigms Workshop, June 25–27, 2002.

3. Trade Studies with Uncertain Information:
Dr. David G. Ullman, President, Robust Decisions Inc.
Brian P. Spiegel, Aerospace Electronic Systems, Honeywell
Sixteenth Annual International Symposium of the International Council on Systems Engineering (INCOSE), July 8–14, 2006.

4. FAA, *System Engineering Manual Version 3.0*, Section 4.6, Trade Studies, Federal Aviation Administration, 2004, www.faa.gov/asd/SystemEngineering/.

5. B.C. Phillips and S.M. Polen, "Add Decision Analysis to Your COTS Selection Process," *Crosstalk*, April 2002.

6. FAA, *System Engineering Manual Version 3.0*.

7. A. Felix, "Standard Approach to Trade Studies: A Process Improvement Model that Enables Systems Engineers to Provide Information to the Project Manager by Going Beyond the Summary Matrix," www.incose.org/so-md/ChapterMeetingMinutes/Presentations/2004NovTrade%20Study%20Brief%20-%20AFelix.pdf.

8. NASA, *NASA Systems Engineering Handbook*, Section 5.1 Trade Studies, NASA SP-610S 1995, dcm.gsfc.nasa.gov/library/Systems_Engineering_Handbook.pdf.

9. Gary Klein, *Sources of Power: How People Make Decisions*. Cambridge, MA: MIT Press, 1996.

10. M. Gladwell, *Blink*. New York: Little, Brown, 2005.

11. J. Arora, *Introduction to Optimum Design*. New York: McGraw-Hill, 1989.

Appendix A

1. L.J. Savage, *Foundations of Statistics*, 1955, 2nd revised edition. Mineola NY: Dover, 1972.

2. R.L. Winkler, *An Introduction to Bayesian Inference and Decision*. New York: Holt, 1972.

3. General Decision-Making Support Method and System, U.S. Patent # 6,631,362, Ullman, D.G. and D'Ambrosio, B., October 2003, Assignee Robust Decisions Inc.

4. K. Claxton et al., "A Pilot Study of Value of Information Analysis to Support Research Recommendations for the National Institute for Clinical Excellence." Centre for Health Economics, Research Paper 4, 2005. And K. Claxton et al., "Bayesian Value-of-Information Analysis: An Application to a Policy Model of Alzheimer's Disease," *International Journal of Technology Assessment in Health Care*, 17:1 (2001), 38–55.

5. F. Yokota and K. M. Thompson, "Value of Information Analysis in Environmental Health Risk Management Decisions: Past, Present, and Future Risk Analysis," *Risk Analysis*, Vol. 24, June 2004, 635.

6. Maxine E. Dakins, "The Value of the Value of Information," *Human and Ecological Risk Assessment*, Vol. 5, No. 2, April 1999, 281–289(9).

7. This is a simplification of the model used in *Accord*.

Index

ISBN 142510956-X

7422515R0

Made in the USA
Lexington, KY
19 November 2010